OPERATION LAST CHANCE

OPERATION LAST CHANCE

One Man's Quest to Bring Nazi Criminals to Justice

Efraim Zuroff

OPERATION LAST CHANCE

Copyright © Michel Lafon Publishing S.A., 2008.

English-language translation copyright © 2009 by Catherine Spencer

All rights reserved.

First published in France as *Chasseur de Nazis* by Michel Lafon

First published in hardcover in 2009 by
PALGRAVE MACMILLAN®
in the United States—a division of St. Martin's Press LLC,
175 Fifth Avenue, New York, NY 10010.

ISBN: 978–0–230–10805–9

Library of Congress Cataloging-in-Publication Data

Zuroff, Efraim.
   Operation Last Chance : one man's quest to bring Nazi criminals to
justice / Efraim Zuroff.
     p. cm.
   Includes bibliographical references and index.
   ISBN 0–230–61730–1 (alk. paper)
   (paperback ISBN 978–0–230–10805–9)
     1. Zuroff, Efraim. 2. World War, 1939–1945—Atrocities.
3. Holocaust, Jewish (1939–1945) 4. War criminals—Legal status,
laws, etc.—Case studies. 5. Fugitives from justice—Case studies.
6. Criminal investigation—Case studies. 7. Simon Wiesenthal Center.
Israel Office—Biography. 8. United States. Dept. of Justice. Office of
Special Investigations—Biography. 9. Nazis—Biography. 10. War
criminals—Biography. I. Title.

D804.3.Z875 2009
364.1'38—dc22   2009039711

A catalogue record of the book is available from the British Library.

Design by Newgen Imaging Systems (P) Ltd., Chennai, India

First PALGRAVE MACMILLAN paperback edition: March 2011

P1

Dedicated to the memory of
Simon Wiesenthal

who refused to allow the Holocaust to be
forgotten. and to the memory of the members of my family
murdered in Lithuania 1941–1944
Rabbi Efraim Zar
Beyla Zar
Eliyahu Zar
Hirsh Zar

CONTENTS

ACKNOWLEDGMENTS

ONE OF THE most rewarding aspects of my activities as a Nazi hunter over the past 30 years has been the wonderful people I have had the privilege to work with, many of whom have become personal friends. So I am particularly pleased to be able to publicly acknowledge their support and thank them for their assistance.

None of the projects and campaigns described in this book would have been possible had it not been for the commitment of the Simon Wiesenthal Center to carry on the mission that our namesake assumed shortly after his liberation from the Mauthausen concentration camp on May 6, 1945. Further, I am grateful to the leaders of our institution—Rabbi Marvin Hier, Founder and Dean, and Rabbi Abraham Cooper, Associate Dean—who entrusted me with that task, and to Executive Director Rabbi Meyer May. From the beginning, in 1986, I have had the support and cooperation of the center's leadership and staff, which proved to be essential to my work. And in that context, I want to especially thank my colleagues Rhonda Barad, our Eastern Region (U.S.) director, and Sergio Widder, our Latin America director, for their particular efforts on my behalf. A special thank you also goes to Steve Mizel, whose support bolstered the Center's Nazi-hunting activities.

Given the global scope of the center's efforts to bring Nazi war criminals to justice, and especially following our launch of Operation Last Chance in 2002, I have had the opportunity to work with energetic and enthusiastic partners from countries all over the world. Those individuals share my vision and determination to hold Holocaust perpetrators accountable for their crimes and deserve mention for their support and assistance. Among them, I especially want to thank, in Croatia: His

Excellency President Stjepan Mesić, Tomislav Jakić, Alen Budaj, Silvio (Shlomo) Jazbec, Zoran Pusić, Lea Šiljak, and Rabbi Kotel Dadon; in Serbia: His Excellency President Boris Tadić, President of the Novi Sad Jewish community Dr. Ana Frenkel, Chief Rabbi Yitshak Asiel, Bishop Irinej, Protosingel Jovan Ćulibrk, Sonja Licht, and Nenad Antonijević; in Lithuania: Shimon Alperovich, Professor Dovid Katz, and Rūta Puišyté; in Romania: Otto Adler, Alex Sivan, Marco Katz, the team at "Tempo Advertising" and especially Eliza Rogalski; in Austria: Samuel Laster, Marianne Enigl, Christine Schindler, Thomas Stern, Dr. Azriel Muzicant, and Raimund Fastenbauer; in Hungary: Szilvia Peto Dittel, Tibor Pecsi, and Márton Rosta; in the United States: Dr. Michael Berenbaum and Dr. Karen Shawn; in Australia: Dr. Colin Rubenstein and the AIJAC team, and Steve Leiblich; in Estonia: Sten Hankewitz; in Spain: Gloria Trinidad; in Denmark: Dr. Vilhjálmur Vilhjálmsson; in Poland: Chief Rabbi Michael Schudrich and Kostek Gebert; in Argentina: Dalila Herbst, Luis Grynwald and Daniel Reisfeld; in Chile: Gabriel Zaliasnik, Edith Blaustein, Marcelo Isaacson, and Joyce Alter; in Brazil: Gabi Milevsky and Rabbi Daniel Tuito; and in Uruguay: Diego Sonnenschein and Sebastian Villa. Many government officials, diplomats, and journalists, whose help proved invaluable in numerous investigations, also belong on this list, but, for understandable reasons, will remain anonymous.

Closer to home, here in Israel, I have often benefited from the sage advice and encouragement of Professor Dov Levin and was given exceptional assistance in various important ways by Dr. Gavriel Bar-Shaked of Yad Vashem and many of his colleagues. In recent years, Aviva Raz-Schecter of the Foreign Ministry has tried very hard to deal effectively on behalf of the State of Israel with Holocaust-related issues, and survivors such as Miriam Aviezer, Yehudit Yaron, Lydia Brenners, and Yosef Melamed have always been ready to help me on specific cases.

Three individuals stand out, however, among all my many co-workers, helpers, and volunteers, and they deserve special mention and gratitude for their extraordinary efforts to help me succeed in my work. The first is Aryeh Rubin, whose financial assistance was critical in launching Operation Last Chance, and whose friendship and emotional support have been invaluable over the years. Whether my destination was Iceland, Costa Rica, or Croatia, Aryeh was always at my side to help out in whatever way necessary. The second is my colleague Dr. Stefan Klemp, our researcher in Germany, who for the past decade has done an excellent job on a wide variety of research projects and whose help on issues related to Germany and Austria has been critical. His outstanding research in the framework of our project to assist the German Welfare Ministry in canceling the special disability pensions of those who violated the norms of humanity during World War II is of historic significance. Over the past decade, we have spent many days together traveling all over Germany and Austria, and I truly appreciate his talents and friendship. Last, but not least, is Talma Hurwitz, my loyal office manager, who has helped keep our campaigns running smoothly for almost two decades. Without her dedicated efforts, we would never have been able to achieve nearly as much as we did, and the center owes her a deep debt of gratitude.

I have tried my best to write a book that will accurately reflect the scope of my work and its motivation; the trials, tribulations, and frustrations, as well as its broader educational, political, and moral implications. My thanks to Sophie Charnavel and Michel Lafon Publishers for being the first in the publishing world to recognize the importance of the subject, and to Alexandre Duyck for helping to bring to life the most significant cases. Thanks also to Catherine Spencer, who translated the original French edition, which was a starting point but which I completely rewrote, and to Alessandra Bastagli and her assistant Colleen Lawrie, who helped me find my voice and reach the English-speaking public.

Finally, my deep affection and appreciation go to my parents, Abraham and Esther, who were wonderful role models and instilled in me the dedication and passion to serve the Jewish people, who continue to be one of the major motivations behind my work. And to my wife and partner, Elisheva, my heartfelt love and gratitude for many years of standing by me through thick and thin and for your encouragement and support. Our children and grandchildren are the best testament to the beauty of our relationship. And to our second and third generations—to our children and their spouses: Avigayil and Tzvika, Itamar and Yael, Elchanan and Talia, and Ayelet—and to our grandchildren: Noga, Aviya, Avishai, Shira, and Michael, and those G-d willing still to come—may you always follow in the footsteps of your worthy ancestors and continue to be a source of pride and joy for all of us.

OPERATION LAST CHANCE

ONE

MILIVOJ AŠNER, A SUSPECTED NAZI AT EURO 2008

JUNE 2008: THE European soccer championship organized in Switzerland and Austria was in full swing. Some of the fans there were thrilled, others unhappy or totally dejected, depending on how their favorite team was doing. This man was one of the cheerful ones. Arm in arm with his wife, Edeltraut, he strolled through the streets of his city, Klagenfurt, in Carinthia, a province in southern Austria, where the Croatian national team was staying. Despite having lived in Austria for almost half a century, he remained a dedicated supporter of Croatia, his native country. At the age of 95, he walked with a lively step, although he never let go of Edeltraut's arm.

Sitting at a table outside a café like ordinary folk, the pair was enjoying themselves, joking with waiters before going off to do some shopping.

Hidden from view, a photographer from the *Sun*, the famous British tabloid, captured every moment of this charming scene. The next day, the two lovebirds' little stroll was on the newspaper's front page under the title "We find wanted Nazi at Euro 2008!"

This man, dressed in a black sweater, white shirt, and canvas trousers, was not just any retired soccer fan. This elderly, respectable-looking gentleman ranked fourth on our list of the world's ten most wanted Nazis.

Surname: Ašner. First name: Milivoj. In Austria he went by the name of Georg Aschner. Year of birth: 1913. Service record: former chief of the Ustasha (Croatian fascist) police in the city of Požega, he was accused of having organized the deportation of hundreds of Serbs, Jews, Gypsies, and Communists to Croatian concentration camps, where most were murdered. Under his command, Požega's great synagogue was burned down, and a concentration camp built in its stead. On the night of August 26, 1941, 300 prisoners were executed for attempting to escape. The mass deportation of Jews then began on December 25, 1941. The men were sent to the Jasenovac camp, the women and children to the camp of Djakovo. Jews had been forced to bring large sums of money and all their valuables to his office. Yet he was smiling broadly as he welcomed the *Sun*'s reporters to his home and claimed that he was not a war criminal. "I didn't have anything to do with it. I was just an officer with the justice department—a lawyer. I never did anything bad against anybody."[1]

THERE HAVE BEEN countries in which our appeals for informants and witnesses to come forward in response to our promise of rewards for information that would facilitate the prosecution and punishment of Nazi war criminals did not elicit any immediate results. This was not the case in Croatia, where even before we officially launched Operation Last Chance on June 30, 2004, one very important target was already in our sights. At the time, he went by the name of Milivoj Ašner. In late May 2004, I had received a report on him in Israel, sent to me by a 27-year-old man, Alen Budaj, a native of Požega, the city where Ašner was chief of police and the scene of his heinous acts.

Budaj lived in Zagreb, where he was fighting to keep memory alive—especially that of his Jewish grandparents, buried in a now-ruined Jewish cemetery that had been abandoned and repeatedly desecrated. In the course of his research for a book on the history of Požega and its Jewish community, Budaj had met an old resistance fighter who had told him that the former local chief of police, a certain Milivoj Ašner, had returned to Croatia in 1991, after having spent a long time in Austria, where he had gone into hiding after the war. For several years, Budaj had been doing research at the Croatian National Archives in Zagreb almost daily. Among the countless documents filed away there over the last 60 years, he found deportation orders and decrees signed by Ašner. The report I received from Budaj was a condensation of his meticulous work: a summary of the case and copies of the original documents proving Ašner's guilt, 60 pages that connected the overwhelming facts. The temptation to move immediately to the next stage and make a public accusation was great. But I had to take certain precautions. I contacted Miriam Aviezer, a friend who was a specialist in the history of the Holocaust in Yugoslavia and who had worked at Yad Vashem, Israel's national memorial and research center dedicated to the victims of the Shoa, and asked her to translate and evaluate the documents. She confirmed their authenticity, and once I was able to read them, it became clear to me that the material sent by Budaj was definitely credible. At the same time, I also got in touch with my good friend Igor Alborghetti, the editor of *Globus*, the leading Croatian weekly newsmagazine, who in mid-June called me to confirm that Ašner was still alive.

The facts of the case were now clear and confirmed, and we could proceed. A lawyer by training, Ašner had served as the Ustasha chief of police of Slavonska Požega. In that capacity, he had written and signed numerous anti-Jewish and anti-Serb decrees that had resulted in the deportation and deaths of at least several hundred people. I was now ready to launch the Croatian chapter of Operation Last Chance and immediately contacted Budaj to arrange a meeting; I wanted to know whom I was dealing with.

On June 29, 2004, I landed in Zagreb in the early afternoon and shortly thereafter met Alen Budaj at the Dubrovnik Hotel. He came with his cousin Salomon (Shlomo) Jazbec, who appeared to be fairly knowledgeable in Jewish affairs and even spoke a little Hebrew. But none of my friends in the Zagreb Jewish community, whom I had called after receiving the dossier, knew either one of them, which naturally aroused my suspicions. I therefore was somewhat hesitant and Budaj himself appeared very cagey—he seemed worried that I might appropriate his work, which was a bit strange considering that it was he who had approached me and asked for my assistance. Clearly these two men were in possession of information of the first order, but they needed me, my networks, my historical knowledge, my experience, and my media skills, and I needed them, because they had brought me the Ašner file. But by the end of our meeting I had, thank G-d, convinced them that I was just as determined as them to see Ašner prosecuted and that I had no intention of stealing the credit for their research. I informed them of my plan to launch Operation Last Chance the next day and we agreed to work together to achieve our mutual goal.

The following day, June 30, I held a press conference. I knew that what I was preparing to do might be a little dangerous, but I did not think at that point that the risk of Ašner's escape was very serious: I therefore revealed Ašner's identity and laid out the charges of which he was accused. I stated that I had his address and telephone number. I also showed two documents from the Ustasha police, dating from October 1941, signed by Ašner. The first was the order of expulsion—in reality, the deportation—from Požega of 26 Jewish and Serbian families. The second was an order of confiscation of all the goods of one Valerija Moskowitz, whose husband, according to the document, was held in a concentration camp for expressing opposition to the Ustasha.

I also showed that Milivoj Ašner, who was a Croatian citizen, had fled at the end of the war to Austria, where he had never been brought to justice, and had returned to live in Croatia in 1991. Ašner had fled in 1946 because the Yugoslav State Commission for the Investigation of War Crimes had documented in detail the events that had occurred in Požega during the war. Among the charges described were "prisoners tortured by being hung upside down, their toenails torn out." The investigators specified that "Ašner, as chief of police, took the decisions concerning arrests, expulsions and deportations."[2]

I ended the press conference by reminding the journalists that Ašner had relatively recently established a political party, the Original Croatian Peasant Party, that had run in the Croatian national elections, so he obviously was in reasonable health regardless of his age, and stated my intention to hand these documents over shortly to attorney general Mladen Bajić. Finally, I announced that, as in all the countries we had previously targeted, an advertisement promising a reward of US$10,000 for information leading to the prosecution and punishment of any Nazi war criminal would be published, in this case free of charge, in *Globus*. Following the press conference, I rushed off to meet with Croatian president Stjepan Mesić, who in a wonderful show of support for our efforts had agreed to meet me on the very day we launched Operation Last Chance in Zagreb. In his office, I asked President Mesić to do everything in his power to help me get Ašner arrested quickly since he was already over 90 years old. He was as determined as I was. It was clear that we were dealing with an important war criminal and a cunning man, and in this respect, Ašner's case was unique. In fact, his name appeared on a list, drawn up in Croatia in 1985, of the names of "all the victims of fascism in Zagreb"—clearly Ašner had passed himself off as a Holocaust victim at the end of the war. Mesić assured me of his determination to help; he called the attorney general, Mladen Bajić, and asked him to see me immediately. Bajic agreed, and that afternoon I gave him the complete file on the Ašner case.

The press conference proved a veritable bombshell. Journalists rushed to Ašner's hometown of Daruvar, to his two-story house with its white walls where he had lived since 1991. His reaction was similar to that of the other alleged war criminals: denial and feigned incomprehension. Hearing the news of the hunt, the contemporary Croatian fascists and neo-Ustasha sprang into action. Now, under the title of the "Anti-Jewish Movement," they were trying to intimidate me and those who wanted to help us in this case.

An anonymous letter was delivered to the Civic Committee for Human Rights in Zagreb, addressed to my friend Zoran Pusić, who was the director. At the bottom of the page was the movement's logo: an enormous U for Ustasha.

"You Jews really are a peculiar nation! You yourselves are looking for a sword that will cut off your heads. What you are looking for is what you Jewboy Zuroff will receive! Leave the Croats in peace. If any Croat will be put into jail because of your sick Jew ideas, we warn you: We'll start murdering your fellow countrymen in Croatia. We know your names and addresses. You decide for yourselves."[3]

They offered rewards for the murder of Minister of Justice Vesna Štare-Ožbolt (US$75,000), of Dr. Zoran Pusić (US$50,000), and of myself (US$25,000) and threatened many other anti-fascist Croatians. Perhaps because I am not a Croat my life was worth less to them than that of the other two.

While I was not scared by these intimidation tactics, they did influence other people such as the former Serbian resistance fighter who explained that he was afraid to tell his story openly 60 years after the events because everyone knows him and Ašner still has his men around Požega. It was Ašner who gave the orders to arrest him on April 12, 1941. He didn't come and do it personally, but the policeman who came for him showed him the warrant with his signature.

The information gathered by Budaj, the confirmation of its authenticity, Mesić's support,[4] Ašner's apparent good health—it all seemed too easy. I should have been on my guard. Instead, I had done something imprudent, which soon proved to be a huge mistake. I had not seriously considered the possibility that Milivoj Ašner might disappear. Going on the run at his age seemed unthinkable: one does not venture to an unknown country to make a new life under a false identity at the age of 91. But that was to ignore the support network the man could draw on; Ašner, whose son lived in Austria, had a landing place, a safe refuge. Knowing that I had the support of President Mesic and the attorney general and that, if he stayed in Croatia, Ašner would certainly face trial, almost certainly prompted his flight. I would have to go to Austria to hunt him down.

IT DID NOT take long for Budaj and Jazbec to find out where Ašner was living: Paulitischgastrasse 8, Klagenfurt, Carinthia, his previous residence in Austria. Doubtless he thought he was safe there, aware that Austria was notorious for its consistent failure to prosecute suspected Nazi war criminals and for its policy against the extradition of its citizens. In fact, he could not have chosen a safer haven.

An international warrant was issued for Ašner's arrest, and Interpol put out a wanted notice, Ref. 2005/29623, along with a photograph of the fugitive, smiling and wearing a striped blazer, dated December 13, 2001. It was to no avail.

I was up against a wall, a wall of silence on the part of the Austrian judiciary and authorities. Meanwhile, Ašner, never short on cynicism, lived in total tranquility, even declaring to an Israeli journalist, "I'm the Croatian Schindler,"[5] tainting the name of the German industrialist Oskar Schindler, who had saved more than 1,000 Jews during World War II. He gave several interviews, stating he had never done any harm, that everything I claimed was false, and that he had never had anything to do with the political police. He repeated endlessly that I simply wanted to harass good Croatian patriots. He also gave an interview to the Austrian news weekly *Profil* entitled "Ach, dieser Jude, ein Lump" (Ah, that Jew, what a rascal) in which he attacked Alen Budaj, who he described as: "Ah, that Jew! A hobo on welfare, a bum paid by Jewish organizations to tell fabricated stories!"[6]

Realizing that the Croatian authorities could not help me further, I turned to the Serbs. Many of their compatriots had been among Ašner's victims, and an extradition request from that quarter would be more than justified. However, Austria was no more cooperative with Serbia than it had been with Croatia.

IN JULY 2005, I returned to Zagreb, where I met President Mesić, who remained as determined as ever: "We shouldn't look at Ašner as an ordinary old man," he said to me. "Old or not, it doesn't matter. We have no reason to protect men like him, fascists who used fascist methods."[7] Shortly thereafter, in September 2005, there was finally some progress on the legal front, as Croatia submitted an official request to Austria for Ašner's extradition to stand trial for his crimes in Požega.

I made numerous trips to Vienna to try to get things moving. In late January 2006, I traveled there to meet with the Austrian minister of justice, Karin Gastinger. Her predecessor, Dieter Boehmdoerfer, had been the personal lawyer of the extreme right leader Jörg Haider, ex-president of the Freedom Party of Austria (FPÖ) from 1986 to 2000, known for his populist and xenophobic policies, and accused several times of anti-Semitism. Karin Gastinger had begun her career in the FPÖ, so I was not at all optimistic about her position on this issue.

As expected, the meeting did not go well. Gastinger informed me that as far as Ašner was concerned it could not accede to the Croatian extradition request since Austria did not extradite its citizens. I argued that since Ašner had obviously lied in his application for Austrian citizenship and concealed the fact that he was a wanted man in Yugoslavia, his citizenship should be revoked. Gastinger rejected my suggestion and also dismissed the possibility of Asner being prosecuted in Austria, since according to the Austrian prosecutors, Ašner's alleged crimes came under the existing statute of limitations. When I pointed out to her that he had signed orders to deport people to their death, Gastinger admitted that the Austrian statutory limitation law was unsatisfactory from a moral standpoint and promised to try and reinvestigate Ašner's Austrian citizenship.

Used to unfulfilled promises by Austrian ministers and officials and therefore unconvinced by her statements, I called a press conference the next day in which I declared: "Austria is a paradise for Nazi criminals." This phrase made the headlines of *Der Standard*, *Die Presse*, and the *Krone Zeitung* and apparently led the Carinthian minister of the interior to announce that Ašner had in fact lost his Austrian citizenship in 1992, when he requested Croatian citizenship without getting prior permission to do so from the Austrian authorities.

Despite this progress, the former police chief in Požega was still not extradited to Zagreb, this time on the grounds that Ašner was not medically fit to be prosecuted. And thus Ašner was comfortably settled in the center of Klagenfurt, where he still lives today. This city of 90,000 inhabitants—famous for its Lake Wörthersee, mountains, many parks, and 23 castles in the surrounding area, and a favorite among tourists—is the capital of the province of Carinthia, which at the time was governed by the right-winger Jörg Haider.

At the end of 2006, I was back in Zagreb for another meeting with the attorney general. He confirmed that his talks with Vienna did not seem to be leading to anything promising. It seemed inevitable that Ašner would die peacefully at home in Austria.

It was under these adverse circumstances that the case again came before the court in Klagenfurt. Every few months, a hearing was called in order to determine whether Ašner was fit to be questioned about his past and possibly extradited. In 2007 came the unsurprising ruling: the Klagenfurt court cited two psychiatric reports stating that Ašner's health was too poor for him to be questioned and stand trial. Too old and weak, he was even said to be suffering from the onset of Alzheimer's.

CONVINCED THAT THE problem might well be the sympathy of the local doctors for the elderly Croatian (Carinthia was known for its high percentage of residents who, like Ašner, held xenophobic and anti-Semitic views, which explains the continued electoral success there of Joerg Haider), we applied to the court to supply our own geriatric expert, but in May 2007 our request for another medical report was refused. Around that time, President Mesić made an official visit to Austria. I begged his foreign affairs adviser to make sure he raised the Ašner case. This is what he wrote to me two days later: "Dear Efraim, the President mentioned the Ašner case in his talks with Prime Minister Gusenbauer, who did not react at all. My personal feeling was that he does not know anything about the case. So I spoke about the whole affair at length with the foreign policy advisor of President Fischer. He promised me he would do everything that is possible…Let us hope that it will have some effect."[8]

BY THE SPRING of 2008, my sense was that the Ašner affair was closed. All our initiatives to overcome Austria's opposition to Ašner's extradition, including a plan to secretly film him in order to prove that he was healthy enough to be prosecuted, had failed for one reason or another. Then an extraordinary succession of events occurred. The team from the *Sun* found Ašner in Klagenfurt. Photos of the alleged war criminal, who according to the court was supposedly too sick to stand trial, depicted him looking, for a man of 95, fit as a fiddle. These images were featured on the front page of the paper on June 16, 2008, and were then published all around the world.

Once again, in media interviews I leveled the accusation at Austria: "This country still constitutes a safe haven for Nazi criminals." If

Ašner was capable of sipping a glass of wine in a sidewalk café, supporting his soccer team, and wandering confidently through the streets on his own, his health was probably good enough to stand trial. I immediately sent an official letter to the Austrian minister of justice, Maria Berger:

> "The photos and video clips...made available to this office make it abundantly clear that Ašner is in good health, lucid and able to get around on his own, in contradiction to the finding of an Austrian court which ruled that he cannot be extradited to stand trial in Croatia due to ill health...Under these circumstances, there is absolutely no justification for the continued refusal to extradite this [suspected] Nazi war criminal to the country where he committed his [alleged] crimes, so that he can finally be held accountable for the hundreds of Serbs, Jews and Gypsies deported to Ustasha concentration camps, where the majority were brutally murdered. Since your appointment as justice minister, there has been a slight improvement in Austria's handling of Nazi war crimes cases, but much remains to be done if your country is to finally disprove its reputation as a paradise for Holocaust perpetrators. The immediate extradition of former Ustasha police chief Ašner would be a very welcome and major step in that direction."[9]

But it was all for nothing. A ministry spokesperson mulishly insisted that "the extradition process to Croatia was halted last year after the presentation of two reports from psychiatric specialists in 2006 and 2007," adding that the procedure could only be reopened if there was a new ruling from the court in Klagenfurt.[10] In turn, the court denied it was protecting any Nazis. "I formally deny that we protect alleged Nazi war criminals. Austria is a legitimate state, not Guantanamo. We do not relinquish our principles for political motives," Manfred Herrnhofer, a judge in Klagenfurt and vice president of the Association of Austrian Judges, declared. This same spokesperson suggested that a foreign specialist be appointed "to silence critics."[11]

On the same day, June 18, 2008, Ašner received the support of Jörg Haider himself. In an interview given to the newspaper *Der Standard*, Haider voiced his opposition to extradition: "He [Ašner] must end his life here. For a number of years, he's been a citizen of Klagenfurt, living peacefully among us. They're a very nice family and we're all very attached to them."[12]

Yet in an interview given to a Croatian television channel and broadcast on June 19, Milivoj Ašner admitted he had ordered the deportation of hundreds of Serbs, Jews, Gypsies, and communists during the war, claiming that nothing ever happened to citizens loyal to the Croatian state. Those who were not loyal, however, had to leave and were therefore sent back to their homelands. "I believe that if you are not a Croat and hate Croatia, then go back to your homeland, go to Belgrade, Vojvodina, to your homeland and let us Croats be…"[13]

In his interview with the *Sun* reporter, Milivoj Ašner said he was ready to face Croatian justice. After dismissing the accusations against him as "hilarious,"[14] he spoke of a possible trial in Zagreb, saying: "I'm utterly convinced that if the judges are honest, they'll acquit me, since I'm a Croat."[15] But he knew perfectly well that the Austrians would not let him down. Over the following days, the new psychiatric report ordered by the Klagenfurt district attorney's office concluded that the subject's senility ruled out any possibility of extradition. Ašner could continue watching the Euro 2008 matches in peace.

Faced by these adverse circumstances, I felt that I had to make one last effort to convince the Austrian authorities to take action, and I asked for a meeting with Justice Minister Berger. We met in Vienna in late June 2008, and I implored her to invite a foreign medical expert to examine Ašner to ensure the objectivity of the examination. At the meeting she refused to do so, but shortly thereafter, the Austrians announced that the Swiss geriatric expert Dr. Marc Graf was going to be invited for the task. But he was unable to do so for technical reasons, and months passed during which the Austrian authorities claimed that financial difficulties were holding up the new examination.[16] It was not until spring 2009 therefore, that a German expert named Norbert Nedopil examined Ašner, but his opinion merely confirmed the results of the three previous examinations, allowing the former Ustasha police chief the luxury of continuing to reside in one of Europe's best paradises for Nazi war criminals.

TWO

FIRST ENCOUNTERS
WITH THE HOLOCAUST

BROOKLYN, SPRING 1961.
My mother, normally a calm person, was unusually excited. She grabbed me and sat me down in the den opposite the television. "Efraim, sit down! You have to see this! Israel kidnapped Adolf Eichmann, one of the biggest Nazis, and his trial is starting today in Jerusalem and they are showing it now on TV. You have to see this!"

At this point, shortly before my bar mitzvah, I had very little idea of what this was all about. I knew that something terrible called the Shoa, or "Holocaust," had been carried out by the Nazis against the Jews in Europe, many of whom were murdered in concentration camps, but I had almost no knowledge of the details or the identity of those responsible, except Hitler. We had not studied it in school, nor was the subject spoken about a lot in our home. But the idea of Jews catching one of the big criminals and putting him on trial in Jerusalem sounded very exciting. I had never heard of Adolf Eichmann and certainly knew nothing about his role in the Final Solution. Only much later did I learn about his crimes, his initial role in the forced emigration of Jews from Nazi-occupied Austria and Czechoslovakia, and his subsequent career as the director of Department IV-B-4 of the Reichssicherheitshauptamt

(Reich Security Main Office) under Reinhardt Heydrich and later Ernst Kaltenbrunner, all of which made him the key operative in the implementation of the Nazis' plan to annihilate all of European Jewry.

As a twelve-year-old, I had little, if any, understanding at this point of what an amazing achievement Eichmann's capture by Israeli Mossad agents in Argentina was, or how important his trial would be. But the story made a strong impression on me, and it was the first time that the Holocaust penetrated my consciousness. Little did I realize what a profound impact it would have.

I FIRST SAW the light of day in New York City on August 5, 1948. The most important person in my life, alongside my parents, was my maternal grandfather, Samuel L. (Shmuel Leib) Sar,[1] who from the very beginning played an extremely active role in my upbringing and even gave me my name. My parents had already chosen the name Moshe for their first-born son, but two days before the official naming ceremony at my *brit milah* (circumcision), a telegram arrived from Paris, where my grandfather had been sent by the Joint Distribution Committee— American Jewry's premier overseas relief organization—to help provide for the religious needs of the survivors of the Holocaust. The terse message was, "Suggest name him Efraim." My parents gladly acceded, knowing of my grandfather's deep affection for his youngest brother, Efraim Zar, who had been murdered with his wife, Beyla, and two sons, Hirsh and Eliyahu, in Lithuania during the Holocaust. Perhaps it was the fact that I was named after the head of the only branch of our immediate family to be murdered in the Holocaust that determined my destiny.

For several years after my birth, we lived in Brighton Beach, but when I was 11 we moved to the Flatbush area of Brooklyn, a middle-class neighborhood populated primarily by second- or third-generation Italians, Irish, and Ashkenazi Jews like us. At this point in time, everyone was focused on the future and had little desire to dwell on the past, however tragic it might have been. Their America was that of John F. Kennedy, space conquest, democracy, and upward mobility. Practically everyone aspired to the "American way of life," with its ideal of the melting pot. My family, however, had no intention of assimilating into the general society and was determined to adhere to Orthodox Judaism, albeit in its "modern" variety, which sought to incorporate those elements of modernity that could enhance our lives but did not contradict *halacha* (Jewish religious law).

In that respect, my grandfather and my parents were excellent role models. Samuel Sar had helped create Yeshiva University (YU), the flagship educational institution of modern Orthodoxy in America, and served there as the dean of men and in many other important capacities during his 43 years of service. My father, Abraham, not only received his rabbinical ordination and his undergraduate and doctorate degrees at YU, but also worked as an educator in its institutions his entire life, primarily as the principal of YU High School for Boys in Brooklyn (known as BTA) and as the supervisor of three additional YU high schools. My mother, Esther, worked at Stern College for Women, the female affiliate of the same YU, as the director of student services, and all three were totally invested in the educational efforts to keep Judaism alive in America. They were convinced that this could only be done by the promotion of modern Orthodoxy, the only type of authentic Judaism that they believed could survive in an open Western society whose ideal was the melting pot.

IN THE AMERICA of the 1950s and 1960s, the Holocaust was not a subject for discussion or preoccupation in Flatbush or anywhere else. Not even for Jews. For my parents, the Holocaust was at this time neither more nor less than the most recent tragedy in a long list of suffering endured by our people. My maternal and paternal grandparents had settled in the United States in the early years of the twentieth century and had therefore been there a long time when World War II broke out.

My paternal grandfather, Aaron Zuriff,[2] had left Kolki, in western Ukraine, in 1907, hoping to raise enough money to pay for my grandmother, Pesyl (Bessie), and their four children to emigrate to the United States. But this plan was delayed by the outbreak of World War I, and it was only in 1920 that my grandfather's family rejoined him in Baltimore, where he had settled and was working as a salesman. My father was the product of their reunion, the only one of their five children born in the United States. Unfortunately, I never really got to know my paternal grandparents because we rarely saw them and because my grandfather spoke only Yiddish, a language I learned only after his death. The fact that he was already well over 70 when I was born was also no doubt a factor. My main memory of them was of our annual trip to Baltimore at the end of the school year. My grandfather would always question me about the portion of the Torah I was studying, and my father would translate his questions from Yiddish. The brief interchange invariably ended with a warm smile and a compliment.

My maternal grandparents were born in Lithuania at the end of the nineteenth century, my grandfather in Ligmiyan (Linkmenys) and my grandmother, Batya (Bertha), in Seduva, both part of czarist Russia. My grandfather was one of six boys, five of whom emigrated before the outbreak of World War II: one to the United States, one to Scotland, two to South Africa, and one to Eretz Yisrael (Palestine). Already married, he arrived in the United States in 1914, settling initially in Baltimore, and moved to New York City in 1919 when he was invited by Rabbi Dr. Bernard Revel to join the staff of what became YU. Since they lived in New York, we saw my maternal grandparents quite often, and they played an active role in our lives. It was at my grandfather's insistence that I was sent for elementary school to the Yeshiva of Flatbush, reputed for the quality of its Hebrew language instruction.

My maternal grandfather, who had high hopes for me to become a rabbi or a scholar of Jewish studies, believed that a solid knowledge of Hebrew was an absolute prerequisite for success in those fields. He therefore convinced my parents to send me there, even though the level of religious studies, especially of the Talmud, left much to be desired and most of the students were not observant. Besides studying Hebrew fairly intensively at school, I also spent eight weeks every summer for seven years at Camp Massad Bet, which was conducted entirely in Hebrew, from sports to theater to dinner menus.

Another important element of my Hebrew-language education was reading books. The librarian at my school, David Birnbaum, was truly extraordinary. The library housed thousands of Hebrew books, all of which he had read. When a child brought a book back, David would ask him a number of very simple questions about it. If the child's answers were correct, he would make a note of the number of pages in the borrowed book and then, at the end of the school year, give a prize to the child who had read the most. To be honest, the competition appealed to my competitive nature, and thus I found myself reading *Uncle Tom's Cabin*, many volumes of the *Tarzan* series, and even one or two books by Jules Verne, all in Hebrew rather than in English. This was quite unusual, to say the least, even for the Yeshiva of Flatbush, but it helped my proficiency enormously.

Our life in Flatbush in the 1960s was pleasant and relatively comfortable. We had moved from a fairly cramped apartment in Brighton Beach to a much more spacious one that occupied the entire second floor of a two-family house at 1191 East 14th Street, which was within walking distance of my school. My sister Elayne, two years my junior, and I had a lot of friends in the neighborhood. My parents liked their jobs very much in spite of the difficulties they faced; they were extremely dedicated to the schools where they worked and, of course, to their parent institution, YU. Although they both had important positions, their salaries were quite modest (miniscule in comparison to those of equivalent positions today), but we made do and never felt disadvantaged.

The main problems I faced growing up as a teenager had to do with my family's "prominence" or "notoriety" (depending on one's vantage point) in our insular community. As the principal of one of the two main high schools serving the modern Orthodox community in Brooklyn, my father was a local personality, and that meant that I often felt that I was living my life under public scrutiny. Any misstep by "Abe's son" or "little Zuroff" was immediately magnified. Add to this my grandfather's prominence as one of the key figures at YU and one of the leaders of the Mizrachi (religious Zionists) in America, and it is not hard to understand why I often felt undue pressure.

Another problem that I faced was my parents' expectations, which, while not unreasonable, posed a problem as I got older. My father had studied with two of the greatest Talmud teachers at YU, Rabbi Joseph

Soloveitchik (often referred to as "the Rov"), the most outstanding religious intellectual figure produced by modern Orthodoxy, and Rabbi Dr. Samuel Belkin, who, as the president of YU, led it to some of its greatest achievements. Naturally, he hoped that I would follow in his footsteps and study with the Rov, and become a rabbi/Jewish educator, but somehow that path never appealed to me. Although I have always been totally committed to modern Orthodoxy, becoming a rabbi was the last thing I wanted to do with my life. A good part of this had to do with my dislike of studying the Talmud, which was the most important subject in rabbinical studies. For some reason, I always preferred Tanach (the Bible) and especially my true love, Jewish history, which ultimately led me in a different academic direction.

I also have to admit to an emotional block against going in my father's footsteps, something very common among children of rabbis, many of whom either accept their "fate" or rebel against religion, at least temporarily. In my case, I developed a very active interest in sports from a young age with the guidance and encouragement of my father, who was an avid fan, and devoted an enormous amount of time to playing many different sports and to following my professional favorites—the Knicks, Nets, Orioles, Colts, Jets, and so on. In fact, my real fantasy while growing up was to be the first Orthodox Jew to play in the NBA rather than devote my life to the rabbinate or to Jewish education. But given my limited skills on the court (I was a starter for most of my senior year at YU on our Division III team with distinctly unspectacular statistics) and the obvious difficulties of remaining observant, that dream never came true.

IN JUNE 1967, the Holocaust entered our home in an unexpected way. Several weeks earlier, the Egyptian president Gamal Abdel Nasser had ordered the United Nations troops to leave the Sinai Peninsula and had blocked the Straits of Tiran, effectively stopping Israeli ships from reaching the southern port of Eilat, while Arab armies assembled on Israel's borders. War was imminent. Sitting in the den on the Sunday morning before the war broke out, I leafed through the *New York Times*. The "Week in Review" section had a map of the Middle East and a statistical summary of the opposing forces. Three columns of figures were given: the number of soldiers, the number of tanks, and the number of planes—those of the Arab countries on one side and those of Israel on the other. On one side there was a long list of figures and on the other small numbers for each category. The balance of power was unequal; the situation looked catastrophic. The thought went through my mind that, G-d forbid, there was going to be another Shoa, and Israel was going to be wiped out. Over the following days, all of us were glued to the news around the clock. In six days, however, Israel, thank G-d, annihilated its enemies. Caught up in the jubilation over the victory, I didn't dwell very much on my instinctive fear of another Holocaust, which was quite strange considering the lack of mention and discussion of that subject while I was growing up. It was only later that I learned that many other young Jews my age all over the world had reacted in the exact same manner. And it was those events of the heady days of June 1967 that propelled all of us in the direction of the Jewish homeland.

It would be hard to describe the depth of the elation and relief experienced by so many American Jews and their coreligionists around the world in the wake of Israel's stunning victory in the Six Days' War, which can only be understood in the light of the deep anxieties that had preceded it. The brazen threats of Arab leaders, who were bent on Israel's destruction and prepared their armies for its annihilation, evoked memories of the Jewish people's greatest tragedy that had been repressed since the end of World War II. Not only had the nascent Jewish state not been wiped off the map, but it had regained parts of the historic homeland of the Jewish people and reclaimed the Old City of Jerusalem and the Temple Mount, Judaism's most holy site. It was as if an antidote of Jewish military brilliance had begun to ease the pain of the losses suffered during the Holocaust.

Needless to say, my family and our close friends shared these feelings of exhilaration, pride, and adulation for Israel. This was hardly surprising, since we were always among the minority of American Jews who were active Zionists and who considered the State of Israel their true homeland. This level of commitment was not shared by most of our coreligionists in the United States, who supported Israel as part of their heritage but considered themselves first and foremost Americans.

This was certainly not the case in my home, where my maternal grand-father set the tone. While he was thankful to the United States, which had helped spare him the fate of his brother murdered in the Holocaust, and was appreciative of America's many advantages and opportunities, he always made it clear that our primary loyalty should be to the Jewish people. And since Judaism was not only a religion but also a national-ity, we therefore would always be American Jews rather than Jewish Americans.

From a very young age, I had internalized this distinction and real-ized that in this regard I was at odds with the majority of my fellow Jews, let alone general American society. One of the interesting dilem-mas I faced as a result came to a head in the fourth grade. At all the assemblies held in the Yeshiva of Flatbush, the custom was not only to sing the national anthems of the United States and Israel, but also to pledge allegiance to both countries. At age nine I suddenly realized that this might one day be a serious problem. What was I going to do if the two countries suddenly went to war? I knew that they were friends at that point, but one can never know what will happen. I opted for Israel in this case, continuing to sing both national anthems out of appreciation and respect for my country of residence, but making only one pledge of allegiance. If anything, these feelings were strengthened at Yeshiva University High School for Boys in Manhattan (MTA) and at college at Yeshiva University.

Given this mind-set, which was reinforced by the Six Days' War and my parents' enthusiastic reports about their first-ever visit to Israel in July 1967, it was only natural for me to decide to spend my junior year of college at the Hebrew University of Jerusalem. And although it meant that I would lose an entire season of varsity basketball, one of my great passions, by this point my interest in sports was definitely second-ary to my desire to experience life in the Jewish state.

IN THE FALL of 1968, I arrived in Jerusalem seeking to broaden my Jewish horizons, both in terms of my study of Jewish history, which had become my primary academic interest, and in terms of getting to know Israelis and Jews from other countries. In both respects, my

year at Hebrew University was incredibly rewarding. I had an opportunity to take courses that opened my eyes to various dimensions of
Judaism and Jewish life that I had hitherto been unaware of, as well
as advanced courses in Jewish history that were unavailable at Yeshiva
College.[3] One course in particular had a profound impact on my life.
Titled "Basic Issues in Contemporary Jewish Life," it was taught on
Sunday mornings at 8 AM, ostensibly the worst possible time slot of the
week, yet the lecture hall was almost always packed to capacity. Taught
by Dr. Michael Rosenak, a top expert in Jewish education who was an
alumnus of YU and had emigrated many years previously to Israel, it
dealt with a wide range of issues facing Judaism in the modern era,
especially in the State of Israel, that I had never even contemplated
while living in Brooklyn. The challenges posed by the establishment
of a modern, democratic Jewish state fascinated me and were among
the factors that encouraged me to seriously consider making Israel my
permanent home.

Outside the classroom as well, life in Jerusalem was very rewarding. My encounters with young Jews from all over the Western world,
as well as with the initial arrivals from the Soviet Union, were exciting, and the shared enthusiasm for Israel was very contagious and
enjoyable. And since I was completely fluent in Hebrew before my
arrival, my interactions with Israelis, who are (to a large extent correctly) considered relatively unfriendly to outsiders and newcomers,
were also relatively successful. Add to that the wonderful welcome I
received from my local relatives and it is not hard to understand why,
in the course of my junior year, I decided that Israel was the place that
I wanted to be and that I would make aliyah (immigration to Israel)
after completing my BA in the United States. One of the most important factors that convinced me to make the move was my feeling that
Israel was the place where Jewish history was being made on a daily
basis, as opposed to life in the Diaspora, where Jews were confined to
being spectators or, at best, cheerleaders in response to the exciting
unfolding events of contemporary Jewish history. What was clear was
that Israel offered a much broader spectrum of options for a fulfill-
ing Jewish life and opportunities for fuller participation in the reality

of Judaism, which was only beginning to become important in the United States.

I was sad to leave Jerusalem, but I knew that it would be for only a year. I returned to Yeshiva College for my senior year full of energy and enthusiasm, which found their primary outlet in campus activism on behalf of Israel and Soviet Jewry. Along with several of my classmates who had also spent the previous year at Hebrew University, I established the first-ever "Israel Aliyah Club" to encourage underclassmen to spend a year studying in Israel (on the assumption that that was the best way to interest them in making aliyah) and took to the streets often to defend Israel or to protest for the rights of Soviet Jews to emigrate there. I continued to play for the basketball team, but by this point, my heart and mind were clearly elsewhere, preparing for aliyah, a fact clearly reflected in my lackluster performance on the court. So after graduating in June 1970 with a degree in history, I made aliyah to Jerusalem, where I began my graduate studies at the Hebrew University. Unfortunately, my maternal grandfather was not alive to see this, but my parents were proud of my decision and gave me their unqualified blessing and support, even though they were sad that I would be far away from them. After all, in this regard, I was definitely a product of their education and ideology.

At this point, my goal was to pursue a career in the service of the Jewish people, and therefore, the university's Institute of Contemporary Jewry appeared to be the ideal choice for graduate studies. It offered the best program in the world on the history, sociology, and demography of the Jewish people in the twentieth century, and what better preparation could I have? The only question was, which specialization should I choose? In practical terms, the large-scale immigration to Israel from the Soviet Union made East European Jewry the obvious choice, but that would have required me to learn Russian, a prospect I did not find appealing because it meant having to master a completely new alphabet. That left the Jews of North and South America, those from Asia and Africa, Zionism, Jewish demography, or the Holocaust.

The mystics would no doubt claim that bearing the name of the Holocaust victim Efraim Zar left me no choice, but the decision was far more prosaic. By this time, it was clear to me that the program at the institute was primarily designed to train academics rather than activists or employees of Jewish defense or relief organizations and that it would take at least three years to complete my degree. Under those circumstances, I opted for the subject that interested me the most intellectually—the Holocaust, and more specifically, how such a disaster could have taken place. Given my activism on behalf of Jewish causes in the United States, I was especially curious about the response of American Jewry to the Shoa and the extent of their efforts to save Jews from the Nazis.

That decision was ultimately critical to my becoming a Nazi hunter, and I have never—not even for a moment—regretted it. Most of the material was fascinating and intellectually stimulating, and I had the privilege of studying with Professor Yehuda Bauer, who besides being an excellent historian was an even more superb lecturer. I used to sit in his classes glued to his every word, and it was he who inspired me (and numerous other students of his) to devote our lives to dealing with the Holocaust in some meaningful way.

IN THE MEANTIME, other aspects of my life were also going very well. In the fall of 1971, after Friday evening services at a Jerusalem synagogue that catered to university students, I was introduced by a female friend named Bracha Rose to a very attractive young woman named Elisheva Bannett, who was her guest for Shabbat. She had just broken up with her boyfriend and was visiting Bracha, who had offered to help her recover by introducing her to another man. But before that meeting could be arranged, however, I thought that I might be interested in her myself, and I tried to engage her in conversation. One of the things that intrigued me and aroused my interest was that she told me she was majoring in math and physics at Bar-Ilan University. That combination amazed me, since I had always considered those subjects to be incredibly difficult; moreover, all the young women I knew were either planning to be teachers or were studying social work or psychology. When Elisheva told me that her parents were Americans who had come to Israel as pioneers in 1950, it only increased my desire to get to know her more intimately. Later on in our relationship, we even discovered that our maternal grandfathers had been friendly with each other in the old country and had both been active in the Mizrachi movement in America.

A year later, we got married at Kfar Haroe, a community of religious farmers and professionals near Hadera, where she grew up, and we began our life together in a tiny apartment in Jerusalem on Hapalmach Street. In early 1974, our eldest daughter, Avigayil, was born, and she was followed by two sons, Itamar (1976) and Elchanan (1981), and another daughter, Ayelet (1984), a foursome that are our pride and joy.

WITH EDUCATION AND love taken care of, what remained to be done was to find employment. My first foray into the Israeli job market proved rather traumatic. I was hired for a part-time job at the Ministry of Religion by Rabbi Zev Gotthold, who was responsible for running a special intensive six-week program for prospective converts to Judaism. The work was fascinating and very challenging, and Rabbi Gotthold, a true renaissance man who combined deep erudition in Jewish sources with extensive knowledge of art and music, was a wonderful boss. The problem was, however, that some of the key officials at the ministry, which was basically controlled by a bevy of benighted political hacks, were not enthusiastic about assisting Christians to convert to Judaism. They therefore decided to make trouble for Rabbi Gotthold by finding all sorts of excuses to refrain from paying me my salary. Luckily, I had no career ambitions in this field and ultimately was paid after I sued the ministry with the active help of Rabbi Gotthold.

By June 1973, I had finally finished my course work for an MA at the institute and began looking for my first full-time job. Friends suggested that, given my specialization, I should apply to Yad Vashem, Israel's national memorial museum to the victims of the Holocaust, which also had the world's premier library, archives, and research center on the subject. Luckily, they were looking at the time for someone who could edit historical research and translate scholarly articles from Hebrew into English, and this part-time job led shortly thereafter to my appointment as assistant editor of *Yad Vashem Studies*, at that time the only annual publication totally devoted to Holocaust research. Besides being the most important place in the world to study the Shoa, Yad Vashem was also a wonderful place to get to know survivors. Indeed, many of the leading lights of the institution—its chairman, Dr. Yitzchak Arad; senior researchers such as Professor Yisrael Gutman; the director of the archives, Dr. Yosef Kermisz; my boss, Dr. Livia Rothkirchen—had all survived in Nazi-occupied Europe, and it was the daily contact and interaction with them that helped clinch my decision to make the Holocaust my life's work, although it was not yet clear at this point exactly what form that would take.

My duties as assistant editor of *Yad Vashem Studies* were basically an extension of my academic studies and therefore quite beneficial, but there were other aspects of my job that I found more exciting. Thus, for example, because of my fluency in English, which was relatively rare at Yad Vashem in those days, I was often called upon to guide visiting VIPs in the museum and teach them the history of the Holocaust. Among the dignitaries whom I accompanied were Anis Mansour, the editor of the Egyptian weekly *October*, who came with Anwar Sadat on his historic visit to Israel in 1978; the Los Angeles mayor Tom Bradley; and the U.S. representative Charles Vanik, whose cosponsorship of the historic Jackson-Vanik Amendment in the U.S. Congress, which linked free trade with freedom of emigration, helped open the gates of the Soviet Union for hundreds of thousands of Soviet Jews seeking to come to Israel. I also was among the guides for the entourage of the U.S. president Richard Nixon. I really enjoyed giving these tours because I felt that I was contributing to Israel's efforts to explain herself to the world more effectively and convincingly.

Although I had a full-time position at Yad Vashem, I was simultaneously continuing my studies and research at Hebrew University. I took my MA exams and wrote a thesis on the American Vaad ha-Hatzala (Rescue Committee), a group established by Orthodox rabbis in November 1939, initially to save rabbis and yeshiva students exclusively; subsequently it expanded its activities to try to save any and all Jews from the Nazis. This project, which dealt with the Vaad's initial efforts, was in certain respects a personal quest, since the question in the history of the Holocaust that preoccupied me more than any other was: What had American Jewry in general, and the Orthodox community in particular, done to help their fellow Jews in Nazi-occupied Europe? Thus, I was thrilled to learn from my mentor, Professor Bauer, with whom I consulted about a thesis topic, that Orthodox rabbis in the United States had created their own rescue agency; that the subject had never been fully researched; and that the Vaad's archives were in storage at, of all places, YU. From my perspective, this was a dream topic, and I enthusiastically started to do the research, part of which I completed for my MA degree in 1975, leaving the rest for a planned PhD thesis.

THREE

"I DID NOT FORGET YOU"

AS I APPROACHED my thirtieth birthday in 1978, life in Jerusalem continued on course. I had obtained approval for the topic of my PhD dissertation, which was to be an expansion and continuation of my MA thesis on the Vaad ha-Hatzala. The official title was "The Response of Orthodox Jewry in the United States to the Holocaust: The Activities of the *Vaad ha-Hatzala* Rescue Committee 1939–1945." The problem was, however, that I had no time to devote to my research. Like most Israeli graduate students in the humanities who were married and had children, I was working at several jobs simultaneously—full-time at Yad Vashem and also at two side jobs, or *chalturot*, as they are referred to in Hebrew. One involved teaching a course on the history of the Holocaust at a yeshiva for post–high school Americans, and the other one involved doing research for Bar-Ilan University on the Holocaust-era archives of a local ultra-Orthodox political party. And if this was not bad enough, it was clear to me that I had to go to the United States and to Switzerland for at least a few months to do archival research before I could start writing my thesis.

Just as I was struggling with these difficult circumstances, a solution materialized out of the blue. I received a phone call from Rabbi Marvin Hier, whom I had never heard of at this point, who had just opened a new Holocaust center in Los Angeles and was looking for a Holocaust scholar to serve as the director. Apparently, someone at YU had recommended me, and he wanted to know whether I might be interested in the job. We agreed to meet one morning at Yad Vashem to discuss his proposal. To be honest, although I was intrigued by the offer, the prospect of taking Elisheva, Avigayil (aged four), and Itamar (aged two) to Los Angeles for an extended period did not sound particularly appealing.

There are, however, few people as persuasive as Rabbi Hier, who has superb marketing skills. Not only did he offer me the challenge of helping create the center's new museum, archives, and library, but he also spoke of his ambitious plans to produce movies on the Holocaust (stressing the center's proximity to Hollywood) and promised that I would also be able to do the necessary research for my doctorate. His condition, however, was that I come to Los Angeles for at least two years. I originally had no such intention, and frankly, Rabbi Hier's vision for the new Holocaust center seemed at least a bit exaggerated, if not bombastic, but as I subsequently learned, he is the kind of person who should never be underestimated. Thus, when he won an Oscar for the best documentary film of 1981 ("Genocide"), my father reminded me of how skeptical I had been of Rabbi Hier's boast, only three years previously, about how the new center would produce uniquely successful movies about the Holocaust. In any event, I went home and discussed the idea with Elisheva, who, to my surprise, did not seem in the least fazed by the prospect of moving to Los Angeles for two years, and that clinched the deal.

Before leaving for California, I met Simon Wiesenthal for the first time. At this point, in late spring 1978, he was the world's most famous Nazi hunter, an individual who, thanks to years of dedicated efforts to track down the leading Holocaust perpetrators, had become the personification of the quest for justice. Perhaps even more important, he was among the few individuals who helped keep alive the memory of the Holocaust during the three decades immediately after World War II, when there was little interest in the subject. As a survivor who, together with his wife, Cyla, had lost 89 family members in the Shoa, he was determined to make sure that the world would never forget it.

He was also one of Rabbi Hier's personal heroes, which was a major reason that the rabbi sought to name the new Holocaust center in Los Angeles after him. In that respect, Rabbi Hier's choice was brilliant since it would give the nascent institution instant name recognition and respectability, which proved to be so important in our political campaigns and fundraising efforts. And even though there was no official organizational link between LA and Wiesenthal's Dokumentationszentrum (Documentation Center) in Vienna, a mutually beneficial relationship was created between the two institutions, and thus it was only natural that Mr. Wiesenthal would want to meet the new director of the Holocaust center that bore his name.

Our meeting took place at Yad Vashem, and it did not begin auspiciously. Assuming that I, a budding Holocaust historian, must certainly know fluent German, Simon began speaking to me in that language. When I responded that I preferred speaking in English because my German was not that good, his disappointment was clearly palpable. "Nicht gut, nicht gut" (Not good, not good), he muttered, and I suddenly felt that perhaps my plan to go to the new Wiesenthal Center was not such a good idea after all. But as soon as we began discussing the history of the Holocaust, the mood changed, the tension eased, and I had the distinct impression that I had passed the history test with flying colors, even though my German was not as good as Simon hoped. I had no idea at this point what influence, if any, Wiesenthal wielded in Los Angeles, but at least I had not lost my job even before I began.

I DID NOT go straight to the United States from Israel; instead, I visited the places that I had studied so much in recent years. For the first time in my life, I went to the concentration camps in Poland. At the time, Poland had no diplomatic relations with Israel; the Poles, following Moscow's lead, had broken off ties with Israel in the wake of the Six Days' War. Luckily, I had an American passport, so I left my Israeli one at the Israeli consulate in Zurich. Thus, I passed for an ordinary American tourist in Poland, whereas in reality I was a Holocaust scholar going to see the death camps of Auschwitz, Treblinka, Majdanek, and

Chelmno. In 1939, there were 3.3 million Jews in Poland. Six years later, there were just 380,000.[1] I don't think the trip could have been any more saddening or depressing. The mountains of shoes at Auschwitz and Majdanek, the terrifying silence in the fields of Treblinka and Chelmno—they would all become permanently engraved within my consciousness.

What shocked me the most in Poland was the almost complete absence of Jews. The emptiness. While there were miniscule communities in the large cities, where tens of thousands of Jews had previously lived, there were none in the smaller towns and villages where Jewish life, despite no small degree of anti-Semitism and increasing economic hardships, had previously existed for centuries. One could wander through Warsaw, Krakow, Lodz, or Lublin and hardly encounter any signs of Jewish life, past or present. I spent a lot of time walking in Warsaw, pacing what had been the most famous ghetto in the world. After the war, the area had been entirely rebuilt and had become an ordinary residential district, its previous identity obliterated to such an extent that I wondered whether the current inhabitants knew what had happened there several decades earlier. I left the country overwhelmed, sad, and depressed, convinced that the only way a Jew should make such a journey was on one's way *to* Israel, not in the opposite direction.

I FLEW FROM Warsaw to Amsterdam, and on the way, the emotions which I had kept inside while in Poland burst out and I found myself crying the tears that I had not dared to shed even in the camps. It was therefore wonderful to meet Elisheva and the kids after such a traumatic and intense experience. We flew from Holland to New York to spend some time with my parents and shortly thereafter, in late August 1978, arrived in Los Angeles, where we settled in a small two-bedroom apartment not far from the Wiesenthal Center and began to try to adjust to life in Tinsel Town. Living in Los Angeles and working at the center were very different from living in Jerusalem and working at Yad Vashem. In some respects, I felt as if I had landed on another planet, but I was determined to try my best, if not to fit in, at least to succeed professionally and realize the goals I came there to achieve.

The distance between Yad Vashem and the Wiesenthal Center became more tangible soon after my arrival in Los Angeles that August, when Elisheva and I were invited, along with the entire staff of the center, to the Hollywood premiere of the film *The Boys from Brazil*, a blockbuster directed by Franklin J. Schaffner, based on a novel by Ira Levin, the author of *Rosemary's Baby*. The film could be summed up as follows: Ezra Lieberman, a famous Nazi hunter who lives in Vienna (and whose character clearly was based on Wiesenthal), receives a call from a young Jew settled in Paraguay. The latter thinks that there is a plot, hatched by former Nazi officials led by Josef Mengele, to create clones of Adolf Hitler all over the world, enabling the coming of the Fourth Reich. The plot is uncovered, and Mengele flees to Canada with Lieberman in pursuit. In the end, the two men meet and fight, and Mengele dies, torn to pieces by the Dobermans unleashed upon him. With a superb cast, it was a good film—even if the screenwriters took a bit too much liberty with historical truth. Regardless, the profits of the premiere were donated to the center and afforded us a massive, unexpected, and free publicity campaign. Still, how far away Yad Vashem seemed to me.

Simon, who was celebrating his seventieth birthday at the time, had come from his home in Vienna especially for the premiere and spent a few days at the Wiesenthal Center, which had prepared several events in his honor. I will never forget the tears running down his cheeks when he joined us for Friday night services and we began to sing "Lecha Dodi," the beautiful song describing how we greet the Sabbath as a beloved bride. Simon, who was not observant, but obviously recalled these songs and prayers from his childhood in Buczacz, Galicia (then Poland, today Ukraine), was overcome by emotion, which in turn moved all those present, myself included.

After our brief encounter in Jerusalem, I was looking forward to my first real opportunity to get to know him and learn more about his life's work. I knew, of course, who he was, but I had never read any of his books, nor had the subject of Nazi hunting been of any particular interest to me. We discussed his ongoing debate with my mentor, Professor Bauer, over whether non-Jews murdered by the Nazis should be counted among the victims of the Holocaust. (Simon thought they should, but Bauer disagreed, claiming that the Jews' fate under the Third Reich was unique, and that was the true meaning of the term "Holocaust," which applied only to the Nazis' Jewish victims.) I also listened intently to his prophetic prediction that the massive exodus of Jews from the Soviet Union would afford us access to a tremendous amount of information, hitherto unknown, about the mass murder of Jews in that geographic region.

I found Simon to be a very clever person with an excellent, if at times slightly off-color, sense of humor. He was an extremely astute observer of politics and the human condition. He also had a wonderful ability to convey principles and important concepts in a phrase or sentence. Thus, I heard for the first time that "those who ignore the murderers of the past, pave the way for the murderers of the future," and agreed very much with his observation that "Democracy is not a present. It must be defended every day."

Best of all was his wonderful explanation of why he chose to become a Nazi hunter rather than returning to his original profession as an architect. Simon related that that he was often asked that question: "Before the war, you were a promising and well-reputed architect. Why did you not resume your profession afterwards? Europe was in ruins and there was so much rebuilding to do! You could have had a great career!" And his reply was: "I am not a religious man, but I believe in a world after this one. I am convinced that after our death we will all go to heaven, and there we will meet the victims of the Holocaust. The first question they will ask us is: 'You were lucky, you survived... You kept your lives like so many gifts. But what did you do with them? What have you done with your life?' Some of us will reply, 'I became a businessman'; others, 'I became a lawyer'; still others, 'I became a teacher.' Me, I want to be able to give them just one answer: 'I did not forget you.'"

More than any other story, observation, aphorism, or joke, that response has remained with me ever since, inscribed in my heart and mind. And when I have to explain why we continue to try to bring Nazi war criminals to justice, I always note our obligation to the victims, something Simon Wiesenthal made sure we would never forget.

FOUR

THE OFFICE OF SPECIAL INVESTIGATIONS AND THE CASE OF KAZYS PALČIAUSKAS

SIMON WIESENTHAL WAS approaching his seventieth birthday when I began working at the Wiesenthal Center, but he was full of energy and still very active as a Nazi hunter. The center bore Wiesenthal's name out of respect and admiration for his work, but the search for Holocaust perpetrators was initially not even on the agenda of our newly established institution, as no one had any intention or desire to replace Wiesenthal. The center's original mission was primarily in the fields of commemoration and education, with some plans to support Holocaust research. In fact, the center's original full name included the words "for Holocaust Studies," and it was envisioned as a standard "Holocaust center," one of many such institutions beginning to be established all over the United States.

This was hardly surprising, considering the backgrounds of the center's leaders. The Wiesenthal Center was the brainchild of Rabbi Hier, an Orthodox Jew born in New York in 1938, who had been extremely successful as a pulpit rabbi in Vancouver, British Columbia, and was known as an excellent speaker and fund-raiser. His trusted associate, Rabbi Abraham Cooper, also an Orthodox rabbi born in New York (in 1950), had headed the educational institutions in Rabbi Hier's synagogue in Vancouver. Both were experienced Jewish educators who viewed the Wiesenthal Center primarily as an educational tool to help raise Holocaust consciousness on the West Coast and simultaneously help strengthen Jewish identity and fight against assimilation. In Rabbi Hier's grand vision, the center was complemented by its sister institution, YU of Los Angeles, which he established around the same time and on the same premises, and which offered an intensive program in Jewish religious studies.

During the two years that I worked at the Wiesenthal Center, however, two very important developments took place that had a significant impact on its evolution from a Holocaust center whose primary goal was education to a classic activist Jewish defense organization, whose major objective is to combat anti-Semitism and racism and defend Jewish rights the world over (though this also has an educational dimension). The first was the arrival of Warren Frazier, a young lawyer with extensive political lobbying experience in Sacramento, who helped Rabbis Hier and Cooper in their initial political initiatives in California. The success of these campaigns on behalf of oppressed and endangered Soviet and Ethiopian Jewry—to defend Israel and fight against anti-Semitism, which was reflected in increased fund-raising, for example—led to greater emphasis on these activities at the expense of topics such as Holocaust research. As the only major Jewish organization with headquarters on the West Coast, the center rapidly filled an important vacuum and attained national prominence.

The second development was the establishment in 1979 of the Office of Special Investigations (OSI) of the U.S. Justice Department, created to take legal action against Nazi war criminals and collaborators living in America. Its establishment marked the culmination of a lengthy process of investigation and political lobbying that had been initiated in the wake of revelations by immigration officials such as Tony De Vito and investigative journalists such as Howard Blum that numerous East European Nazi war criminals and collaborators had immigrated to the

United States after World War II. The political struggle to ensure that legal action would be taken against these individuals was led by two members of the U.S. House of Representatives, Elizabeth Holtzman of Brooklyn and Joshua Eilberg of Philadelphia. The practical implication of this development for the Wiesenthal Center was that once Nazi war criminals in the United States became an important public issue, the center naturally sought to become involved.

A key element of the OSI's work was to find and interview Holocaust survivors as potential witnesses, but its initial efforts to do so proved to be much more problematic than it had originally anticipated. That is what brought the OSI investigator Bill Crane to my office in Los Angeles in the spring of 1979. He had come to California to meet with Holocaust survivors but had not imagined it would be so difficult. The survivors refused to speak to him, either because they were suspicious or because they did not want to talk about their traumatic memories. Who was this man, claiming to defend them, when he was not even Jewish? No one had heard of the OSI. The survivors worried he was a spy, a journalist, or an informer. Crane therefore came to ask for our help, hoping that those he sought to question would be more communicative if he came to them with the recommendation of the Wiesenthal Center.

Bill hardly had to ask me to help him: I was dying to. This charming man was obviously sincere in his efforts. He was not Jewish, and his family had not suffered from the Holocaust in any way, yet he could not bear the idea of Nazi criminals living peacefully in the United States. I wrote a letter for him to present to survivors, which included the following statements: "Without witnesses, there can be no trial. Without trials, these assassins will continue their happy and peaceful existences, living out a tranquil retirement, laughing at the powerlessness of the Jewish people and of all those who support justice and morality."

With hindsight, I realize that Bill Crane was among those who helped turn me into a Nazi hunter and motivated my increasingly active involvement in this area in the United States. In fact, in the wake of our meeting, I launched the first-ever attempt to create a database of all the Holocaust survivors living in North America in order to help find potential witnesses for the cases being investigated by the OSI.

SEVERAL MONTHS LATER, in October, I went to Washington, D.C., to meet the director of the OSI, Walter Rockler. Given my excellent working relationship with Bill Crane, I was expecting to meet a man every bit as sympathetic and passionate. But Rockler seemed completely indifferent to what I was saying to him. I was flabbergasted. He seemed to know relatively little about the Holocaust, he confused cases, and he mistook names—he even confessed that he had never been to Israel and, what is more, despite being a Jew, said he didn't understand why anyone would want to set foot there. I left his office saying to myself that if this man was in charge of hunting down Nazis in the United States, the war criminals had nothing to worry about. They could continue gardening and playing peaceful rounds of golf.

A year later, I was invited by CBS in Los Angeles to take part in a program. While I was waiting in the studios before the show, I was unpleasantly surprised to find that I would be on air with Walter Rockler. I prepared to endure the worst day of my life. But things turned out differently; I was face-to-face with another Rockler. He proved to be not only friendly but also very erudite, with a good command of the events of the Holocaust and the fate of the Nazis who had escaped after the war. He told me that he had recently returned from Israel, where he had gone for the first time in his life, and that the trip had greatly impressed him. I couldn't believe it. Did he suffer from a split personality? Had he been playing with me when I had met him in Washington?

When the program was over, I told him that my posting in Los Angeles was about to come to an end and that I was going back to Israel. Working with the OSI had fascinated me, and I was sorry that our collaboration was ending. So I made him a proposition: "It would be very advantageous for you to have someone on the ground, in Israel. There are so many witnesses to the Holocaust there and so many archival documents to which you don't have access at present. Besides, I know the subject quite well and have a graduate degree in the history of the Holocaust from Hebrew University, the world's best such program."

He agreed to hire me as a researcher for the OSI, initially for a duration of two months.

IN THE SUMMER of 1980, I returned to Jerusalem, delighted to be back. To be honest, as a historian, I had not learned much during my stint as director of the Wiesenthal Center, which had no operations to focus on scholarly research. At the same time, living so close to Hollywood had enabled me to discover the world of the media: how it worked, what its expectations and interests were, how to approach it, and how best utilize it. I learned that, thanks to the media, it is possible to reach the widest public possible and, through that connection, to advance one's ideas. And I fully intended to use this new knowledge in Israel.

I accepted a second job in addition to my assignment with the OSI: I was the second-in-command of a department of the Jewish Agency that dealt with Jewish education for religious youth in Israel and abroad. I gradually realized, however, that this job did not suit me at all. On the one hand, I was wasting my expertise as a Holocaust scholar; on the other hand, I realized that my chances of making a meaningful contribution at the Agency were really minimal. The organization was too bureaucratic and hidebound. Even if I had devoted myself to it 24 hours a day, I would not have made one iota of progress. I therefore handed in my notice and began to work for the OSI full-time.

Working full-time for the OSI had several extremely positive aspects. Most important, I really loved what I was doing and found my job deeply satisfying, especially when the documents or the information I found in Israel proved helpful for the successful prosecution of a suspect, as it did in the case of Kazys Palčiauskas, the mayor of Kaunas, Lithuania. Additional advantages were the opportunity to expand my knowledge of the Holocaust, the flexibility of the job (I was paid by the hour), and the salary, certainly good by Israeli standards.

There were, however, several issues that I found problematic. One was that I had been hired as a contract researcher, which meant that I was employed for a maximum of only six months at a time and had absolutely no job security or any of the benefits given to regular government employees. Another was the OSI's refusal to allow me a more public profile in Israel, which I believed could considerably improve our chances of finding potential witnesses. This decision was apparently a result of the OSI's desire not to "trespass" on the territory of the

Israeli police and its Nazi War Crimes Investigation Unit, whose job it was to find potential witnesses in Israel. The physical distance from Washington also played a negative role, since it would be many months before I met the attorneys I was working for, and very often the flow of information was only in one direction, from Jerusalem to the United States, and not vice versa.

Despite these drawbacks, I very much enjoyed the research and investigative aspects of the work and learned a tremendous amount about the role played by East European collaborators in the implementation of the Final Solution. This was one of the very important historical aspects that had been relatively ignored until then by historians, who naturally focused on the main German and Austrian initiators and implementers of the Holocaust. The fact that the vital role played by the Nazis' East European accomplices in Lithuania, Latvia, Estonia, Ukraine, Belarus, and Croatia, and so on had not been accorded sufficient scrutiny partly explains how so many Holocaust perpetrators succeeded in immigrating to the four largest Anglo-Saxon democracies (the United States, Canada, Australia, and Great Britain) in the immediate aftermath of World War II. In fact, within less than a decade after the end of the war, many thousands of Nazi war criminals and collaborators had succeeded in fooling the immigration authorities of these countries and had begun new lives for themselves and their families far away from the scene of their crimes.

To these cases, which can only be explained by a combination of ignorance, bureaucratic incompetence, and apathy (manifest in the utter failure to catch those who lied about their wartime activities), we must add a small number of German rocket scientists who had committed war crimes by working inmates to death in the creation and manufacture of the V-2 rockets in the Dora concentration camp. They were knowingly brought to the United States by the American authorities to exploit their scientific expertise and for fear that they might be abducted by the Soviets. Another group in this category comprised individuals who were recruited as potential anti-Soviet spies by U.S. and Allied intelligence agencies. The number of such persons was, however, relatively small in comparison to the total number of Nazi war criminals admitted as refugees to the United States.

Among the Nazi war criminals admitted, there was a wide range of culpability and complicity that spanned the entire spectrum of Nazi criminality, from high-ranking initiators of mass annihilation to lower-level functionaries whose involvement did not include personal participation in murder. The criminals could be roughly divided into two major categories: those who directly facilitated or committed murder or actively assisted in an act of execution, and those who participated in persecution but were not actively involved in actual murder.

Those in the first category must be divided according to the severity of their crimes, that is, whether they were mass murderers or were killers of individuals. The mass murderers included either commanders of concentration camps, such as the Estonian Karl Linnas of the Tartu camp, or those who were actively involved in mass annihilation over a wide geographic area and for a considerable length of time, such as the members, and especially officers, of murder squads run by those such as Major Antanas Impulevičius, the commander of the infamous Twelfth Lithuanian Auxiliary Police Battalion. The killers of individuals included those who committed murder in a specific geographic area during a limited time period and whose crimes therefore differed quantitatively from the crimes of those in the initial group.

Those in the second category—those who played an active role in the persecution of Jews but did not personally commit murder—can also be divided into several subcategories. At the top of the list are the leaders of quisling collaborationist regimes or administrations that facilitated the implementation of Nazi directives and German rule. A second subcategory is high- or middle-level administrators who implemented the Nazis' discriminatory policies against the Jews but did not personally commit murder, such as Kazys Palčiauskas. Their assistance in the preliminary stages of the Final Solution was critical, but stopped short of participation in murder. The final subcategory is of the propagandists, those who conducted the war of words against the Jews and other enemies of the Reich and helped pave the way for their annihilation, such as the Romanian Valerian Trifa or the Russian Vladimir Sokolov-Samarin.

As might be expected, there were relatively few in the category of Nazi leaders or mass murderers who opted to seek refuge in the United States. The most notorious were the Croatian minister of the interior and justice Andrija Artuković, who was responsible for the network of concentration camps established by the Croatian fascist Ustasha to carry out the genocide of the local Serbs, Jews, and Gypsies; and the above-mentioned Major Impulevičius, whose unit murdered tens of thousands of Jews in Lithuania and in Belarus during the years 1941–1943.

The preponderant majority of those who found haven in the United States were members of the local and police security units and concentration camp guards who implemented the Final Solution in countless cities, towns, and villages all over Eastern Europe. They were virtually anonymous individuals whose crimes in the service of the Nazis were motivated by anti-Semitism fueled by patriotism, greed, jealousy, and political opportunism. Posing as innocent refugees, they fled to the bastions of Western democracy believing that they would never be held accountable for their crimes, either because they assumed that their identities and misdeeds remained unknown or because of their sterling anti-Communist credentials in a world dominated by the Cold War. But that assumption held true only for the first three and a half decades after the war. Once the OSI was established and began working effectively, the situation changed dramatically.

MY ASSIGNMENT FOR the OSI had two components. My primary task was archival research for documents, testimony, and information that could help clarify the wartime activities of the suspects being investigated by the OSI. It was relatively rare that I was able to find any specific references to the subjects of our investigations, but I was often able to provide a lot of background material on the events of the Holocaust in the place where the subject operated. My success or failure in this regard usually depended on the size of the Jewish community in that location. The larger the number of Jews in the pre-war community or who lived there under Nazi occupation, the greater the chances of finding relevant material and survivors who might be potential witnesses. The search for the latter was the investigative or "detective" component of my job, since many of the accounts or interviews I read did not indicate the address of the survivor. In other cases, the information had been recorded many years previously, which made it difficult to track down the potential witness.

I spent the overwhelming majority of my time in the archives and library of Yad Vashem, Israel's national remembrance authority for the victims of the Holocaust. Established by a law of the Knesset (Israeli parliament) in 1953, it combined a historical museum and memorial with the world's largest library and archives on the history of the Holocaust. Having worked at Yad Vashem for almost five years before going to Los Angeles to work at the Wiesenthal Center, I felt completely at home there and was the beneficiary of the generous assistance of many of my former colleagues, who were willing to go out of their way to arrange for me to stay in the building after hours or to circumvent bureaucratic regulations to facilitate my research.

In retrospect, I have to admit that on a certain level, the results of my work at Yad Vashem, as well as at the other Israeli Holocaust archives where I did research—Lohamei ha-Gettaot (Ghetto Fighters' House), Moreshet, Wienner Library at Tel Aviv University, and Bar-Ilan University—were relatively disappointing, because it was extremely rare to find any direct references to the subjects of our investigations or even to the police units or concentration camps that many of them served in. There were several reasons for this phenomenon, which I initially found surprising, since Yad Vashem was reputed to be the place to search for all the answers to any questions related to the Shoa. As I learned the hard way, however, that was not the case.

The most important reason for the lacunae in the Yad Vashem archives regarding the perpetrators was the fact that as the central remembrance authority established by the State of Israel on behalf of the entire Jewish people, its primary focus was on documenting Jewish responses to Nazi oppression rather than on the intricacies of the process of mass annihilation and the identities of the perpetrators. The Jewish responses were considered uniquely important since they had been ignored or distorted during the initial three decades after the war by historians such as Raul Hilberg, who based his monumental, pioneering study of the Final Solution, *The Destruction of the European Jews*, almost exclusively on Nazi documents. Hilberg's book painted a particularly unflattering picture of the response of Jewish leaders and communities to the Nazi onslaught. Yad Vashem, therefore, considered it a holy mission to counter the misleading image of excessive Jewish passivity and made documenting Jewish responses the primary focus of its archival acquisitions.

Another reason for this emphasis on how Jews reacted in the face of Nazi oppression was the initial obsession in Israel with the question of armed resistance by Jews against the Nazis. Anxious to disprove the canard that Jews went to their deaths "like sheep to slaughter," Yad Vashem and numerous Israeli Holocaust researchers sought to prove the opposite by documenting every possible instance in which Jews under Nazi occupation fought against their oppressors. This explains why practically every survivor interviewed by the institution was asked, "Who smuggled the first gun into the ghetto?" Practically no one, however, was questioned about the identity of the local collaborationist police chief and the role played by his policemen in the roundups, deportations to death camps, or the murders by his policemen.

Yet another very important reason was that, in many cases, those who survived did not know the identities of the killers. This was particularly true of those who escaped murder by the Einsatzgruppen (mobile killing units) and their collaborators from local killing squads. In such cases, there was virtually no possibility that they could identify the murderers, with whom they had never had any contact either before or after the murders. This was less the case when the murders were carried out by local police forces, some of whom were known to the Jews in that community, although in such cases, the larger the town or city, the less chance there was that local Jews could identify the key perpetrators.

Despite these obstacles, there were cases in which the material I found in Israel was very helpful in the investigation of criminals living in the United States. One of the most important such cases was that of Kazys Palčiauskas, the mayor of the city of Kaunas (Kovno in Yiddish and Hebrew), Lithuania. The interwar capital of Lithuania

(Vilnius was then part of Poland and was disputed territory between the two countries), Kaunas was home to 30,000 Jews. It was the country's second-largest Jewish community and a most important center of Jewish political and religious activity, learning, and culture. Starting immediately after the retreat of Soviet troops (Lithuania had been occupied by the Soviet Union in June 1940) and even before the arrival of the first Nazis, large-scale pogroms, in which hundreds were murdered, were carried out against the Jews of the city by gangs of anti-Semitic, ultranationalist Lithuanian vigilantes. On July 10, 1941, Palčiauskas, who had been appointed the mayor of Kaunas and who was a prominent member of the Lithuanian Activist Front, which represented the local Lithuanian population, issued orders for all the Jews living in Kaunas to move into a ghetto in Viliampole, the most run-down section of the city, by August 15, 1941, and to wear a yellow star on their clothing. In addition, he forbade them from walking on the sidewalks and supervised the confiscation of local Jewish property.

In the meantime, the mass murders that began with the killing of 900 Jewish men seized at random and 500 "intellectuals" liquidated in August culminated with the massacre of close to 10,000 Jewish men, women, and children on October 28, 1941, by Lithuanian security police units in the Ninth Fort, one of a series of fortifications built on the outskirts of the city by Russian czar Alexander II. The remaining Jews were confined to the ghetto established by order of Palčiauskas, where they were subjected to terrible treatment. Enlisted for very difficult forced labor, they were made to subsist on totally inadequate rations of inferior quality. Housing and sanitary conditions were substandard, and epidemics were a constant danger.

Palčiauskas served as the mayor of Kaunas until May 1942, during which time at least half of the Jews in the city were murdered by the Nazis and their Lithuanian collaborators. He then went to work for the Sodbya dairy cooperative and, toward the end of the war, escaped with the retreating Nazis to Germany, where he posed as a refugee and received the status of a displaced person. During the entire application process for immigration to the United States, he never mentioned his term as the mayor of Kaunas. He listed his occupation as "office clerk" and lied about holding jobs at the Ministry of Meat and Milk and working as a manager at the Union of Cooperatives. He arrived in Boston on April 19, 1949, and lived for many years in Chicago, prior to his retirement in St. Petersburg, Florida.

Palčiauskas's residence in the United States was known to the American immigration authorities even before the OSI was established. When questioned about his wartime activities, he denied any wrongdoing, claiming at first that he was merely a figurehead for the Germans, who made all the decisions. He even asserted at one point that his resignation from his post had led to accusations that he was pro-Jewish and to threats on his life.

Although there is abundant literature on the Kaunas ghetto, due in part to the relatively large number of survivors (who were only a minuscule percentage of the original community), when I began researching the case, I found almost no information on the Lithuanian municipal administration. Thus, for example, Leib Garfunkel, who wrote *Kovnah ha-Yehudit bi-Churbana* (The Destruction of Jewish Kovna), one of the most important memoirs of the Holocaust in Kaunas, mentioned the mayor three times, but without naming him. His book did, however, lead me to the conclusion that my best bet of finding incriminating evidence against Palčiauskas was to locate members of the Judenrat (Jewish council) or people who had worked for its administration. I discovered that two of the former were reportedly still alive—Zvi Levin in Tel Aviv and Yaakov Goldberg in Johannesburg—but as luck would have it so often in such searches, by the time I reached them, Goldberg had passed away and Levin was too ill to answer any of my questions. Luckily, I was also able to find two other survivors, a man and a woman who had worked for the Judenrat and were alive, healthy, and living in Tel Aviv, and they ultimately testified at the trial.

My most important contribution to this case was, however, finding a collection of documents at Yad Vashem that clearly proved the role and activities of Palčiauskas as the mayor of Kaunas. The story behind the creation of the collection is important because it reveals a lot about the incredible resilience and unflagging spirit of the leaders of the local Jewish community. Despite the terrible hardships they suffered at the hands of the Nazis and their Lithuanian henchmen, they were determined to document their tragedy decree by decree, protocol by protocol. Thus, the collection included documents on the process of ghettoization, the inadequate food supply, and the use of Jews for forced labor. The Judenrat succeeded in hiding the documents in the ghetto as long as it still existed and smuggled them to a trustworthy Lithuanian prior to the final liquidation of the Jewish community of Kaunas in June 1944. When a few survivors returned to the city after the war, they retrieved the entire collection, which subsequently had to be smuggled out of Soviet Lithuania and deposited in its rightful place, the Yad Vashem archives.

It would be hard to describe the elation I felt when I found Palčiauskas's name in one of the documents that explained his role in the forced transfer of all the Jews of Kaunas into the ghetto. Those feelings of satisfaction and validation were reinforced on March 23, 1983, in Tampa, Florida, by Judge Robert Morgan, who stripped Palčiauskas of his American citizenship after finding that it was "beyond dispute" that he had participated in the creation and administration of the ghetto and the fact that he had concealed his role in the Nazi occupation clearly proved that he "lacked the good moral character required for [U.S.] citizenship."[1]

Palčiauskas died of a stroke several years later as he faced deportation from his adopted homeland. And although he did not receive a punishment entirely commensurate with his crime, due primarily to legal constraints in the United States, there is no question that a significant measure of justice was achieved. The fact that the spiritual bravery of the leaders of the Kaunas ghetto helped make it possible only makes Palčiauskas's defeat in court that much more meaningful.

FIVE

THE SEARCH FOR DR. MENGELE AND ITS UNEXPECTED BONUSES

THE FIRST HALF of the 1980s began with very exciting developments for my family. We returned from Los Angeles to Jerusalem in the summer of 1980, and our third child (and second son), Elchanan, was born in January 1981. By this time, I was already working full-time for the OSI (U.S. Justice Department's Office of Special Investigations), and my contracts were being renewed on a semiannual basis, which was the best arrangement available to overseas contract researchers. In August 1983, we left Jerusalem for our first (and only) house in the new settlement of Efrat, where I became quite active in local politics, sports, and cultural affairs and was even twice elected to the municipal council. Less than a year later, Elchanan underwent successful open-heart surgery for a congenital condition called valvular pulmonic stenosis, and two weeks after that, in April 1984, our fourth child (and second daughter), Ayelet, was born, completing our family.

Despite my absolute moral and emotional commitment to my work for the OSI, as the years went by, my enthusiasm began to wane. One of the reasons was that the paucity of relevant documentation in Israel on the cases being investigated in the United States had left me with a sense of futility about my research efforts. Another reason was the increasing preference of the OSI, for obvious (financial) reasons, to whenever possible use American Holocaust survivors as witnesses rather than Israeli survivors. In that respect, the Palčiauskas case had been exceptional. If there had been more investigations in which documents and witnesses from Israel had been so helpful, I obviously would not have felt as frustrated as I did. In addition, as time went by, the cases began to repeat themselves; this was only natural, since once a decision had been won against a person who served in a specific unit, it was much easier to prosecute another person who had served in the same formation.

This was especially true in the United States, which was prosecuting the Nazi war criminals in America not for any crimes committed during World War II, but for lying on their immigration and citizenship applications. Legal constraints that prevented prosecution for crimes committed outside the United States in which the victims were not Americans made this necessary. In these cases, which were civil (not criminal) proceedings, proving that a person had concealed the fact that he or she had served in a Nazi unit that engaged in the persecution of civilians was sufficient cause to strip the accused of his or her American citizenship. Prosecutors did not have to prove that an individual had personally participated in murder, although had they been able to do so (which was relatively rare), it would have been very helpful.

As my frustration with the work for the OSI grew, I began thinking of possible alternatives. One of the things that had become increasingly clear to me over the years was the need for a computerized database of all Nazi war criminals. The lack of such an important tool for Holocaust research was so obvious, in fact, that it was surprising that such a project had never been undertaken, although it would no doubt have been a very expensive project to launch. In any event, in the early spring of 1986, I decided to suggest such a project to Rabbi Hier at the Wiesenthal Center. According to my proposal, the headquarters would be established in Jerusalem, and there would also be offices in Los Angeles and Washington, D.C. The Jerusalem office would also function as the Wiesenthal Center's base in Israel, which would kill two birds with one stone, since unlike all the other major American Jewish defense organizations, the Wiesenthal Center had still not opened its own office in Israel. Rabbi Hier's initial reaction was noncommittal. He said that the idea sounded interesting, but that he had to think about it carefully and would let me know in due course.

At least two or three months passed without any answer from Rabbi Hier. In the meantime, I was deeply engrossed in what turned out to be one of the most intriguing but frustrating cases I ever worked on at the OSI. An investigation had been launched in the wake of the Wiesenthal Center's publication of an April 26, 1947, letter found in the National Archives from an American counterintelligence corps (CIC) officer named Benjamin Gorby. Gorby indicated that one of his agents had received information that Dr. Josef Mengele, the notorious "Angel of Death" from the Auschwitz death camp, had been arrested and released by the American authorities in Vienna in late 1946. In light of this revelation, the U.S. attorney general William French Smith announced on February 6, 1985, that the government would conduct a full-scale inquiry to determine whether Mengele had indeed been arrested and released by the United States in 1946, to find out whether he had ever entered the United States, and to identify his current whereabouts. The first two questions were assigned to the OSI, and I was one of the researchers who participated in the investigation. We ultimately learned that the Auschwitz doctor had indeed been held briefly in 1945 in two prisoner-of-war camps but was released because the U.S. Army never learned his real identity. The story that Gorby recorded turned out to be merely a rumor.

Ironically, it was the investigation of that rumor that ultimately produced two very important results. The first was the discovery that Mengele, probably the most wanted Nazi war criminal during the previous three decades, had drowned in the Atlantic Ocean near São Paulo in 1979 and had been buried in nearby Embu under the name of Wolfgang Gerhard. This sensational discovery was revealed by a search conducted in the office of Hans Seidelmayer, the Mengele family's attorney. The sad and infuriating truth was that, had the same search been conducted a decade earlier, Mengele could have been caught and prosecuted for his crimes. The fact that it was only in the wake of the involvement of the Americans, who were shortly thereafter joined by the Israelis and the Germans, that the search in Seidelmayer's office was carried out, points to a major failure of the previous investigations undertaken in this case by the Germans.

The second by-product of the Mengele investigation was totally unexpected, but as the Jewish saying goes, "*mitzvah goreret mitzvah*" (one good deed leads to another). One of my assignments in the case was to try to find a Polish Holocaust survivor named David Freimann, who had been an inmate clerk at the Hygiene Institute in Auschwitz and apparently was the source of the information regarding Mengele's arrest and release by the Americans. This proved to be a very difficult task since his name was fairly common—in fact, there were quite a few survivors named David Freimann. In addition, we had no idea where he was living; whether he had come to Israel, as many survivors had; and whether he had Hebraized his family name, which was a fairly common practice among European immigrants.

IMPATIENT WITH MY slow progress, I discussed the investigation with David Silberklang, a friend working at Yad Vashem, who suggested that I take a look at the files of the International Tracing Service (ITS), a collection that I had never hitherto consulted, probably because I was under a very mistaken impression regarding its contents. For some reason, I thought that it was primarily a collection of lists of Jews who had lived in Europe during World War II and hence of little value in the search for incriminating evidence against Holocaust perpetrators. In reality, it proved to be an extremely important collection with incredible potential for my research (and which also provided some clues on the whereabouts of David Freimann, who had died in Germany in 1976).

Established by the Allied High Commission in Germany shortly after the end of the war and housed in the town of Arolson, the ITS, which comprised 3,915 microfilms with a total of 16,268,291 frames, was a veritable gold mine of biographical information on the fate of Jews and non-Jews who had lived in Europe during the war. Of unique importance was the data in its files on the postwar immigration of displaced persons. Thus, for example, many of the cards included information on the country of immigration, the ship sailed on, and the date of departure of such persons. In the cases of those who had immigrated to the United States, there was even an American address listed. I knew from years of research that the overwhelming majority of the Nazi war criminals who had fled to Western democracies had done so as displaced persons posing as innocent refugees fleeing Communism. It therefore stood to reason that the ITS almost certainly had an enormous amount of critical data on the escape to the West of numerous Holocaust perpetrators. And what made this revelation even more significant, for me in particular, was the fact that the original documents housed in Arolson were virtually inaccessible to researchers, whereas the microfilm copies at Yad Vashem were completely open to the public.

In order to test my theory, I compiled a list of 49 Lithuanians and Latvians accused of committing crimes against civilians during World War II and searched for their names in the files of the ITS. I found entries for sixteen of them, and in ten cases, I found detailed information regarding their postwar immigration to the West. In practical terms, that meant that almost one-third had escaped from Eastern Europe to Germany after World War II and had obtained refugee (or displaced person) status and that at least ten had subsequently left for the United States, Canada, or Australia. It was immediately clear to me that this discovery had enormous implications. Now, for the first time ever, it would be possible to verify within minutes whether an East European Nazi war criminal or collaborator had escaped from his or her country of origin and emigrated to a Western democracy. And although this method was not entirely foolproof, since there obviously were cases in which the killers changed their names, our experience had shown that the overwhelming majority of the Lithuanian, Latvian, Estonian, Belarusian, Ukrainian, *Volksdeutsche* (Eastern Europeans of German ancestry), and Croatian Holocaust perpetrators who escaped to the West did not adopt new identities, most probably because they assumed that their crimes would never be discovered in their new homelands.

It was obvious from the very beginning, therefore, that the potential of these files for helping to find Nazi war criminals was almost limitless. All I had to do was find the names of perpetrators or suspects from other reliable sources (the ITS cards did not contain information regarding a person's wartime activities unless they had been incarcerated in a concentration camp, which hardly ever happened to Nazi war criminals) and run a search through the ITS files, and I would be able to determine whether they had escaped to the West. And while it was already clear that many of the people whom we hoped to find were no longer alive, our chances of finding those we could still bring to trial had just improved exponentially. The question now was, how could I best maximize the impact of this fantastic research tool?

At this point in early spring 1986, only one of the governments that could benefit from the findings in the ITS files was already in a position to do so. The United States was the only country to which numerous East European Nazi war criminals had escaped that already had a legal mechanism in place to prosecute and punish them (albeit unfortunately, not for the crimes themselves, as noted earlier) and had established a special office, the OSI, to investigate and try these cases. Canada and Australia had already initiated governmental investigations to determine whether Holocaust perpetrators had indeed emigrated there and were currently resident in those countries, but had still not decided whether to take legal action against them, let alone open a special office for that purpose. Great Britain and New Zealand had still not taken any steps whatsoever to even investigate the matter or to opt for legal action of any sort.

Under these circumstances, it became clear to me that the most important objective at this point was to prove to Canada, Australia, Great Britain, and New Zealand that numerous Nazi war criminals had entered those countries posing as refugees and to convince them to take legal action against those individuals, hopefully using a special office established exclusively for that purpose. The question was, how best to advance those goals? I obviously could not do so while working as a contract researcher for the OSI, so my first thought was to turn to the Wiesenthal Center, not only because of my previous tenure and connections there, but because I believed that its activist stance on the issue of Nazi war criminals, the fact that it bore the name of the person who symbolized the quest to bring Holocaust perpetrators to justice, and its proven expertise in arousing public opinion made it the organization best suited to assume this historic task.

Ironically, several weeks after I discovered the potential of the ITS files, Rabbi Hier called to inform me that he wanted to accept my proposal to establish a computerized database of Nazi war criminals. Imagine his surprise when I told him that in view of the potential of the ITS files, we should forget about the database and concentrate instead on convincing the Anglo-Saxon democracies besides the United States to initiate the prosecution of the Nazi war criminals residing in their countries. Rabbi Hier immediately agreed, excited about our prospects of making history, and thus the Wiesenthal Center's campaigns for justice in Canada, Australia, Great Britain, and New Zealand were launched and I became the Center's first Israel representative.

Leaving my job at the OSI, which was the pinnacle of practical research a historian could do to facilitate the prosecution of Nazi war criminals, to go work for a private nongovernmental organization (NGO) without the power to prosecute anyone was undoubtedly a gamble. My gut feeling was, however, that only a major international campaign orchestrated by an activist organization such as the Wiesenthal Center could convince governments to take action. The truth was that I could be replaced at the OSI by another historian or researcher (which was indeed the case), but unless we convinced Canada, Australia, Great Britain, and New Zealand to move quickly against the Holocaust perpetrators in their midst, these criminals would die in peace and tranquility with their crimes unpunished, a thought that was simply unbearable.

SIX

NAZIS DOWN UNDER

IN NOVEMBER 1943, Roosevelt, Churchill, and Stalin met in Moscow to discuss the Allied efforts to defeat Nazi Germany. One of the subjects they dealt with was the steps to be taken after the war to punish those who had committed war crimes and atrocities against civilians. Their determination that these criminals should be held accountable was unequivocally expressed in the Moscow Declaration, issued following their meeting, in which they clearly asserted that "most assuredly the three Allied powers will pursue them to the uttermost ends of the earth and will deliver them to their accusers in order that justice may be done."[1]

I often think of that declaration, and especially of the phrase about pursuing Nazi war criminals to the "uttermost ends of the earth," in relation to the Wiesenthal Center's efforts to facilitate the prosecution of the many Holocaust perpetrators who had emigrated to Australia and New Zealand after World War II. If there is a region that fits that description, it surely is Oceania. Its remote geographic location was undoubtedly one of the factors that prompted so many Nazi war criminals to emigrate down under. Like the United States and Canada, Australia was an attractive destination for many of Hitler's East European henchmen because it was far away from the scene of their crimes; it was an anti-Communist country not likely to extradite them to their countries of origin, which were at that time part of the Soviet Union; it was a country that had not suffered a Nazi invasion; it was a country of economic opportunity that was open to new immigrants; and it was a country that already had émigré communities ready to help the newcomers, regardless of which side they had supported during World War II.

When we began our campaign to find these fugitives, in early fall 1986, our focus was on the three major Anglo-Saxon democracies that had still not decided to take legal action against the Nazi war criminals in their midst—Australia, Canada, and Great Britain. (As far as New Zealand was concerned, I initially found very few suspects who immigrated there, which severely limited our chances of convincing the government to take legal action against them and made the problem less of a priority.) At this point, the scope of the problem in these countries was still not clear. The first two had already initiated official governmental inquiries, whereas the issue had still not surfaced in Great Britain. In Australia, the problem had reached the headlines for the first time in April 1986 in the wake of an Australian Broadcasting Corporation radio series entitled *Nazis in Australia*, produced by the Sydney journalist Mark Aarons, and a television documentary, *Don't Mention the War*. Both claimed that numerous Nazi war criminals had entered the country as legal immigrants, in certain cases because British and American intelligence agencies had withheld information from the Australians regarding their wartime activities. In response, the government established an official commission of inquiry headed by the veteran civil servant Andrew C. Menzies to investigate the allegations and make recommendations vis-à-vis government policy.

That was the situation when I began to compile my lists of suspects based on the cross-referencing of names of Nazi war criminals with the ITS files. I already had one such name from my original experiment with the ITS, but it was not difficult to find additional suspects who had emigrated to Australia. Within several weeks, I already had the names of 25 Latvians, 13 Lithuanians, 1 Pole, and 1 Ukrainian. Who were these people? For the most part, they were typical Baltic Nazi war criminals, members of the infamous Latvian Arajs Kommando, which had murdered at least 30,000 Jews in Latvia and later was sent to Minsk to continue its bloody activity, as well as men who had served in other Latvian and Lithuanian security police units that had actively participated in the mass murder of Jews in different locales in their countries of origin. While two were over 80, the majority were under the age of 75, and a few were under 65. About half were in their seventies. I had found most of their names in documents from the Yad Vashem archives, and a few were named in Soviet publications, such as *Documents Accuse, Daugavas Vanagi: Who Are They?* and *'Political Refugees' Unmasked!*, designed to embarrass Western democracies that had admitted Nazi war criminals.

Rabbis Hier and Cooper gave the list to the Australian foreign minister Bill Hayden in a meeting at the United Nations on October 1, 1986, along with a letter to Prime Minister Bob Hawke, in which they requested that the charges be investigated and necessary legal action be taken. It was likely, they noted, that I would ultimately discover "at least several hundred suspected Nazi war criminals...believed to be living in Australia,"² a prophecy that turned out to be remarkably accurate. Despite intense pressure from the media, Rabbi Hier decided not to publicize the names of the suspects in order to give the government an opportunity to take the necessary measures against them, to reduce the chances of the suspects escaping, and to avoid possible cases of mistaken identity.

As it turned out, this list was only the first of a total of 18 different lists of Australian suspects, totaling 487 men, that I compiled on behalf of the Wiesenthal Center over the course of the last 23 years. They ranged in numbers of suspects from 1 to 94 and were overwhelmingly made up of Lithuanians (336) and Latvians (117), a reflection of the extremely large number of local perpetrators in those countries and the relative abundance of documents on the crimes committed by those nationals in their own countries and elsewhere in Eastern Europe.

The key that linked these suspected criminals to Australia was their immigration data in the ITS. In late 1986, the Menzies Commission completed its investigation, which confirmed the existence in Australia of a serious problem of suspected Nazi war criminals, at least 70 of whom were alleged to have committed "crimes involving the murder of many persons, in some cases hundreds of persons, in circumstances of the utmost cruelty and depravity." Most important, it made it clear that "the argument that the culprits, by coming to this country, have turned their backs on such events has, in my view, no validity" and therefore recommended that the government "take appropriate action under the law to bring to justice persons who have committed serious war crimes found in Australia."[3]

It took slightly more than two years for the Hawke government to implement that recommendation by passing the Australian War Crimes Amendment Act in early 1989, which mandated the criminal prosecution in Australia of suspects accused of war crimes in Europe (a proviso pushed by the Liberal Party to exclude the possibility of prosecuting Australian servicemen for crimes committed in the Pacific). While the struggle to pass this legislation was proceeding in Australia, I continued my research, finding more and more Australian suspects, which on occasion I revealed in a manner designed to increase the pressure on the government to take legal action.

At Rabbi Cooper's suggestion, for example, I used the occasion of Prime Minister Hawke's January 1989 visit to Israel to highlight the issue by requesting an opportunity to meet him so that I could submit to him an additional list of suspects. When the Australian ambassador refused to arrange such a meeting because of "programming constraints," it was not hard to turn the incident into a prominent news story that catapulted the issue, which otherwise could have been virtually ignored, into the front pages of the leading Israeli and Australian newspapers. Add a press conference on the submission of the list of 15 new suspects and my op-ed in the popular Israeli daily *Ma'ariv* entitled "An Open Letter to a True Friend," and we had focused maximum public attention on the need for Australia to prosecute its Nazi war criminals and turned the issue into one of the key elements of Prime Minister Hawke's visit to Israel. None of these "gimmicks" would have been necessary had this issue been a high priority of the Israeli government, but, unfortunately, that was not the case; it therefore became necessary for the Wiesenthal Center to step into this void, a void that we faced on many occasions.

A **YEAR AND** a half after the passage of the bill enabling the criminal prosecution of Nazi war criminals in Australia, the first prosecution was about to commence in late July 1990 against a Ukrainian Nazi collaborator named Ivan Polyukhovich, who was charged with the murder of 24 Jews and involvement in the killing of an additional 850 Jews in the town of Serniki in the Volhynia region of Ukraine. On the morning of the trial, however, the suspect, who was free on US$20,000 bail, was found shot in the chest about a block from his suburban Adelaide home. I will never forget the furious, expletive-filled harangue I was subjected to at 5:30 AM at home from one of the most respected leaders of the Australian Jewry, who gave me the news and warned me not to "meddle" in this issue or "dare say anything" to the local media, since the suspicion was that Polyukhovich had been shot by a Jewish avenger, and he did not want any "outsiders" getting involved in this very sensitive issue.

This tension between locals and outsiders was almost a permanent feature of our campaigns to facilitate the prosecution of Nazi war criminals in different countries. Our modus operandi was to seek the partnership of the local Jewish community, but in many cases, especially, although not exclusively, in smaller communities that perceived themselves as particularly vulnerable to anti-Semitic attacks, this proved to be quite difficult. I often had to undertake a delicate balancing act to achieve my goal without angering or alienating the local Jewish leadership. This proved to be extremely difficult at times, and there were instances, as I will later in the book explain, in which all our efforts to address the concerns, and especially the fears, of our fellow Jews failed, and we had to seek different partners. And while there were obvious advantages to having non-Jewish allies, whom we always welcomed, I always believed that part of our mission in these campaigns was to empower weaker Jewish communities and raise their profile and self-confidence, so when they refused to join forces with us, or at least support us, it was very sad and disheartening.

As it turned out, Polyukhovich had not been shot by a local Jewish extremist but had tried to kill himself. This was by no means a welcome development. His suicide attempt was not interpreted by the public as an admission of guilt and, in fact, led to costly delays in the trial. A month later, there was more bad news as Attorney General Michael Duffy announced that the Special Investigations Unit (SIU), which had been established in May 1987 to carry out all the Nazi war crimes investigations in Australia, would be closed down on June 30, 1992. Until that date, the unit would concentrate on the 12 cases identified by its director, Robert Greenwood, as most likely to result in prosecution and could investigate up to 5 additional cases.

While this decision was primarily dictated by financial considerations, it was no doubt also influenced by the staunch political opposition to prosecution by the local émigré communities (whose members were the suspects in question), right-wing extremists, and anti-Semites, as well as by various politicians and public figures. In Australia, as in every country in which we tried to facilitate the prosecution of Nazi war criminals, the battle for justice required not only sufficient evidence against the criminals but also winning over public opinion as a means of achieving what ultimately had to be a political victory, since without the support of the local politicians, the prosecution effort would never have been launched and subsequently maintained and given the resources necessary to succeed.

In practical terms, the decision to close down the SIU was a total disaster for two major reasons. The first was that it was being closed down at the very time that the pertinent archives in the former Soviet Union and post-Communist Eastern Europe, which is where the overwhelming majority of the crimes by the suspects living in Australia had been committed, were finally being opened, with full access granted to Western prosecutors. Just as our chances for successful prosecutions in Australia had increased immeasurably, the government was closing down the agency entrusted with the task. The second reason was that prosecutors trying these cases had to acquire expertise that usually only comes with experience. At the time that the decision was made to close down the SIU, not a single case had yet been tried in court. It was clear that the politicians had lost their will to bring Nazi war criminals in Australia to justice and were pulling the plug way too soon.

The Australian government responded to our criticism of this decision by claiming that the closure of the SIU would not necessarily end the pursuit of Nazis, since, at least in theory, the Australian Federal Police (AFP) could fulfill the same function. It was clear to me, however, that this was merely lip service, because once the specialized Nazi-hunting agency established by the government was shut down, the chances of a successful prosecution were minimal. This also meant that several of our strongest cases would most probably never be brought to court, a scenario that I found infuriating, especially considering the fact that Greenwood had specifically indicated that several of them had excellent potential for prosecution. The thought that people like Leonas Pažūsis, who had served in the infamous Ypatingas būrys, a notorious Lithuanian murder squad that was responsible for the mass murder of an estimated 70,000 Jews at the Ponar (Paneriai) killing site outside Vilnius, my great-uncle Efraim and his family most likely among them, would escape justice was too much to bear. And he was only one of several such mass murderers whose names were on the lists I compiled and had submitted to the Australian authorities.

Subsequent developments, unfortunately, bore out my pessimistic assessment. Two other cases brought to court floundered (one for medical reasons, although after his case was dropped, the defendant, Heinrich Wagner, who was charged with participation in the murder of 104 Jews in Israelovka, Ukraine, was clandestinely filmed doing arduous physical tasks), and even Polyukhovich was acquitted when his trial resumed, following his recovery from his suicide attempt, almost three years later. Although his collaboration with the Nazis was clearly established, it was not entirely clear whether he, or either of the two other Nazi collaborators by the same name, had personally committed murder. That left one major case that the government had promised to continue even after the SIU had been closed down, that of the Latvian Arajs Kommando officer Kārlis Ozols, whom I had named on our first list of Australian suspects.

Ozols was one of the highest-ranking alleged Nazi war criminals living in Australia at this point and the person accused of the most serious crimes, including the murder of thousands of Jews. He also was the most famous suspected Nazi and certainly one of the best known in the Melbourne Jewish community, since he was a very successful chess player who had won the Victoria Chess Championship nine times and had many Jewish students in the chess classes he taught in the 1950s and 1960s in the St. Kilda neighborhood in Melbourne.

The main allegations against Ozols related to his service in Minsk, Belarus, from July 24 to September 27, 1943, as a lieutenant in the Arajs Kommando. Ozols commanded a company of 100 Latvians that carried out the mass murder of thousands of Jews, primarily from the Minsk ghetto, in the killing sites of Gut Trostinets and Maly Trostinets, either by shooting or by asphyxiation in gas vans used especially for this purpose. The company is also accused of participating in the liquidation of the Slutzk (Belarus) ghetto and the mass murder of 2,000 of its Jewish inhabitants on February 8–9, 1943. Despite extensive evidence (including eyewitness testimony by fellow perpetrators under Ozols's command) and very strong recommendations from legal experts, including those from the SIU, that he be prosecuted for genocide, the government refused to approve the completion of his investigation and in 1997 closed the case for financial reasons, thereby sparing Ozols an almost certain conviction.

All our efforts and those of our wonderful partners at the Australia-Israel Jewish Affairs Committee (AIJAC), led by the extremely able Dr. Colin Rubenstein, to change this outrageous decision unfortunately failed, allowing a notorious murderer to escape justice. Ozols died unprosecuted on March 26, 2001, at the age of 88 and was cremated three days later at a secret ceremony at a Melbourne funeral parlor, a chilling testimony to the failure of the Australian government's efforts to hold the Nazi war criminals residing in their country accountable.

In the years following Ozols's death, four additional cases of Holocaust perpetrators surfaced in Australia, mostly as a result of my research and lobbying together with AIJAC and the efforts of the journalist Mark Aarons, whose pioneering work in the field was indispensable. The most unique of these cases was undoubtedly that of the Latvian Arajs Kommando officer Konrad Kalejs, whose postwar odyssey provides us with insight into, and a rare opportunity to compare the attitudes of the four Anglo-Saxon democracies that had admitted the largest number of Nazi war criminals—Australia, the United States, Canada, and Great Britain. Despite the existence of substantial evidence implicating Kalejs in the mass murder of civilians during his service with the Arajs Kommando in Riga, at the Salaspils concentration camp, and on the Eastern front in 1942, he was allowed to immigrate to Australia under the displaced persons scheme. Arriving in October 1950, his first job was as a documentation and processing clerk at the Bonegilla migrant camp for new arrivals to Australia, a position in which he might well have been able to assist his fellow Latvian Nazis. He moved to Melbourne in 1957 and, two years later, immigrated to the United States, where he was a very successful businessman in the Chicago area.

In the mid-1980s, however, the OSI discovered that he was residing in the United States and set out to deport him (he had never acquired American citizenship and thus could be immediately deported). An American court found that he had concealed his wartime service with the Arajs Kommando, which included the murder of civilians in various locations, among them Riga, and the Salaspils concentration camp[4] ordered his deportation to Australia, which finally took place in April 1994 after the U.S. Supreme Court rejected his final appeal.

The Australian authorities had no intention of taking any legal action against him, but within two months, Kalejs again left Melbourne, this time for Canada, where he remained until May 1995, when the local immigration authorities suggested that he return to Australia. He returned to Canada again, however, in September, after which the Canadians began deportation proceedings against him. (Unlike the United States, which has a watch-list that effectively bars Nazi war criminals from entering the country, such persons can sometimes enter Canada, which subsequently seeks to deport them.) Throughout the proceedings, Kalejs resided in an upscale condominium in the North York suburb of Toronto, which had numerous Jewish residents, among them several Holocaust survivors. When word got out about the identity of their newest neighbor, some would pointedly leave the building's swimming pool when Kalejs came for a dip. In the

summer of 1997, the Canadian judge Anthony Iozzo reached the same
basic conclusion as his American counterpart Anthony Petrone nine
years earlier, that Kalejs had committed serious crimes in Latvia, and
ordered him deported to Australia, where his arrival ignited considerable media attention.

Once again, despite the unequivocally damning judgment against
Kalejs in Toronto, the Australian judicial authorities saw no reason to
attempt to prosecute him. Nonetheless, Kalejs soon left Melbourne,
this time for England, where at least in theory due to the passage of
special legislation, he could have been brought to trial for his World
War II crimes. His clandestine departure from Australia was discovered by researchers for the television program *20/20*, which was in the
process of preparing a documentary on Nazi war criminals in Australia.
Kalejs, it turns out, was living in Catthorpe Manor, a luxurious Latvian
retirement home in Rugby. I was able to inform Acting Constable Mike
Brewer of the Warwickshire police force of the identity of the new resident and urge that he be prosecuted for his crimes or expelled from
Great Britain.

Two days later, I wrote to Home Secretary Jack Straw to urge the
British authorities to investigate Kalejs's entry into the country and
suggested that Great Britain establish a watch-list similar to the one
used with great success in the United States. Straw did indeed launch an
inquiry on December 30, 1999, and four days later, Kalejs was ordered
deported from Great Britain, from where he once again returned to
Australia, the only country where, in the lamentable, but accurate,
words of the Australian justice minister Amanda Vanstone, he was welcome, as an Australian citizen, to enter.

In the wake of Kalejs's deportation from a third Anglo-Saxon
democracy, the wheels of criminal justice finally began moving in his
case. This time, however, I tried to get his homeland of Latvia, where
many of his former inmates had already testified against him, to press
charges against him. My thinking was that if such an initiative were
to succeed, it would help achieve two extremely important objectives.
The first was holding the trial of a local Nazi war criminal, in this case

an officer of the most important Latvian collaborationist unit, for the first time ever in democratic Latvia. The second was facilitating the first-ever successful legal action taken in Australia against a Holocaust perpetrator residing in the country.

Despite the reluctance of the Latvians to cooperate at first, the pressure from the United States, Israel, and the Wiesenthal Center ultimately produced results, initially in the form of a meeting of representatives from the United States, Canada, Australia, Germany, Great Britain, and Israel held in Riga on February 16–17, 2000, to discuss the Kalejs case. (A representative of the Wiesenthal Center was not invited, ostensibly since we are an NGO, not a government, but more likely due to the deep-seated resentment of the Latvians in response to our efforts to get them to bring Latvian Holocaust perpetrators to justice.) In the wake of the meeting, at which the three verdicts against Kalejs, as well as the other available evidence, were presented, the Latvians finally charged him with war crimes in September 2000 and asked for his extradition from Australia to stand trial in Riga.

Although the Latvian request was approved in May 2001, Kalejs used every legal option available to him to avoid being extradited to his homeland. And that is precisely what happened. He died in Melbourne on November 8, 2001, while still appealing his extradition, making Australia the only Anglo-Saxon democracy to have passed a law enabling the prosecution of Nazi war criminals that, more than a decade later, had still not taken successful legal action against a single Holocaust perpetrator.

This being the case, there was one positive judicial decision achieved as a result of the Australian efforts to prosecute local Nazi war criminals, although it did not take place in a court in Australia. In the wake of the investigation conducted in Australia against Heinrich Wagner, who in 1992 was charged with participation in the massacre of 104 Jews from Israelovka, Ukraine and with having personally murdered at least some of the 19 half-Jewish children aged 4 to 11 of the village, the German authorities in 1995 arrested Ernst Hering, who served in the Gendarmerie Ustinova, the same Ukrainian auxiliary police unit as

Wagner. In December 1997, he was convicted in a Cologne court for aiding and abetting murder and was sentenced to one year and eight months on probation. According to Judge Paul Schwellenbach, Hering was on guard duty when the children were taken to be murdered. "Although he witnessed the increasing fear of the crying children, he stayed at his post."[5]

SEVEN

NAZIS IN GREAT BRITAIN

OF ALL THE campaigns launched by the Wiesenthal Center in the various Anglo-Saxon democracies, the one we initiated in Great Britain meant the most to me. For a variety of reasons, the situation there was different from that in other countries, and the challenges we faced were much greater, which made whatever success we achieved that much more gratifying. To begin with, it was the Wiesenthal Center that exposed the presence of suspected Nazi war criminals in Great Britain, information that was previously unknown. By comparison, at the time that we began compiling lists of suspects for Australia and Canada in fall 1986, each of those countries had already initiated its own official governmental inquiry to determine whether there was indeed such a problem, and, if so, the scope and possible remedies available to the government.

Another problem we faced in Great Britain was the limited potential of the ITS files, which included relatively little information on the displaced persons who had immigrated there, in contrast to the abundant information they contained on the enormous number of East Europeans who went to the United States, Canada, and Australia. Also frustrating was the length and the intensity of the campaign we had to conduct to convince the British government that the problem even existed and that legal action had to be taken, and later to assist in the passage of a special bill that enabled the prosecution of Nazi war criminals in Great Britain. Due to these factors, the Wiesenthal Center played a much more active role in the British campaign than in the efforts invested for the same purpose in other countries.

This part of the story begins on October 22, 1986, when Rabbis Hier and Cooper met in Los Angeles with the British consul Donald Ballantine and submitted a list that I had compiled in Jerusalem of 17 suspected Nazi war criminals who had immigrated to Great Britain after World War II. The crimes attributed to the 11 Latvians and 6 Lithuanians on the list ranged from mass murder while serving in death squads (3 Lithuanian suspects), to serving in the collaborationist administration established by the Nazis in Latvia, to supervising the drafting of men for the Latvian SS legion, to the recruitment of Latvians for forced labor in Germany. The list was, of course, accompanied by the center's request, addressed to Prime Minister Margaret Thatcher, that the British authorities investigate the allegations and "if necessary create the required legal apparatus to deal with them."[1] None of us imagined at that point how difficult it would be to achieve even that modest goal.

Almost four months passed before the British government responded, but it was clear from the beginning that there was little willingness in London to address the issue. Thus, even before we had our first meeting with Home Secretary Douglas Hurd in early March 1987, Rabbi Hier had received a letter from Charles Powell, Prime Minister Thatcher's private secretary, asserting that despite the prime minister's "deep revulsion at the atrocities committed during the Nazi era," it was most likely that legal constraints would prevent the prosecution of Nazi war criminals in Great Britain.[2]

When we finally met Home Secretary Hurd on March 2, his message was crystal clear. The only question that the British government was ready to investigate was whether any of the suspects had violated local immigration law. As far as the government was concerned, the information we had submitted was not sufficient to induce the authorities to launch their own investigation, and if we wanted them to do so, we would have to come up with more substantial evidence.

Having said that, even if the Wiesenthal Center had been able to obtain such evidence, the options available to the British authorities for legal action were fairly limited. Prosecution was limited to crimes committed in Great Britain, and extradition to either the Soviet Union or Israel was impossible because of the lack of an extradition treaty with the former and the provisions of the existing extradition treaty with the latter. It was immediately clear that Hurd's position was merely an elegant way of absolving the government of having to take any action in these cases. Given the fact that all the crimes allegedly committed by the suspects had taken place in areas that were currently part of the Soviet Union, it was virtually absurd to expect a Jewish NGO that had been extremely active on behalf of Soviet Jewry to be able to obtain the cooperation of the Soviet authorities even though, in theory, we shared a mutual interest in these cases. It seemed fairly clear that under the circumstances, we were facing very formidable obstacles. And to make matters worse, the more conservative press fully supported the government's refusal to take action and tried to portray our attempts to bring Nazi war criminals to trial in Great Britain as vengeance, not justice.

Thus, for example, on the day following our meeting with Hurd, an editorial in the *Times* reminded its readers that "Britain is a Christian country...[whose] laws enshrine principles of justice tempered with mercy not vengeance" and concluded that "it is wise and humane to let matters rest."[3] The next day, an editorial in the *Daily Telegraph* referred, in the most negative terms imaginable, to the efforts to hold Holocaust perpetrators accountable: "Nazi-hunting has become a new and frankly distasteful blood sport. It is no reflection of anti-Semitism or of indifference to past atrocities, to feel an overwhelming revulsion against the notion of further war crimes trials, almost half a century after the alleged horrors took place. There is a futility, a sterility, about continuing a search of vengeance beyond certain limits of time and space."[4]

And Peter Simple, a journalist at the *Daily Telegraph*, summed up the erroneous arguments of our detractors in the same newspaper as follows: "The more I hear about this meeting between the zealots of the Simon Wiesenthal Center and Mr. Hurd, the more sorry I feel for

Mr. Hurd whose duty it evidently is to placate them even in their most outrageous suggestions, such as changing the fundamental laws of this country. In their enthusiasm for more and more show trials they seem almost to have forgotten what country they are in. So much so that British Jews themselves are showing signs of uneasiness and fears, by no means unjustified, of a 'backlash.' Many of them may well be wishing that the zealots of the Simon Wiesenthal Center had never come here at all, and that they would go back to Los Angeles and stay there."[5]

Under these circumstances, we had to reassess our original strategy. In other countries, once we had submitted the allegations against the suspected Nazis, the local governments had assumed the burden of further investigation, but in Britain the government had refused to do so, thereby putting the entire onus on us. The British had, however, helped us in at least one respect by verifying the current whereabouts of the suspects, six of whom were confirmed to be living in Great Britain, while three others who had been residing in the country were no longer alive. The government supplied us with the names in question, which was of considerable assistance in our efforts.

As luck would have it, one of the suspects alive and well in Great Britain was Anton Gecas, otherwise known as Antanas Gecevičius, who had served as an officer in the infamous 12th Lithuanian Auxiliary Police Battalion, which had carried out the mass murder of thousands of Jews, initially in Kaunas, Lithuania, and later in several locations in Belarus, among them Slutzk, Kletzk, Rudensk, Dukara, and Koidanov. Gecas had already been living in Edinburgh, Scotland, for several decades, and his case and his residence there ultimately had a profound effect on the campaign to bring Nazi war criminals to justice in Great Britain for two major reasons. The first was the severity and enormity of his crimes and the other was that his presence in Scotland so infuriated the top-flight journalists Bob Tomlinson and Ross Wilson of Scottish Television (STV) that they became extremely involved in our campaign, and Tomlinson especially became our most valuable partner. Together with the All-Party War Crimes Group established by Greville Janner, MP, probably the most outstanding Jewish leader in Great Britain at the time, and headed by the former home secretary

Merlyn Rees, MP, they were to play a critical role in convincing the British government to take legal action against local Holocaust perpetrators.

In the meantime, I decided, in consultation with Rabbi Heir, that while in London I should attempt to obtain permission to do research in the Soviet archives in Lithuania and Latvia. The center had, in the past, attempted to obtain visas for a team of researchers from Soviet officials in the embassy in Washington, but with no success. There was no Soviet embassy in Israel, but I now had an opportunity to try to convince the Soviet diplomats in London to help us. What gave us grounds for guarded optimism was the fact that after the center submitted its list of Nazi war criminals living in Great Britain to the authorities, the Soviet embassy in London had leaked the names of an additional 34 suspects to STV and had provided some assistance to them on the Gecas case.

Nevertheless, I had reason to be cautious. Just a mere 18 months previously, I had traveled to Moscow, Riga, Vilnius, and Leningrad posing as an American tourist to meet with Jewish "refusniks" (Jews refused permission by the Soviet authorities to emigrate to Israel, many of whom were harassed and persecuted by the Soviet authorities), teach them about Judaism and Jewish history, and encourage them in their struggle to make aliyah. There was no doubt in my mind, moreover, that the Soviets knew exactly who I was, since my companion, Dr. Menachem Gottesman, and I had been twice stopped by the KGB (once in Riga and once in Vilnius) and had been interrogated and warned that our intentions were fully known to the authorities. And if that was not sufficient to earn a file in the KGB, following my return from the Soviet Union, at my initiative, the city council of our town of Efrat had "adopted" Dr. Ari (Leonid) Volvovsky, who was at that time serving a three-year sentence in Yakutsk, Siberia, for spreading anti-Soviet propaganda, but in reality was being punished for his activities as a teacher of Judaism, Zionism, and Hebrew. So to be entirely honest, the thought of going to the Soviet embassy to meet First Secretary Guennadi Shabanikov sent shivers down my spine and conjured up images of bugging devices and kidnappings.

As it turned out, the meeting was relatively cordial. I updated Shabanikov on our dealings with the British government, stressing the critical need for Soviet assistance in the search for evidence, but he was noncommittal. Although we were able to agree on the necessity to bring the "scoundrels," as he put it, to justice, all he would say was that he would pass on my request for a visa to the pertinent authorities in Moscow. Interestingly, he was quite anxious to discuss other subjects, such as Israel's attitude toward the Soviet Union, but that was not the object of our meeting.

I never received a reply from the Soviets, but about a month later we received an indirect answer when Bob Tomlinson informed me that he had received permission to do research on Gecas in the Soviet Union. I again turned to Shabanikov to request a visa, an appeal strengthened when we were informed by the British authorities that an additional three suspects on our list were found living in Great Britain—but all for naught. Luckily, however, the cooperation denied the Wiesenthal Center was extended generously to STV. In June 1987, Bob Tomlinson returned from Lithuania with excellent evidence against Gecas and with information on an additional suspect (Kiril Zvarich) from the list originally leaked by the Soviet embassy. When Tomlinson sought to present the documents to the Home Office, however, he was informed that the Wiesenthal Center was the exclusive agency for research on war crimes committed by current residents of Great Britain during World War II. Thus, ironically, despite the refusal of the Soviets to allow me to search for evidence in the Baltics, it was we who submitted the damning evidence against Gecas and Zvarich to the British government. We also provided additional documents I had discovered regarding Gecas's unit, and important material prepared by our researcher, Robert Rozett, on Pauls Reinhards and Janis Skujevics, both of whom had served as senior civil servants in the collaborationist Latvian self-government under the Nazi occupation and were on our original list of suspects, and were currently alive and living in the UK.

Our meeting with Deputy Undersecretary of State David Faulkner and Home Office officials was timed to coincide with the nationwide screening of *Crimes of War*, the latest STV documentary on Britain's failure to address the issue of Nazi war criminals. (STV's first film on the subject, *Britain: A Nazi Safe House*, had been shown in January 1987.) The heart of the film was the testimony of three Lithuanians, Juozas Aleksynas, Motiejus Migonis, and Leonas Mickevičius, who had served under Gecas's command in the 12th Lithuanian Auxiliary Police Battalion and personally witnessed on several occasions how he not only ordered his men to line up Jews on the edge of a pit and to shoot them, but also jumped into the pit along with other officers to personally finish off anyone who was still alive. These shootings of Jews took place in the vicinity of several towns and cities in Belarus, such as Kletzk, Minsk, and Koidanov. Another such site was the city of Slutzk, where Gecas's unit carried out the mass executions of Jews in late October 1941 together with a German unit headed by Franz Stahlecker. One of the documents submitted at the Nuremberg Trials was a letter from Carl,[6] the German Gebietskomissar (senior administrator of the area) of Slutzk, to his superiors in Minsk, complaining about the brutality of the Lithuanian unit and imploring, "I beg of you to grant me one request: in the future keep this police battalion away from me by all means."[7]

The screening of the film was followed by a symposium entitled "Crimes of War: Time for Justice," which sought to examine the moral, legal, religious, and historical aspects of the problem of war crimes and to which I was invited as a participant. Prior to traveling to Glasgow for the program, I was approached by Brian MacLaurin, the director of public relations for STV, who suggested that I go to Gecas's home in Edinburgh to try and confront him. Despite my general reluctance to engage in staged theatrics, I felt that I had to agree to do so for "the good of the cause," regardless of whether I liked the idea or not. Ultimately, Gecas was either not home or refused to open the door, so I held an impromptu press conference on his lawn at 3 Moston Terrace in Edinburgh, in which I said that unlike Gecas, who never gave his innocent victims a chance, we were willing to allow him to prove his innocence.

In the meantime, pressure was mounting on the British government to take legal action against Gecas. In August 1987, the Soviets submitted an extradition request for Gecas, and the All-Party War Crimes Group and other interested organizations intensified their efforts to change the official British policy on Nazi war criminals. The first concrete step in that direction was taken on February 8, 1988, by Home Secretary Hurd, who announced the establishment of an independent inquiry to investigate the evidence against the Nazi war criminals living in Great Britain, which was to be carried out by Sir Thomas Hetherington, the former head of the Department of Public Prosecutions in England and Wales, and his Scottish counterpart, William Chalmers, the former Crown Agent in Scotland. Their mandate also included advising the government regarding the steps that might be taken if the evidence warranted a change in the existing policy. This announcement by the same home secretary who, a year previously, had basically told us that we were wasting our time, was quite a victory, but our battle was only beginning.

CONCURRENTLY, THE CENTER continued its research, adding 13 new suspects to our list, and the All-Party War Crimes Group published two very important reports on the issue of Nazi war criminals. The first showed how governmental apathy facilitated the entry into Great Britain of numerous Holocaust perpetrators during the years 1945–1950, and the second examined the various legal options available to the British government for the prosecution of war criminals and recommended changing the current law to enable it. Six months later, on July 24, 1989, when Home Secretary Hurd announced the inquiry's findings, that was their unequivocal recommendation. After examining in depth seven cases, out of a total of 301 allegations received by the government, Hetherington and Chalmers concluded that in four cases there was "a realistic prospect of a conviction for murder on the evidence available were the jurisdiction of the British courts to be widened"[8] and that additional investigations were required in the other three cases. In addition, they found 75 cases in which further investigations were recommended. The rest of the allegations could be dismissed since the suspects had either died (56), left Great Britian (13), apparently never resided in Great Britain (25), or had not committed murder or manslaughter (49).

In terms of legal remedies, the inquiry considered four possible options: denaturalization and deportation, extradition, prosecution in military courts, and passing legislation to enable criminal prosecution in Great Britain. They rejected options one and three as unsatisfactory and rejected extradition since almost all the crimes had been committed in areas that were presently part of the Soviet Union. The inquiry therefore recommended the introduction of legislation to enable prosecution in Great Britain and urged that such a step be implemented as quickly as possible in view of the advanced age of the suspects and potential witnesses. Hetherington and Chalmers also addressed the potential objections that they were certain would be raised against their recommendations and beautifully corroborated what we had been saying all along: "The crimes committed are so monstrous that they cannot be condoned; their prosecution should act as a deterrent in future wars. To take no action would taint the United Kingdom with the slur of being a haven for war criminals."[9]

In the wake of this unequivocal recommendation, the question now was, when would the government propose the appropriate legislation to enable prosecution, and would it be approved in the House of Commons and then in the House of Lords? The process began on the right footing, as Commons voted overwhelmingly (348–123) in favor of a change in the current prosecution law, and on March 19, 1990, a bill introduced by the new home secretary, David Waddington, with provisions for taking evidence overseas on video and which approved the statements of persons no longer alive, passed by a vote of 273–60. At the same time, the government announced the establishment of a special unit of nine police officers to carry out the necessary investigations. A month later, the bill passed a third time, paving the way for its final approval in the House of Lords.

The problem was, however, that there was very strong opposition to the bill among the Lords, and the possibility existed that if they did not pass the bill the government would drop its initiative. That did not happen, thank G-d, but the Lords did reject the bill twice. I have to say that listening to the arguments of those opposed to the legislation (I was in the gallery for one of the debates) was absolutely

painful and frankly bordered on anti-Semitic. Thus, for example, one
of the claims made was that the bill was "racist," since it only dealt with
Nazi murderers. Luckily, however, public opinion polls taken in the
wake of the first defeat of the bill in the House of Lords clearly showed
that there was very widespread support for the prosecution of Nazi
war criminals in Britain, and thus the bill was eventually resubmit-
ted to the House of Commons, where it was passed by a huge margin
(254–88) and was signed by Queen Elizabeth II on May 9, 1991, when it
became the law of the land. During the latter stages of this battle, most
of the political lobbying was done by the All-Party War Crimes Group
under the charismatic leadership of Greville Janner, MP, and by local
supporters. Our role was confined to continuing the search for additional suspects, which we submitted to the new War Crimes Unit of the
Metropolitan Police Service established for this purpose at Scotland
Yard. Our lengthy struggle, of almost five years, to convince the British
to acknowledge the presence of Nazi war criminals in the country and
enable their prosecution, was finally crowned with success.

In the meantime, Gecas lost a huge libel suit that he had launched
against STV, and on July 17, 1992, the judge in the case, Judge
Milligan, branded him a "war criminal." We hoped that this decision
would pave the way for his prosecution according to the new law, but
surprisingly, this did not happen. Despite the overwhelming evidence
against Gecas, Lord Roger Earlsferry, the Lord Advocate, announced
on February 3, 1994, that there was insufficient evidence to launch a
criminal prosecution against any of the Scottish suspects. When it was
subsequently revealed that Gecas had worked for British intelligence
in Scotland as an informer, this infuriating decision was suddenly not
that surprising.

IN ANY EVENT, I did not give up on the case, and several years later, I
finally convinced the Lithuanian authorities to ask for Gecas's extradition for war crimes. That request was submitted to the Scottish authorities on March 26, 2001, but, unfortunately, the process proceeded very
slowly, and by the time a warrant was issued for Gecas's arrest in late July
2001, he was already in failing health, which ultimately saved him from

extradition and prosecution. He died in Edinburgh on September 12, 2001, and was buried six days later in a secret funeral under a false name (A. Smith) lest the ceremony be targeted by anti-Nazi protesters. There was a small degree of comfort in the fact that this mass murderer, so many of whose Jewish victims were buried anonymously in unmarked graves, met his fate under a false name, but the fact of the matter is that even though he was the best suspect uncovered in Great Britain and enormous efforts were made to hold him accountable for his crimes, he ultimately eluded justice.

THE CAMPAIGN WE launched in Great Britain was not all for naught. On April 1, 1999, a court in London convicted Anton (Anthony) Sawoniuk of two counts of murder for his crimes during the Holocaust as a Belarusian policeman in his hometown of Domachevo. Sawoniuk, who was notorious for his hatred of the Jews, would routinely humiliate the inhabitants of the local ghetto. In 1942, a few days after Yom Kippur, he ordered 15 Jewish women to strip naked and stand on the edge of a pit before opening fire on them with a submachine gun. Sentenced to life imprisonment, he died on November 6, 2005, in Norwich Prison, unfortunately the only Nazi war criminal ever to be convicted and punished in Great Britain.

In summation, although the results achieved in Great Britain in practical judicial terms were minimal, the campaign waged and the passage of a law enabling the prosecution of local Nazi war criminals are of important educational, moral, and legal significance.

EIGHT

NAZIS UNDER THE MAPLE LEAF

THIS BOOK WOULD not be complete without at least several stories and insights into the history of Nazi war criminals in Canada. Like the other major Anglo-Saxon democracies, Canada opened its gates in the immediate aftermath of World War II to admit a massive influx of immigrants, among them numerous East Europeans who had collaborated with the Nazis. These people came to Canada for the same reasons, noted previously, that attracted their countrymen to the United States, Australia, and, to a lesser extent, Great Britain. They hoped to leave their homelands, now occupied by the Soviets or under Communist rule, and the scenes of their crimes far behind and to begin new lives for themselves and their families in safe and potentially prosperous environments, where the chances of being held accountable for their crimes were minimal or nonexistent. In that context, Canada was certainly a good choice, at least until the late-1980s.

The Wiesenthal Center's efforts to facilitate the prosecution of Nazi war criminals in Canada were helped and hindered by two unique factors that had a significant impact on its ability to influence events and on my own role in the process. The first was that a governmental commission of inquiry—the Deschênes Commission (named for the judge who headed it, Jules Deschênes) had already been established in Canada more than a year and a half before we began to submit the lists I compiled using the ITS files. That fact in itself was not unique since the Australian inquiry had also already been established before our campaign there began. What were unique were the circumstances of the establishment of the commission, which adversely affected the relations between the commission and Sol Littman, the director of our Canadian office.

The second factor was the existence of a Wiesenthal Center office in Toronto, which was headed by Littman, a veteran journalist with very good connections, who had been actively campaigning for the prosecution of Nazi war criminals long before the Canadian government ever dreamed of dealing with the issue. On the one hand, Sol Littman was the right person in the right place at the right time, but his justifiably aggressive tactics in response to government inaction on the issue soured Ottawa's relations with the Wiesenthal Center and severely limited our ability to assist the authorities in their efforts to locate and find evidence against the Holocaust perpetrators living in Canada.

In fact, the main reason that the Canadian government finally established the Deschênes Commission in February 1985 was a rumor, brought to its attention by Sol Littman, that Dr. Josef Mengele, the infamous Auschwitz doctor, may have entered Canada. Thus, the opening paragraph of the Minute-of-Council establishing the commission begins: "Whereas concern has been expressed about the possibility that Dr. Joseph Mengele, an alleged Nazi war criminal, may have entered or attempted to enter Canada...." Only afterward does the document refer to a far more convincing argument for the establishment of an official governmental inquiry, the concern that "other persons responsible for war crimes related to the activities of Nazi Germany during World War II...are currently resident in Canada."[1]

In that context, it is illuminating to recall that for many years Simon Wiesenthal refused to even visit Canada because of the government's refusal to take legal action against the numerous Nazi war criminals he asserted were living there, whose number he estimated to be approximately 3,000. Canada, it should be noted, was hardly any different in this regard from the United States, Australia, and Great Britain, all of which had failed miserably in the immigration screening process, ignored the issue for decades, and had to be literally embarrassed into investigating the Nazi war criminals issue and taking legal action against the Holocaust perpetrators living in their countries.

The circumstances that led to the establishment of the Deschênes Commission were just the beginning of a fundamentally flawed investigation that naturally produced a totally inadequate analysis of the essence and scope of the problem. For example, even though a large majority of the suspects living in Canada were East Europeans, the commission refused in principle to send the names of the suspects to any East European government, a decision that a priori doomed practically every such case to failure. The commission explained that its decision stemmed from a fear that the recipient countries might "publicize the names of the individuals and attempt to give the impression that the Commission or the Government of Canada had somehow conceded that these individuals were war criminals"[2]; this fear was baseless, however, as none of these countries, who had been dealing with the OSI on exactly the same issue, had ever done any such thing. The negative consequences of this flawed approach are evident in the case descriptions published in its final report. In more than 80 cases the conclusion presented is as follows:

1. Should the Government of Canada not wish, as a matter of policy, to submit the name of the subject to the Yad Vashem archives, to the relevant Eastern bloc government or the appropriate archival center, the file ought to be closed.
2. Should, however, the government of Canada decide to submit the subject's name to the Yad Vashem archive, to the relevant government or to the appropriate archival centers, the matter ought then to be reassessed and a final decision taken, depending upon the result of such inquiry.[3]

This clearly shows that in these cases the most basic and absolutely necessary historical investigations were not carried out, which enabled numerous Nazi war criminals to escape prosecution.

Another highly controversial decision was the refusal of the commission to investigate any of the members of the Ukrainian Galicia Division of the Waffen-SS, many of whom were living in Canada. The justification for the decision was that the commission was not created to indict "one or several particular groups of Canadians" or "to revive old hatreds which once existed between communities which should now live in peace in Canada."[4] But given the serious allegations against the unit, such reasoning is problematic and is tainted by irrelevant political considerations. Other faults in the research could be attributed to a lack of expertise. Thus, for example, descriptions of cases of East European suspects list several German archives that were consulted, but in practical terms, research in these archives was a total waste of time: they had no pertinent documentation on these suspected Nazis, who were neither Germans nor Austrians.

Under these circumstances, I suppose we have to be quite pleased that the Deschênes Commission actually found 20 cases of suspected Nazi war criminals living in Canada that, in its opinion, deserved urgent action and an additional 200 cases on which they recommended further research. Those findings, announced on March 12, 1987, led to the passage in mid-September of the same year of Bill 71, which amended the criminal code to enable the prosecution in Canada on criminal charges of Nazi war criminals.

During the initial seven years following the passage of the bill, four cases were brought to court, all of which failed for one reason or another, but the first case, that of the Hungarian gendarmerie officer Imre Finta, deserves particular scrutiny. Finta, who had the rank of captain, was the commander of the Hungarian gendarmerie in the city of Szeged. In that capacity, he was responsible for the ghettoization in spring 1944 of 8,617 Jews in a local brick factory under appalling conditions. During the period from June 24 to June 30, Finta organized the deportation of all the Jews in the Szeged ghetto from the Rokus railway station to the Auschwitz death camp under extremely harsh conditions, resulting in several deaths. On December 1, 1987, Finta became the first person charged under the new legislation. Yet despite the fact that he did not contest the prosecution's claims regarding his role in the events in

Szeged, he was acquitted on May 25, 1990, by a jury in Toronto on all eight counts of war crimes and crimes against humanity. The primary reason for his acquittal was that the jury accepted his arguments that he was merely following "superior orders" and that in the violently anti-Semitic atmosphere in Hungary at the time, it was not absolutely clear that the orders to deport the Jews of Szeged were illegal.

Given that the legal argument of "superior orders" had hitherto never been accepted in any Nazi war crimes trial and that the anti-Semitic decrees in Hungary were clearly against the Hungarian constitution—which Finta, as a lawyer, should have been well aware of—Finta's acquittal was particularly shocking, especially in view of the fact that he had already lost two libel cases in Canadian courts in connection with the same accusations against him. But appeals by the government against the verdict were rejected, Finta was never punished, and starting in 1994, when his acquittal was upheld by the Canadian Supreme Court, the Canadian government was forced to abandon its attempts to prosecute Holocaust perpetrators living in Canada on criminal charges since all would have been automatically acquitted based on the Finta precedent. The alternative chosen was the method of denaturalization and deportation for immigration and naturalization violations, which had been used successfully by the OSI. In Canada, however, only 8 persons were denaturalized prior to 2009 (compared to 75 in the United States), of whom not a single one has yet been deported, as compared with 60 deported from the United States.

DURING THE INITIAL years of the Canadian war crimes investigations, I compiled numerous lists of suspects who had immigrated to Canada, and Sol Littman was also involved in the research effort. Time and again, we met together or separately with the Canadian officials in charge of the unit carrying out the investigations (William Hobson and Peter Kremer) to try to facilitate maximum cooperation to help them find documents or witnesses regarding the crimes committed by the suspects in Canada, but these overtures were repeatedly rebuffed. At no point were they willing to share information or arrange a framework for mutual cooperation that could enhance their efforts.

The obvious frustrations inherent in this situation prompted me to try a more innovative, but potentially problematic, method of obtaining incriminating evidence against Canadian suspects. In early 1995, through a mutual acquaintance in Israel, I met a New York detective named Steve Rambam, who sought the center's support to conduct a wide-scale undercover operation in Canada to locate suspected Nazi war criminals and attempt to get them to incriminate themselves by confessing to their crimes. Initially, I cooperated with Rambam, but there was serious internal debate at the center about whether we should join the project, partly due to Rambam's extremely abrasive personality and his tendency to control every aspect of the operation, and partly due to legal and financial considerations. Rabbi Cooper and Sol Littman had very serious and legitimate reservations about Rambam, and the fact that he had a shady past did not help. In the end, Rambam was not given the center's official blessing, but he did receive a lot of names of suspects from me, which no doubt helped him carry out his planned operation.

Posing as Salvatore Romano, an assistant professor from a nonexistent institution named St. Paul's University of the Americas, located in Belize, for which he had especially prepared a school sweatshirt, complete with an invented logo, and a fake faculty card, Rambam went knocking on the doors of suspected Nazis. He claimed that he was writing a doctorate on the "interchangeability of civilian and military forces in a law-enforcement support role during wartime"[5] and was looking for background information. According to an extensive story in the *Jerusalem Post* by Robert Sarner and Steve Leibowitz, who accompanied Rambam on a few visits to suspected Nazi war criminals, the New York detective claimed to have located about 150 such individuals in Canada and actually visited 60 of them. The conversations he conducted in which he hoped to get the suspects to admit their crimes were clandestinely taped, but virtually none of the persons he interviewed ever made any self-incriminating confessions, although a few did acknowledge the murder of the Jews in their countries.

Despite the paucity of any hard evidence obtained by Rambam, his operation received extensive media coverage and earned him exceptional publicity, including numerous television stories and an appearance on *60 Minutes*. Part of the reason for the widespread media attention was a single relatively detailed interview he obtained from a former Lithuanian police chief whose name and current city of residence (Hope, British Columbia), along with details on his crimes, I had given to Rambam at a time when I thought that the center would enter into some sort of partnership with him.

The suspect in question was Antanas Kenstavičius, who had served as the chief of the Lithuanian police in the Švenčionys district in northeastern Lithuania. In the early fall of 1941, the Lithuanian police had rounded up approximately 8,000 Jews from the entire district and had incarcerated them in a former Polish army barracks named Polygon in a secluded wooded area outside the town. Initially, the men and young boys were murdered, and the women, children, and the elderly were killed about two weeks later. Kenstavičius described the shootings in a chillingly matter-of-fact manner, as if he were describing the most mundane event imaginable. His wife, Stella, also participated in the conversation, occasionally supplying some details.

In the final part of the interview, after Kenstavičius had described how the men and boys were shot in pits with infantry rifles, Rambam asked him about the women and children:

KENSTAVIČIUS:	After there were no mens.
RAMBAM:	OK. First the men and then the women?
KENSTAVIČIUS:	After, womens. The women in separate camp. Separate barracks.
RAMBAM:	What about the kids?
KENSTAVIČIUS:	The kids go with wives.
RAMBAM:	So the kids were with the women?
KENSTAVIČIUS:	With womens.
RAMBAM:	Now this is...
KENSTAVIČIUS:	First party, I look, after I no want to see. I sit there, and no want to see.
RAMBAM:	OK, let me ask you...
	(*Wife speaks in Lithuanian.*)
KENSTAVIČIUS:	And then, 9 November, one o'clock, finished. Uh...9 October, 1941, no more Jews."[6]

The words "one o'clock, finished... no more Jews" sent a shiver down my spine when Rambam played the tape for me the first time. I did not need to listen to the interview to learn the details of the murders. I knew them from my research on the case. I had even been to Polygon and had recited the Kaddish and memorial prayers for the victims at the site, among them Jews from Ligmiyan, my grandfather's shtetl. It was the blasé tenor of Kenstavičius's voice that terribly unnerved me and enraged me at the same time. It was the kind of "encounter" that I draw upon for inspiration and motivation when things are going badly.

As shocking as the tape was, it did not have any practical value, since Kenstavičius had already been charged by the Canadian government. I had already submitted his name to the Deschênes Commission in 1985, and long before he described the murders to Rambam in January 1996, I had compiled a list of potential witnesses against him as well as a dossier with witness statements taken immediately after the war, which Sol Littman and I had submitted in October 1990 to Peter Kremer, the director of the Canadian war crimes unit. Thus, the Lithuanian police chief was well known to the Canadian authorities, which had already initiated legal action against him. In fact, his trial was scheduled to begin exactly two months after a few segments of his interview were published in the *Jerusalem Post*. Unfortunately, however, Kenstavičius died on the day that his trial was to begin, about six months after his ninetieth birthday.

The irony of the story is that while Rambam's well-publicized operation did not lead to a single prosecution or legal action of any sort against any Nazi war criminal living in Canada, it was instrumental in the prosecution and punishment of a Holocaust perpetrator in Germany. Thus, in response to Rambam's public call for individuals with information regarding Nazi crimes to contact him, an economics professor at Concordia University in Montreal named Adalbert Lallier approached him. A Romanian *Volksdeutsche*, Lallier had been drafted at age 17 into the Waffen-SS and had been sent to serve in the Theresienstadt ghetto/concentration camp not far from Prague.

In March 1945, he was assigned to guard the inmates of the camp, who were taken to Leitmeritz, where they were forced to dig an antitank ditch as part of the attempt to halt the advance of the Red Army. At the end of the day, his commanding officer, the SS lieutenant Julius Viel, opened fire on the inmates, killing seven of them: Ladislav Kras (aged 27), Wilhelm Kauffmann (aged 29), Viktor Schulz (aged 42), Viktor Stern (aged 33), Josua Baruch (aged 23), Vlastimil Seerin (aged 48), and Robert Friedmann (aged 45). Viel, who had a successful career as a journalist after the war, had previously been investigated by German prosecutors but was never prosecuted because of a lack of evidence. Lallier's testimony, which was a direct result of Rambam's operation, led to Viel's conviction on April 3, 2001, in Ravensburg, Germany, for the murder of the 7 Jewish inmates and his being sentenced to 12 years in prison.

Unfortunately, this important and unqualified victory stands practically alone in the annals of the Canadian efforts to hold Nazi war criminals accountable. Although since 1994, when Canada switched to denaturalization and deportation, eight persons have been stripped of their Canadian citizenship for concealing their wartime activities, not a single one has hereto been deported from the country. Given the fact that the Holocaust perpetrators living in Canada have the same exact biographical profile as those in the United States, the OSI's numerous successes underscore the failure to date of the Canadian prosecution effort and point to a serious lack of political will in Ottawa (certainly as compared to Washington) to take successful legal action against the Nazi war criminals and collaborators living under the maple leaf.

NINE

A NEW OFFICE AND THE FALL OF COMMUNISM

FALL 1990 BROUGHT a positive development, a vote of confidence from Los Angeles. Rabbi Hier gave the green light for me to rent an office in Jerusalem and to set up a proper headquarters for our operation. Until this point, I had done most of my work at Yad Vashem and, when absolutely necessary, had access to an office in the home of the journalist Chaim Mass, who was a personal friend of Mr. Wiesenthal. In view, however, of the rapid expansion of our activities all over the globe and the importance of a permanent Israeli address for the center, the decision was made to establish an Israel office—at 1 Mendele Mocher Seforim Street in the Talbiah section of Jerusalem, a very nice residential neighborhood, walking distance from the center of the city, all the major hotels, and even the Old City.

This also meant that I could finally hire a full-time office manager and thereby increase the effectiveness of our activities. There were many candidates for the job, since there is a certain allure to working for the Wiesenthal Center and since many people fantasize about helping to catch Nazis, but our bottom line was not such dreams but cool-headed efficiency, which is why I chose Talma Hurwitz. A former kibbutznik with a very good work ethic, Talma has, for the past 19 years, been an anchor of stability and efficiency in our office. And although we come from totally different political and religious backgrounds, we have worked together in friendship and harmony for almost two decades.

Several months after we opened our office in Jerusalem, a watershed series of events radically altered the political map of Eastern Europe and created a totally new reality as far as the Nazi war crimes issue was concerned. I am referring to the breakup of the Soviet Union and the fall of Communism. The transition from totalitarianism to democracy opened up new possibilities to locate and bring to trial Holocaust perpetrators that were previously unimaginable. Even though the Soviet Union and other Communist regimes categorized themselves as "antifascist" and frequently reiterated their determination to bring Nazi war criminals to justice, in practice that was not always the case. They never allowed open access to the pertinent archives or to potential witnesses. The government officials were the ones who decided which documents and witnesses would be provided and which cases were worthy of their attention. Given the likelihood that some of the criminals who escaped to the West might have agreed to serve as spies in return for immunity from prosecution, this was a very undesirable situation, which, thank G-d, finally came to an end in 1991.

Given the historical significance of the Holocaust crimes committed in Eastern Europe, which far outnumbered those committed elsewhere, and the extensive scope of the collaboration of the local population in the annihilation process there, the political changes in the area created a very good opportunity to bring Holocaust perpetrators to justice, locally and abroad. In that context, it is important to remember the nature and scope of local collaboration with the Nazis, who tried for both ideological and practical reasons to maximize the number of locals actively involved in the implementation of their anti-Jewish policies. From an ideological perspective, this assistance ostensibly proved that there was broad support for the persecution of the Jewish population. From a practical point of view, it spared German and Austrian manpower, which could be used for other tasks. Furthermore, the assistance provided by locals was critical in the implementation of the anti-Jewish decrees, since their ability to identify Jews trying to pass as non-Jews or hide was obviously greater than that of the Nazis, who were neither well acquainted with the local conditions nor fluent in the local language. In addition, the logistic support they could provide in the implementation of the Final Solution was also quite significant, for the same reasons.

In practice, the Nazis' efforts to enlist local help for their anti-Jewish policies were quite successful. In fact, there was not a single country occupied by, or allied with, the Third Reich in which the Nazis did not succeed in enlisting the help of at least some local collaborators to help in the persecution of the Jews. It is important to note, however, that there was a highly significant qualitative difference between the nature of the collaboration in Eastern Europe and the help provided by locals to the Nazis elsewhere. Whereas the local participants in the implementation of the Final Solution in western, southern, northern, and central Europe helped carry out the initial stages of the process—the identification, the Aryanization of property, and the concentration and deportation of the local Jews—their role stopped at the train station, where the Jews were forced into trains that would deliver them to Nazi death camps in Poland. The French police did indeed round up the French Jews for deportation, as did their Dutch, Belgian, Norwegian, Greek, and other counterparts, but they did not personally kill the Jews. Their crimes were undoubtedly terrible, but were not as reprehensible as those of many of the collaborators in Eastern Europe.

In Eastern Europe, the situation developed differently, and the role played by local collaborators in the implementation of the Final Solution was of much greater significance. Unlike the situation elsewhere, the Nazis incorporated local collaborators in the process of mass annihilation throughout Eastern Europe (with the exception of Poland) and made extensive use of special murder squads they established specifically for the mass murder of Jews. Nowhere was the role played in the murders by the locals as important and extensive as in the Baltic states. In Lithuania, Latvia, and Estonia, the locals played a major role in the mass killings, and their participation contributed significantly to the extremely high percentages of Jews murdered in these countries, which were the highest in Europe (all over 95 percent). In the Baltic states all of the following phenomena took place during the Holocaust:

1. large-scale local collaboration in the mass murder;
2. the deportation to these three countries of thousands of Jews from central and/or western Europe to be murdered there, in many cases by local killers;
3. the employment of local security police units to assist in the mass murder of Jews in other countries, especially in Belarus and Poland.

Thus, the breakup of the Soviet Union and the transition to democracy created new possibilities not only for prosecuting Holocaust perpetrators living in Eastern Europe (although many of those guilty had been put on trial by the Soviets or the Communists in the immediate aftermath of World War II), but also for obtaining the necessary evidence to secure convictions against East European Nazi war criminals who had escaped to the West and especially to the Anglo-Saxon democracies. In fact, the cataclysmic changes in Eastern Europe breathed new life and vitality into our efforts to secure justice and created new challenges that led to the expansion of our activities to include the fight against local anti-Semitism and the struggle to preserve the accuracy of the accounts of the events of the Holocaust in the new history books and textbooks being written in the post-Communist countries of eastern Europe.

TEN

LITHUANIA

A STRUGGLE FOR JUSTICE AND TRUTH IN THE LAND OF MY FOREFATHERS

ON JUNE 19, 1991, I landed at Riga International Airport on my way to Vilnius, the capital of newly independent Lithuania. I was full of curiosity and anticipation regarding the upcoming week that I was going to spend in the ancestral home of my forefathers. Along with a group of members of the Knesset (the Israeli parliament) and representatives of world Jewish organizations, I had been invited to attend the dedication of an impressive new monument at Ponar (Paneriai in Lithuanian), the site of the mass murder of the Jews of Vilnius. Approximately 70,000 Jews had been murdered there during the years 1941–1944, making it one of the largest sites of Jewish murder during the Holocaust, outside the death camps.

As an extremely proud Litvak (Jew of Lithuanian origin), I was naturally very pleased to have the opportunity to come to Lithuania so soon after the fall of Communism, but there was also a personal element to my anticipation. My namesake, my great-uncle Efraim Zar, and his family had been murdered in Vilnius, and I hoped, during the trip, to learn the details of their fate, about which we knew almost nothing. There were several articles on my grandfather's family in a memorial volume, published in the sixties, dedicated to their shtetl, Ligmiyan, among other towns, which mentioned that his brother Efraim had been murdered at Ponar, but we had no details or corroboration of this information, which was apparently based on hearsay. I hoped that the trip would allow me to verify the details of the tragic fate of Efraim and his family.

I had originally thought about this possibility when I was visiting the United States and decided to try to find potential witnesses who might have been with Efraim during the Holocaust. I knew that prior to World War II, he had been the *rosh yeshiva* (head) of a Talmudic academy in eastern Poland, but that in September 1939, after this area had been occupied by the Soviets, he, like hundreds of Polish rabbis and yeshiva students who feared the repression of Jewish education by the Communists, had fled to Vilnius, which at that point belonged to the independent republic of Lithuania. And it was there that he, his wife, Beyla, and sons, Hirsh and Eliyahu, had been murdered.

I also knew that Efraim had been an *illui* (prodigy) who had studied for many years at the Radin Yeshiva, one of the world's most famous Talmudic academies, and thought that I should begin my search by trying to find survivors from that yeshiva, whose rabbis and students had also fled to Vilnius following the Soviet occupation of eastern Poland. My inquiries yielded the name of a survivor living in Jerusalem named Kalman Farber, who had studied in Radin as a youth and had escaped to Vilnius, where he survived the Holocaust. I only had a few days between my return from the United States and my departure for Lithuania and was so busy that I could not even try to track down Farber, which upset me, but I assumed that if worse came to worst I could always find him upon my return home.

As I stood outside the Riga terminal waiting for the bus that would take us to Vilnius, my eyes started scanning the numerous suitcases of my fellow travelers lined up on the sidewalk. All of a sudden, a name tag caught my attention. I could not believe my eyes. The name was "Kalman Farber." This was too good to be true. Was he here with us, on his way to Vilnius? I waited to see who would pick up this suitcase, and when the bus arrived, a young man of about 30 reached over to take it. "Are you by any chance Kalman Farber's son?" I asked hopefully.

When he replied in the affirmative, I inquired whether his father was a member of our group. Before he could confirm the fact, an elderly man came over, whom the son introduced as his father. "Shalom, did you study at the Radin Yeshiva?" I asked. "Yes, I did," he replied. I introduced myself as we boarded the bus and explained why I was so happy to meet him. Unfortunately, the name Efraim Zar did not ring a bell with him, and so I went to find a seat on the bus, painfully disappointed.

About 15 minutes later, however, Farber came over to me and invited me to sit down next to him. "Tell me," he asked, "what shtetl was Efraim from?" When I told him Ligmiyan, his eyes lit up. "Efraim Ligmiyaner. Of course, Efraim Ligmiyaner. At the yeshiva we never knew our fellow student's family names. We used to refer to each other by the name of the shtetl that we came from." My heart skipped a few beats. "So you knew him?" "Of course," Farber replied, and began to tell me about my great-uncle, whose name I bear. He confirmed the family lore that Efraim had indeed been an outstanding student who was considered to have great potential in the world of Torah learning, a fact that I thought might have been exaggerated due to his tragic death. In addition, he said that Efraim had a very sunny disposition and was considered to have had a very good personality.

Efraim and Farber went their separate ways after Radin, but they met again in late 1939 or early 1940 in Vilnius, to which both had escaped from Poland. But the Efraim of Vilnius was quite a different person. According to Farber, he was very depressed and no doubt worried about the precarious situation of the Jews in the wake of the outbreak of World War II and the uncertain future that faced the rabbis and yeshiva students who were refugees in Lithuania. Since very few of his own students had fled to Vilnius, Efraim studied with a group of rabbis who had also escaped there. On the fast day of the seventeenth of the month of Tammuz (established to mark the Romans breaching the walls of the city of Jerusalem in the year 70 CE, leading to the burning down of the Second Temple three weeks later), which in 1941 was observed on July 13, Efraim was seized by a gang of Lithuanians who were roaming the streets of Vilnius looking for Jews with beards. They took him to Lukiškės Prison, to this day the central prison in the city, where he disappeared, never to be seen again by his family or friends. The assumption was that shortly thereafter he was taken from there to Ponar, where he was murdered.

"What about his family? Did you know his wife, Beyla, and his sons, Eliyahu and Hirsh? What happened to them?" Farber unfortunately had no information about their fate, which still remains a mystery. All we know is that they were living in Vilnius at Sopena 3, apartment 19, and that they did not survive the war. I asked him whether there were other survivors who might have known the family in Vilnius, but he did not know. I wrote down all the information on a piece of paper that, to this day, I keep in my wallet. I thanked Farber profusely for his help and went to sit by myself, trying to absorb the details that had just come to light, almost exactly 50 years to the day that Efraim had been seized by Lithuanian Nazi collaborators in the streets of Vilnius.

THE DEDICATION CEREMONY of the monument at Ponar took place the next day, June 20. On the surface, it was ostensibly a symbol of the important positive changes that had taken place in the wake of Lithuanian independence. In the Soviet Union, the events of the Holocaust were often manipulated for propaganda purposes to stress the sterling antifascist credentials of the Soviet Union and its role in the defeat of Nazi Germany. Invariably, the identity of the Nazis' primary victims—the Jews—was concealed, as was the ethnic identity of the local killers. In places like Ponar, the monuments bore inscriptions such as "To the victims of fascism," and the books published locally about the Holocaust spoke of the bourgeois or Hitlerite fascists who murdered peace-loving Soviet citizens. One of the hopes of the Jewish world in this regard was that the countries that had been part of the Soviet Union would start to tell the truth about the events of the Holocaust, and especially regarding the central role played by local murderers in the annihilation of Jewish communities.

Yet anyone who had followed the controversies surrounding the construction of the new monument and had carefully listened to the speech of the Lithuanian prime minister Gediminas Vagnorius should have understood that while some of the problems caused by

Communist rule may have ended with the fall of the Soviet regime, we now would be facing new variations of the same very serious difficulties. In this respect, the impressive official ceremony attended by leading Lithuanian officials could not hide the deep-seated issues concerning Holocaust history, justice, restitution, and education that would soon rise to the surface.

The debates began long before the ceremony. The text proposed by the Jews, whose initiative and funding helped create the monument, named "the Nazis and their local collaborators" as responsible for the murders, a formulation rejected by the Lithuanian authorities, who refused to approve the use of the adjective "local" in reference to the murderers, since in their opinion it constituted an indictment of the entire Lithuanian people. In the end, that word did not appear in the Lithuanian, Russian, Hebrew, or Yiddish texts on the monument. This controversy was merely the tip of the iceberg—the initial manifestation of a very bitter ongoing struggle over Holocaust history in Lithuania, which I continue to actively wage to this very day.

Gediminas Vagnorius, the first prime minister of an independent Lithuania in more than half a century, was the featured speaker at the dedication ceremony. I will never forget his speech, which I felt was an urgent danger signal regarding the future and which impressed upon me the difficult reality I was up against in my efforts to bring Lithuanian Holocaust perpetrators to justice. "Let us not forget that this tragedy lasted for more than the wink of an eye, but at least three months," the prime minister solemnly intoned, reducing the scope of the Holocaust by 87 percent—from three years to three months in one fell swoop. Even more objectionable was his attempt to minimize the enormous responsibility of Lithuanian collaborators in the tragedy by claiming that the (in fact extremely limited) assistance provided by Lithuanians to Jews during the Holocaust and the joint efforts of Jews and Lithuanians to help the country achieve political independence prove that "a group of criminals cannot outweigh the good name of a nation, nor can it rob it of its conscience and decency."[1] Thus, instead of admitting the fact that thousands of Lithuanians from all strata of society—from intelligentsia and clergy to criminal elements—had been active participants in the mass murder of Jews both in Lithuania and outside her borders, he chose to whitewash the historical record by creating a false symmetry between those few brave individuals who helped Jews and the many thousands who murdered them. So if any of us had high hopes that the truth about the Holocaust in Lithuania would now become the accepted narrative and that an honest effort would be made to bring Lithuanian murderers to justice, his words, like the downpour that drenched the participants during his speech, washed away all our illusions.

The dedication ceremony at Ponar was, in that respect, a litmus test for the intentions of the Lithuanian government in regard to a whole range of Holocaust-related issues that it, and its fellow post-Communist democracies, was forced to face, almost immediately in the wake of independence. Under different circumstances, these issues would not have been granted priority, but several factors considered critical by these new East European states catapulted Holocaust-related subjects to near the top of the political agenda. For fear of the Russians, all of these governments viewed membership in NATO and the European Union as their primary foreign policy objective, and virtually all of them believed that their success in achieving these goals would be seriously influenced by their relations with the Jewish people and the State of Israel.

In other words, the paths to Washington and Brussels went through Jerusalem. It was clear to these leaders, however, that to enlist Jewish assistance, they would have to mend their fences with the Jewish people (represented primarily by Israel, American Jewry, and their own local Jewish communities), a critical element of which involved dealing with the crimes of their compatriots during the Holocaust. In essence, these countries faced six major issues directly connected to the destruction of European Jewry:

1. acknowledgment of guilt and apology for crimes;
2. commemoration of the victims;
3. prosecution of perpetrators;
4. documentation—rewriting the historical narrative;
5. education—writing new textbooks; and
6. restitution.

In retrospect, as someone who has devoted a large part of the past 18 years to these issues in post-Communist Europe, I would distinguish between the issues that proved to be relatively easy, such as the acknowledgment of guilt and commemoration, and those that have proven to be the most difficult, such as prosecution and restitution. Practically all East European leaders were willing to acknowledge the participation of their compatriots in Holocaust crimes, apologize for them, and express deep regret, but very few, if any, invested any real effort in seeing to it that those still-unprosecuted Holocaust perpetrators would be brought to trial. Another important point, especially from my perspective, is that of all these issues, only one, prosecution, is time-sensitive and must be dealt with while the murderers are still alive. All the others, including restitution, should obviously be dealt with promptly, but if worse comes to worst can be postponed and initiated at a later date.

My focus, therefore, was first and foremost to facilitate the prosecution of as many local Nazi war criminals as possible, a task that proved to be extremely difficult and incredibly frustrating. In Lithuania, these efforts began on a related subject that was initially not on our agenda. In May 1990, as Lithuania approached independence, the parliament passed a special law permitting the rehabilitation of individuals (including those no longer alive) wrongly convicted by the Soviets, in many cases for political crimes. These individuals had their convictions erased and were granted financial compensation of 5,000 rubles and the return of property confiscated upon conviction. Although the law clearly stated that persons who had "participated in genocide" were ineligible for rehabilitation, I was informed by a Holocaust survivor named Rivka Bogomolna living in Vilnius (originally from Butrimonys) that two individuals who had actively participated in the mass murder of the Jews of her shtetl, Juozas Krasinskas and Kazy Grinevičius, had been granted such pardons. During my trip to Lithuania for the dedication of the Ponar monument, I met with Knesset Speaker Dov Shilansky and other Members of the Knesset, along with the Lithuanian prosecutor general Arturas Paulauskas, to protest the pardons given to these killers, but no real progress was made.

TWO AND A half months later, however, I was able to achieve a breakthrough with the help of Professor Shmuel Kuklianskis and his daughter Faina, who provided me with the trial records of 12 Lithuanians who had been granted rehabilitations despite having been convicted shortly after the end of World War II for their active participation in the mass murder of Jews. For example, Aloizas Juodis, who had served in the notorious 12th Lithuanian Auxiliary Police Battalion, which murdered many thousands of Jews in Lithuania and Belarus, openly admitted to his participation in a mass murder of Jews in a village near Minsk, for which he was originally sentenced to 25 years' imprisonment. Ignas Asadauskas, who served as deputy chief of the Lithuanian police in Oran, was sentenced to death for his active participation in the mass murder of close to 200 members of the local Jewish community, which was liquidated in the summer of 1941. Julius Nevera was sentenced to 25 years in prison for his participation in the execution of close to 800 Jews in the town of Kupiskis in the summer of 1941. I sent the documents to Rabbi Hier, who submitted them to the *New York Times*, which ran a front-page story by Stephen Kinzer on this shocking development on September 5, 1991—ironically, the day after Lithuania was admitted to the United Nations.

The initial reaction of the Lithuanians to these embarrassing revelations was total denial. Prosecutor General Paulauskas denied that Juodis or Nevera had been granted rehabilitations and claimed that an investigation had proven that Asadauskas had not participated in the murders. The Lithuanian president Vytautis Landsbergis criticized the report in the *New York Times* and denied that thousands of Holocaust perpetrators were being "legally absolved as patriots of Lithuania."[2]

Within less than a week, however, the same Landsbergis suggested to Knesset Speaker Shilansky the establishment of a joint Lithuanian-Israeli commission of inquiry to investigate the issue. Shilansky accepted the offer, but due to elections both in Israel and Lithuania, there was at first no progress on the matter. The election as president in late 1992 of the former Communist leader Algirdas Brazauskas, who was much more sympathetic to Jewish concerns on Holocaust issues, apparently helped finally move things forward. Thus, in June 1993, the former Israeli justice minister MK Dan Meridor, Professor Dov Levin, a Lithuanian Holocaust survivor who had fought with the anti-Nazi Soviet partisans and later became the world's preeminent expert on the fate of Baltic Jewry during the Holocaust, and I traveled to Vilnius to represent Israel in the negotiations regarding the commencement of the investigations by the joint commission of inquiry.

The primary issues on the agenda were our demand to receive full access to the files of all the estimated 35,000 persons who had been granted rehabilitation and the clarification of the term "participation in genocide," which, according to Lithuanian law, denied individuals from being granted rehabilitation. On both counts we were successful. President Brazauskas himself promised full access to the archives (which Lithuanian officials had hitherto categorically refused to grant) and indicated that all persons involved in any way in the persecution of Jews would be denied rehabilitation. If any legal obstacles might prevent such action, Brazauskas endeavored to issue the necessary presidential decree to facilitate the cancellation of pardons granted illegally.

The investigation was scheduled to begin in fall 1993, but due to bureaucratic delays in Israel, our delegation, which had been appointed by Foreign Minister Shimon Peres and consisted of the retired judge Aryeh Segalson, the advocate Yosef Melamed (both Lithuanian Holocaust survivors), and I, arrived in Vilnius only in late January 1995. By this time, I already had a list of 58 individuals who had participated in genocide yet had been granted rehabilitation. It was clear to me, however, that this figure was merely the tip of the iceberg, and we therefore hoped that the Lithuanians would keep President Brazauskas's promise to grant us full access to all the rehabilitation files.

Upon our arrival, we learned that local opponents of the process were already at work, among them a Lithuanian member of the commission named Vidmantas Vaicekauskas, who not only gave a very negative interview about the commission to the *Respublika* daily, but even contacted the families of those on our list of 58 illegal rehabilitations to ask whether they agreed to allow Israeli researchers to examine their relatives' files. The fact that Vaicekauskas was the director of the special

department for war crimes in the Office of the Prosecutor-General is a
clear indication of the problems we faced in our task. (He was removed
from the commission but not from his job.) We received another powerful reminder of the strong public opposition to the commission the
next day when an enraged Lithuanian burst into the room where we
were working and screamed at us: "Who gave you permission to come
here and investigate? These people [the KGB] murdered Lithuanians.
All the Jews should be taken away and shot. Why did they leave any
alive? I will take an automatic weapon and kill all of you and your president" (he apparently meant Brazauskas, not Weizman). Luckily, he was
unarmed and was quickly removed by a policeman.

After several days of research, we met with our Lithuanian counterparts to discuss the practical aspects of the continuation of the
investigation. The key problems were obviously the reluctance of
the Lithuanians to provide us with all the pertinent documentation
and the lack of transparency in the rehabilitation process. Thus, for
example, they only provided 40 of the 59 files (an additional name was
added to our original list) that we had requested, and, with one exception, there was no explanation in any of the files why rehabilitations
had been granted in cases in which individuals had been convicted for
the murder of civilians. Our primary request, therefore, was to receive
a complete list of all those who had been granted rehabilitation, since
in order for us to be sure that no murderers of Jews had been pardoned,
we obviously had to receive all the names of rehabilitation recipients.
The Lithuanians responded that this would be an infringement of their
sovereignty.

Eventually, we reached a compromise whereby they would initially
send us the names of all those indicted for the persecution and/or
murder of civilians who had been granted rehabilitation (approximately 10 percent of the total of 50,000 Lithuanians pardoned). We
would then add the names of the perpetrators known to us who did
not appear on their list, and we would be able to review all the files
of the individuals on this master list. The meeting ended without
resolving how disputes would be decided and what legal mechanism

would be used to cancel the illegal rehabilitations. But the three of us left Vilnius with the sense that at least the investigation process had finally been launched. Having said that, it was clear to us that the success of the investigation process would depend primarily on the cooperation of the Lithuanians, a factor that clearly was at best uncertain.

Fourteen years later, I can relate that the Lithuanians did not keep a single promise made to the Israeli delegation. In fact, they never sent us the list of those indicted for the murder of civilians who had been granted rehabilitation, and the joint investigative process never got off the ground. What did take place was a review carried out exclusively by the Lithuanians, who to date have cancelled approximately 225 rehabilitations illegally granted to individuals who were ineligible for pardons. But this very important achievement must be tempered by the fact that the local media have virtually ignored this story. Nor is it clear whether the individuals whose rehabilitations were cancelled have been forced to return the funds and property they received or have been prosecuted for false declarations. In other words, a highly significant victory in the battle for truth about the Holocaust in Lithuania, which was achieved primarily due to international pressure, was purposely minimized by the Lithuanian authorities and the local media.

Since Lithuanian independence, my activities there became the source of much hostility, which was directed both at me and the Wiesenthal Center, to the extent that I often felt that I was the most hated Jew in the Baltic states in general and in Lithuania in particular. Whether it was visually unflattering caricatures in the local media, very nasty talkbacks in the news portals, or attacks by right-wing politicians who demanded that I be declared a persona non grata, the message was abundantly clear. For many Lithuanians, my call upon them to honestly acknowledge the scope of the complicity of their compatriots in the mass murder of Jews during the Holocaust, both in Lithuania and outside her borders, and to bring their hereto unprosecuted killers of Jews to justice was simply unacceptable.

IN ASSESSING THE impact and results of our campaign to help bring local Holocaust perpetrators to justice, several historical facts must be borne in mind. The first is the enormous scope of Lithuanian complicity in the murder of Jews, which was a vital factor in the extremely high percentage of Jews annihilated in Lithuania during the Holocaust. Of the approximately 220,000 Jews who were living in the country under the Nazi occupation, only about 8,000 survived, a victimology rate of 96.4 percent, the highest in Europe with the exception of Estonia, where the minuscule figures involved make the statistics far less significant. In that context, the logistics of the annihilation process in Lithuania played a highly critical role. Unlike the situation in most of the rest of Europe, from where Jews were deported to be murdered elsewhere, the mass murders in Lithuania were carried out close to home with the active participation of local helpers in every single location.

The second is that the many thousands of Lithuanians who actively participated in the murders came from all strata of Lithuanian society, including the clergy and intelligentsia, which makes it impossible to dismiss local collaboration with the Nazis as a phenomenon limited to the marginal elements of Lithuanian society. On the contrary, it truly reflected the ethos of World War II Lithuanian society. In fact, Lithuania is the only country in Europe in which a special term was coined for the "shooters of Jews" (*žydšaudžiai*), another proof that the phenomenon was hardly marginal.

The third is that the Soviets prosecuted many of the Lithuanians they caught who collaborated with the Nazis and meted out relatively harsh sentences. These trials, which were undoubtedly painful for the Lithuanians as a people, created the illusion that justice had been fully served and that local collaborators had been sufficiently punished. Forgotten or ignored was the fact, however, that many of the major perpetrators and those who had served in the notorious Lithuanian murder squads (Ypatingas būrys, which carried out the mass murders at Ponar, and the 12th Lithuanian Auxiliary Police Battalion, which murdered many thousands of Jews in Kaunas and in Belarus) had escaped punishment by fleeing to the West, primarily to the Anglo-Saxon democracies. As it turned out, this last fact was to have a profound impact on the prosecution of local Nazi war criminals in Lithuania.

The country that over the past three decades has had the greatest success in the prosecution of Nazi war criminals has been the United States, and among the Holocaust perpetrators prosecuted there have been numerous Lithuanians. In fact, they are probably the ethnic group against which the U.S. authorities have had the greatest success. With one exception, all the Lithuanians denaturalized by the OSI and deported from the United States have returned to Lithuania. Since these criminals could not be prosecuted for genocide, war crimes, or crimes against humanity in the United States (because the crimes were not committed on American territory, nor were the victims Americans) and in view of their return to Lithuania, an ideal possibility was created for the prosecution of quite a few Holocaust perpetrators in the Baltic republic. The fact that several of the Lithuanians denaturalized and deported from the United States had occupied fairly prominent positions in the Lithuanian security police or served in murder squads increased the potential for criminal prosecution in their country of origin.

Over the past 18 years, I have tried very hard to facilitate the prosecution of Nazi war criminals in Lithuania, one of the countries in which the Wiesenthal Center invested much effort. Our primary focus was on the leaders of the Saugumas (Lithuanian security police) in the Vilnius district—the commander, Aleksandras Lileikis and his deputy, Kazys Gimžauskas. The Saugumas played a very important role in the Nazis' plan for the systematic annihilation of the Jews of Vilnius. They guarded the Vilnius ghetto to prevent Jews from escaping and any non-Jews from providing help. Jews caught by the Saugumas were turned over to the Ypatingas būrys unit to be murdered. Among the Jews whose execution was ordered by Lileikis were six-year-old Fruma Kaplan and her mother, Gita, who were murdered on December 22, 1941, at Ponar. Gimžauskas also personally ordered the arrest and imprisonment of civilians, mostly Jews, many of whom were turned over to the Nazi murderers. Although neither of these men could be prosecuted in the United States for those crimes, the OSI historian Michael MacQueen did an excellent job of researching their role in the implementation of the Final Solution in Vilnius, which provided a solid basis for their prosecution in Lithuania.

The problem was, however, that the Lithuanian authorities were in no hurry to press charges against the two Saugumas officers. Their stance was extremely worrying and caused me considerable anguish, because besides my obvious desire to see them prosecuted, I had personally played a key role in seeing to it that Lileikis returned to Lithuania, a story revealed here for the first time. My involvement began on May 24, 1996, the day that he was stripped of his American citizenship. Having closely followed the case and being well aware of its significance due to the important role Lileikis played in the murders in Vilnius, I called the OSI director Eli Rosenbaum to congratulate him on the decision, expecting him to be elated. I was therefore extremely surprised to find him rather dejected, which he explained was due to his pessimistic prognosis regarding the continuation of the case. Lileikis had indeed been stripped of his U.S. citizenship but, given his advanced age (he was born in 1907), it was doubtful whether the OSI would succeed in having him deported, a fact that clearly frustrated Rosenbaum enormously, for obvious reasons.

Upset by this turn of events, I thought about the existing options and came up with a plan. Lileikis would naturally have preferred to stay in the United States, but what if there was a possibility of his extradition to Israel to face genocide charges? Under those circumstances, he most probably would prefer to be in a country such as Lithuania, which would refuse to extradite him for trial. I knew that Israel, which was still traumatized by the ostensible failure of the Demjanjuk trial, would not be willing to seek Lileikis's extradition, but he probably wasn't aware of that fact. It might be enough, therefore, to simply convince him that the Jewish state was seriously considering that option. So I decided to bluff. I called Irit Kahn, the director of the international department of the Ministry of Justice, and explained the situation, noting that all Israel had to do to help was to make known that it was seriously considering the Lileikis case with a view to possibly requesting his extradition. I would do the rest. Irit, who understood the situation perfectly, immediately agreed, and I then called Judy Rakowsky, the legal affairs correspondent of the *Boston Globe*, who had covered the Lileikis case from the beginning, to inform her of the latest development. I was sure that if the *Globe* would report on Israel's interest, Lileikis, who lived in Norwood, Massachusetts, near Boston, would find out about it and take the necessary measures to prevent extradition. Sure enough, Rakowsky called Irit Kahn, who confirmed the story, and within less than two weeks, Lileikis departed from the United States forever. Thus, my plan had solved the problem from an American perspective (and Eli Rosenbaum's pessimistic prognosis was averted), but the question now became whether Lithuania had the political will to prosecute the high-ranking Saugumas commander and his deputy.

In theory, Lileikis and Gimžauskas, who had already arrived in Lithuania in 1993, should have been immediately arrested upon arrival in Vilnius and prosecuted as quickly as possible, especially in view of their advanced age. That is what would have happened had the Lithuanian government been determined to hold its Holocaust perpetrators accountable, but that was not the case. On the contrary, despite President Brazauskas's promise to the Knesset in 1995 that his country would prosecute Lithuanian Nazi war criminals "publicly, consistently and conscientiously,"[3] years passed before any action was taken. Thus Gimžauskas was only indicted on November 20, 1997, and more than a year and a half passed before Lileikis, who landed in Vilnius in June 1996, was charged on February 6, 1998, in both cases only after they were ruled medically unfit to stand trial. Neither was ever incarcerated for any length of time, nor was either of them ever obligated to appear at a single session of their trials (although Lileikis briefly appeared once of his own volition on November 5, 1998).

During this period, the Lithuanian Seimas (parliament) passed three special laws in response to pressure from the United States, Israel, and Jewish organizations to prosecute Lileikis and Gimžauskas. The laws permitted the investigation of medically unfit genocide suspects, the indictment and prosecution of such suspects, and the conducting of the trials of these suspects via video hookup. The truth was, however, that instead of turning the trials into watershed educational events that would have a significant impact on Lithuanian society, the Lithuanians basically turned them into a farce that only reinforced the prevailing reluctance to confront the scope of Lithuanian complicity in Holocaust crimes. Lileikis, who wrote his memoirs while under indictment, died on September 26, 2000, before his trial was completed, and by the time Gimžauskas was convicted on January 14, 2001, he was too ill to be punished, outcomes that only strengthened those elements of Lithuanian society that considered these "desk murderers" (individuals who gave orders that resulted in deaths but did not personally pull the trigger) patriots and heroes.

MORE RECENTLY, THERE have been new developments that clearly prove that if anything, at least in judicial terms, Lithuania is farther away from facing the truth than ever before. For example, on March 27, 2006, Algimantas Dailide, a member of the Vilnius Saugumas, was convicted in Vilnius for his role in the persecution of Jews and Poles during World War II and sentenced to five years in prison, the first time ever that a Lithuanian healthy enough to be tried and punished was convicted by a local court. The judges, however, refused to implement his sentence on the grounds that he was old, his wife was sick, and Dailide did not pose a danger to society. Outraged by this show of compassion for a person who had no sympathy whatsoever for his innocent and helpless victims, I pressed the Lithuanian prosecutor to appeal the verdict, as did many others. After more than two years of delay, the prosecutor's appeal was rejected when, on July 4, 2008, the court ruled that Dailide was not medically fit to serve his sentence, although he had not been obligated to appear in person for an examination by the experts who reached this dubious conclusion. Journalists who more recently have visited Dailide in Kirschberg, Germany, where he currently resides, have found him in reasonable health, taking care of his wife, who was indeed very ill and has since died.

As frustrating and infuriating as the Dailide case was, it pales in comparison to the latest efforts by the Lithuanian judiciary to prosecute Jewish anti-Nazi Soviet partisans for war crimes during World War II. On September 10, 2007, prosecutors announced that they were opening an official investigation against an Israeli citizen for war crimes committed during World War II and sent a request to Israel for judicial assistance in the case. Although this was not the first such request, the identity of the suspect was shocking, to say the least. The allegation was that the well-known Holocaust scholar Dr. Yitzchak Arad, who had served for many years as the chairman of Yad Vashem and previously had been the chief education officer of the Israeli Army, had committed war crimes against Lithuanian civilians while serving with the anti-Nazi Soviet partisans. In the wake of this investigation, armed Lithuanian plainclothes police went to private addresses in Vilnius looking for former Jewish Soviet partisans Rochel Margolis and Fania Brantsovsky, both of whom served in Soviet anti-Nazi units. These steps were accompanied by vicious anti-Semitic articles by Lithuanian academics, one of which referred to Dr. Arad as a terrorist and to Brantsovsky as a murderer who should be brought to trial. When various Jewish groups protested the mistreatment and singling out of Jewish partisans, the prosecutors said that Margolis and Brantsovsky were merely sought as "witnesses," but were unwilling to promise that they would not be prosecuted. Only in the wake of a vigorous international campaign was the investigation against Dr. Arad officially dropped (although the prosecutor, at the same time, called upon the public to supply any existent incriminating information against him).

This incident sent a clear message that Lithuania was determined to delegitimize the quest by Jews like myself to bring Lithuanian Holocaust perpetrators to justice by leveling equally horrible charges against Jewish heroes. Add a governmental campaign to equalize Communist and Nazi crimes and disseminate the false "double genocide" theory (which claims that the Soviets carried out a systematic policy of genocide against the Baltic peoples similar to the Nazi policies against the Jews), and it is clear that Lithuania is a country that has unfortunately learned very little from its Holocaust past.

ELEVEN

LATVIA

A MASS MURDERER AS
A CONTEMPORARY HERO

LATVIA'S HOLOCAUST HISTORY has many similarities with Lithuania's, the only major difference being the size of its Jewish community during the Nazi occupation, which was less than one-third that of its neighbor. Approximately 70,000 Jews stayed in Latvia under the Nazis (out of a prewar community of 90,000), and only 3,000 of them survived the war. The Latvians collaborated extensively with the Nazis in the implementation of the Final Solution at a local level as well as in other countries, primarily in Belarus. In Latvia, too, a notorious murder squad, the infamous Arajs Kommando, played a leading role in the mass murders and was also sent elsewhere to carry out killing operations.

When Latvia became independent in 1991, it was forced, like Lithuania, to face the same difficult issues related to the extensive scope of local collaboration with the Nazis, but there has been little political will in Riga to prosecute Latvian Holocaust perpetrators and honestly confront the past. In Chapter 6 I related the story of the Arajs Kommando officer Konrad Kalejs, who is, to date, the only Latvian ever charged with Holocaust crimes in independent Latvia. In his case, only after extensive pressure was applied by the United States, Israel, and Jewish organizations such as the Wiesenthal Center and an international conference of researchers and experts from six countries was convened in Riga did the Latvian prosecutors agree to indict him and seek his extradition. In that respect, the fact that Kalejs had been deported from the United States and Canada and expelled from Great Britain obviously had a positive impact on the decision to seek his extradition, just as the prosecution of all three Lithuanians tried in Vilnius (Lileikis, Gimžauskas, Dailide) was possible because they had previously been denaturalized in the United States and ordered deported by the OSI. Had other prominent Latvian Nazi war criminals such as Kārlis Ozols and Argods Fricsons, the head of the Latvian security police in Liepaja, immigrated to America rather than to Australia, where the government failed to prosecute them despite their active participation in mass murder, it is highly likely that we could have succeeded in getting Latvia to seek their extradition. (The same applies to the Ypatingas būrys unit member Leonas Pažūsis, who might well have been extradited to Lithuania had he emigrated to the United States rather than to Australia.)

A second issue that I dealt with in Latvia was the rehabilitations, accompanied, as in Lithuania, by various financial benefits, illegally granted to Latvian Nazi war criminals—who in theory were ineligible to receive these pardons. In mid-1999, I was informed by Miriam Zalmanovich, our researcher in Latvia, that numerous men who had served in the Arajs Kommando and other Latvian units that had participated in the persecution and murder of Jews, and had been convicted after the war by the Soviets, had been granted rehabilitation following the reestablishment of Latvian independence in 1991.

For example, Peteris Butlers, who had been convicted for participation in the mass executions of Jews in the Bikerniki Forest (in Riga) and other locations as a member of the Arajs Kommando, and had been sentenced to 20 years' imprisonment, was granted rehabilitation in 1994. Alfreds Kaulins, who had originally been sentenced to death for his participation in mass killings outside Latvia and for his role as a guard at the Salaspils and Lenta concentration camps while serving in the Arajs Kommando, was pardoned on October 9, 1997. Rehabilitations were also granted to individuals who had participated in the persecution and murder of Jews in Liepaja, Jelgava, Preili, Aizpute, Subate, and the districts of Dobele, Ilkuste, Rezekne, and Tukums, all in Latvia, as well as to quite a few members of the Arajs Kommando who had participated in some of the numerous mass executions carried out by the unit in Belarus. In all, the list that I compiled consisted of 41 such names; among them, 18 were members of the Arajs Kommando.

On June 20, 1999, I sent a preliminary list of names to the Latvian president Guntis Ulmanis and asked him to take the necessary steps to address the situation. Ulmanis, however, was already close to the end of his term, and thus the problem was inherited by his successor, Vaire Vike-Freiburga, an émigré Latvian professor who had lived most of her life in Canada. We met in Stockholm on January 26, 2000, at the local Latvian embassy to discuss this issue as well as Latvia's poor record on the prosecution of Nazi war criminals. It was a very tense meeting since we were at an impasse on the issue of Konrad Kalejs, whom the Latvians were refusing to extradite for prosecution, and the Latvians were upset and embarrassed by our exposure of the rehabilitations granted to convicted Holocaust perpetrators. Yet despite the deep differences of opinion, President Freiburga indicated that the Latvian judicial authorities would review the problematic cases in which pardons may have been granted illegally.

The real question was whether the pertinent officials, many of whom were staunchly opposed to our initiative, would back that assertion with the necessary action. The fact that President Freiburga, my colleagues Shimon Samuels (Paris) and Mark Weitzman (New York), and I were all in Stockholm for an international conference on Holocaust education attended by many heads of state and world leaders only increased my suspicion that the promises made to us by the Latvian officials were for the benefit of the international media. (In practice, an investigation subsequently carried out by the Latvian judicial authorities, whose quality we were unable to evaluate for lack of information, concluded that mistakes had indeed been made in two of the cases on our list. These two rehabilitations were cancelled, but we never received any details regarding the process, nor were the cancellations publicized in Latvia, as they should have been.)

At the conference the next day, Freiburga spoke about the events of the Shoa in Latvia from her perspective. Interestingly, but not surprisingly, after acknowledging the loss of 90 percent of Latvian Jewry, she first mentioned the numerically negligible (although no doubt heroic) Latvians who helped save 300 Jews and only then dealt with the much larger problem of Latvian Nazi war criminals. Freiburga attributed the participation of "Latvian citizens" (a term that includes members of all ethnic groups, even Jews, and shields ethnic Latvians from blame) in the Holocaust to an "aggressive campaign of racist anti-Jewish propaganda [by] the Nazi German regime,"[1] as if there had never been any anti-Semitism in Latvia and as if otherwise, no Latvians would have ever killed any Jews during the Holocaust—a gross distortion of the historical reality.

SUCH ATTEMPTS TO whitewash or minimize the crimes of local perpetrators, almost all of whom it should be noted were volunteers, are a permanent feature of public life throughout post-Communist Europe, especially in the Baltic states, and are often accompanied by efforts to equate Communist and Nazi crimes by creating false parallels between them. Time and again, I wrote op-ed pieces and spoke out against these misrepresentations of the historical facts and distorted views regarding the Holocaust. On numerous occasions, it meant publicly opposing pronouncements of Baltic leaders and prominent intellectuals, which hardly helped my popularity and that of the Wiesenthal Center.

A typical example was an op-ed I published in the *Baltic Times* in February 2004 in response to a speech by President Freiburga at the International Forum for Preventing Genocide, an offshoot of the 2000 Stockholm conference on Holocaust education, sponsored by the Swedish prime minister Goran Persson. In her remarks, Freiburga focused almost exclusively on Communist crimes, mentioning the Holocaust or Jews only once, and merely as a backdrop to her assertion that the Communists had committed genocide against the local population in Latvia (and elsewhere). According to Freiburga, "Genocide can happen through many forms of execution: a gun, a knife, or a machete, it can take place in a gas chamber, but it can also be brought about by a slow death on a Siberian plain from hunger, from cold and exhaustion from forced labor. The result is the same—death on a massive, genocidal scale."[2]

In my response, I explained that as horrible as the crimes referred to by Freiburga (the mass deportations of Latvians by the Soviets before and after World War II) were, they did not constitute genocide and did not have to be categorized as such to be worthy of a proper response. Further, by creating a false historical symmetry between Holocaust and Communist crimes, the Latvian president was doing a disservice not only to the Nazis' victims but also to her own cause. The problem in Latvia was not that Communist crimes were not recognized as genocide, but rather that Holocaust crimes by Latvians were being ignored or minimized, and Freiburga's speech was only one small example of that. In my words, "Unpunished in Latvian courts, unmentioned in public pronouncements by Latvian leaders (even at a conference to prevent genocide), [these] crimes continue to damage the fabric of Latvian-Jewish relations and the prospect of future cooperation."[3]

As could be expected, the local responses to my critique of President Freiburga's speech were, in many cases, abusive and blatantly anti-Semitic. Among them were calls for me to be shot. Some of those responding did so under names such as Kalejs, Josef Stalin, Arajs, SS, and Dr. Mengele. But that is precisely why what I am trying to achieve in these countries is so important, not so much for me, as I have pointed out countless times, but for these societies themselves.

ONE ADDITIONAL STORY that will clearly illustrate this point concerns Herberts Cukurs, a gifted pilot who, in prewar Latvia, was a national hero like Charles Lindbergh, but during World War II Cukurs served as deputy commander of the Arajs Kommando. After the war, Cukurs escaped to Brazil. The Soviets sought his extradition, but Brazil refused to hand him over, claiming that he could only be extradited to Latvia, which no longer existed as an independent state. Under these circumstances, and facing an impending statute of limitations on the prosecution of Nazi war criminals in Germany, which would have eliminated another possibility for his prosecution, a team of Mossad agents executed Cukurs on February 23, 1965, while he was on a business trip in Uruguay. Israel never officially admitted involvement, but in 1997, the key operative published a book entitled *Chisul ha-Talyan mi-Riga* [The Liquidation of the Hangman from Riga] under the pen name Anton Kuenzle, explaining the rationale and describing the implementation.

Ironically, it was Cukurs's assassination that ultimately enabled his family and Latvian nationalists to launch their effort to restore him to his former glory. Since his involvement in the mass murder of Jews had never been confirmed by a court of law, Cukurs's supporters ostensibly had a basis for questioning his personal guilt. In the fall of 2004, right-wing nationalists from the Union of National Power Party distributed envelopes bearing his photograph throughout Latvia. His family asked the Prosecutor-General to declare him innocent of war crimes, and in May 2005, a large exhibition on his life entitled "Herberts Cukurs— Presumed Innocent" was opened in his hometown of Liepaja.

The opening of the exhibition attracted considerable public attention. It was accompanied by interviews in the local media with Latvia's two leading historians of the Holocaust who, unfortunately, reinforced the legitimacy of the efforts to restore Cukurs's hero status by questioning his personal guilt, though neither denied that he served in the Arajs Kommando. One of them, Andrew Ezergailis, was quoted in the media as saying that there was no evidence that Cukurs had been at the pits at Rumbula, the site of the mass murder of approximately 30,000 Riga Jews, and that, in any event, it had not been proven that he was "the most eager shooter of Jews in Latvia,"[4] as if to say that less zealous murderers deserved rehabilitation.

Even worse, in response to the Jewish community's protest against the exhibition, Aleksanders Kirsteins, the chairman of the Saiema (Latvian parliament) Foreign Affairs Committee, warned the Jews of Latvia "not to repeat the mistakes of 1940 and openly cooperate with the enemies of the Latvian people,"[5] a reference to an accusation popular in nationalist circles that Jews "welcomed" the Soviet enemy. Kirsteins was expelled from his People's Party and forced to resign his post, but the exhibition remained open, as does the Cukurs case itself in the eyes of the Latvian public. On the anniversary of his assassination, the daily *Latvijas Avize* commented that although Cukurs had spoiled his reputation by serving in the Arajs Kommando, there was no evidence of his "direct participation" in murder or in the theft of Jewish property.

I knew that the only way to put an end to this outrageous attempt to rehabilitate one of the biggest Latvian murderers of the Holocaust was to produce and publicize the evidence of his crimes. At Yad Vashem, I found quite a few testimonies of survivors taken immediately after the war that told the true story of Herberts Cukurs's prominent role in the mass murder of Jews. Rafael Shub, for example, noted that on July 2, 1941, Cukurs burned to death eight Jews in the new Jewish cemetery: the synagogue sexton Feldheim, his wife and four children, and Cantor Mintz and his wife. Abraham Shapiro, a survivor who had been incarcerated at the headquarters of the Arajs Kommando at 19 Valdamaras Street after Cukurs had taken over his family's apartment, related that the deputy commander had personally murdered two Jews, one of whom was named Leitmann, who failed to appear at a lineup as ordered. He also witnessed Cukurs and his fellow Latvian officers sexually molest and torture a young Jewish girl while he played piano at a command performance ordered by Cukurs in the apartment he had seized from the Shapiro family.

The most damning evidence was supplied by Max Tukacier, who on September 23, 1948, testified that he was among a group of Jews arrested by the Arajs Kommando and taken to their headquarters, where he witnessed how numerous Jews were tortured and subsequently shot on Cukurs's orders. On July 15, 1941, he personally saw Cukurs order an elderly bearded Jew to rape a 20-year-old Jewess in front of a crowd of Latvian police and prisoners, and when he proved incapable of doing so, forced the man to kiss the naked girl all over her body again and again. Those prisoners who could not bear to watch this ugly sight— some 10 to 15 of them, including several women—were beaten to death by Cukurs with the butt of his pistol. Tukacier also testified to Cukurs's active role in the mass murders of November 30 and December 8, 1941, noting that he beat and shot men, women, and children who could not keep pace on the death march to Rumbula.

On June 1, 2005, I sent copies of these and other testimonies to Janis Osis, who was in charge of the Cukurs file at the office of the Prosecutor-General. In addition, I published an op-ed entitled "Herberts Cukurs—Certainly Guilty" in *Diena*, Latvia's largest and most important daily, as well as in the English-language weekly the *Baltic Times*. The exhibition was not closed down, but the good news is that Cukurs was not posthumously rehabilitated. In that respect, the fight for justice in the Baltic states is clearly far more than a judicial matter. It is a struggle to preserve the accuracy of the historical record and clearly identify those who bear responsibility for the crimes of the Shoa. And, as proven by the case of Herberts Cukurs, it will undoubtedly continue long after the perpetrators are no longer alive.

TWELVE

ESTONIA

THE BEST JUSTICE MONEY CAN BUY

ON APRIL 1, 2009, Scotland was scheduled to host Iceland in a qualifying soccer match for the 2010 World Cup, which is to be held in South Africa. What better occasion to interview Johannes Edvaldsson, the former star of the Icelandic national team, who had played professionally for Celtic, one of the top teams in the Scottish league, and who was currently living in Linwood, Scotland? But instead of discussing the prospects for the game or reminiscing about his soccer career in both countries, Edvaldsson had a different subject on his mind. "Nazi Link Killed My Dad, Says Ex-Celt" was the headline of the article in the *Paisley Daily Express*, in which Edvaldsson asserted that his father, Evald Mikson, or Edvald Hinriksson as he was known in Iceland, had died as a result of false accusations leveled against him by the Wiesenthal Center (or, to be more precise, by me) regarding his wartime activities in Estonia. Mikson was accused of being a Nazi collaborator who murdered 30 people and was responsible for the deaths of 150 more, but Edvaldsson denied all the charges, claiming that we had accused his father to justify our continued existence even though "all the old Nazis were gone." But "it was all lies. Rubbish." Even worse, "It killed [Mikson] in the end." As far as

Edvaldsson was concerned, far from being a killer and collaborator, his father "was actually a freedom fighter who fled to Iceland after the war."[1]

This incident—which was in many respects a repeat performance of an interview that Johannes's brother, Atli, had given to an Icelandic newspaper on the occasion of his appointment as the Icelandic national soccer coach several years before—is an excellent introduction to a chapter on the third Baltic republic, Estonia.

Prior to World War II, Estonia had a very small Jewish community, and 3,500 of its 4,500 Jewish inhabitants were either deported by the Communists or needed to flee to the Soviet interior before the Nazis' arrival in mid-summer 1941. Nonetheless, despite the comparatively minuscule size of its Jewish community, Estonians were as guilty of collaboration with the Nazis during the Holocaust as their Baltic neighbors. Nine hundred and ninety-three of the 1,000 Jews who remained in Estonia under the Nazi occupation were murdered. Numerous Estonians participated in the persecution and murder of Jews there, as well as outside its borders. Thousands of Jews, primarily from Central Europe, were deported to Estonia to be murdered, in some cases by local Nazi collaborators, and Estonian security police units were sent to Belarus and Poland, where they actively participated in the implementation of the Final Solution.

The first Estonian case that I dealt with was that of Johannes and Atli Edvaldsson's father, the so-called freedom fighter Evald Mikson, whose residence in Iceland was brought to my attention in the fall of 1991 by Yaakov Kaplan, an Estonian Jew living in Israel. An amateur historian whose special interest is the history of Estonian Jewry, Kaplan was astonished to read an interview with Mikson—whose role in the mass murder of Estonian Jews was well known to him—in an Estonian newspaper. Advised by Hebrew University Professor Dov Levin to contact me, he sent me information regarding Mikson's Icelandic name (Edvald Hinriksson) and details of his crimes, including the alleged rape and murder of 14-year-old Ruth Rubin, the niece of the famous Zionist leader Chaim Arlozoroff. In Kaplan's words, "It is unthinkable that the son of a bitch will continue to live in peace and tranquility."[2] The rest was up to me.

Several months later, I found out that the Icelandic prime minister David Oddsson was scheduled to visit Israel. By this time, my research had already revealed that Mikson had been involved in the persecution and murder of Jews and other civilians in three different capacities—as the leader of the Omakaitse (a nationalistic vigilante squad) in the Vonnu district, as an investigator at the Tartu concentration camp, and, most important, as the deputy chief of the Estonian political police in the Tallinn-Harju district. The only question left was whether he was still alive and healthy. I invited Kaplan to my office so that we could call Mikson on the pretext of inviting him to a reunion of World War II members of the political police in Estonia that summer. Mikson's enthusiastic positive response was music to my ears.

Unfortunately, I had only learned of Oddsson's visit to Israel a day before his arrival, and, naturally, all my efforts to obtain a meeting with him were unsuccessful. I therefore prepared a package with the pertinent materials on Mikson's crimes, along with a letter calling upon Iceland to stop granting shelter to the Estonian Nazi war criminal and to investigate whether any other Holocaust perpetrators were living there, and left it at the King David Hotel for the prime minister. I also made the package available to the local and foreign press. In this manner, the Mikson case was turned overnight into the major focus of Oddsson's visit, which otherwise would have been totally uneventful. Oddsson told his hosts at Yad Vashem, whom I had fully briefed on the case, that my accusations would be investigated. However, others in Iceland, such as Foreign Minister Jon Baldvin Hannibalsson, rushed to Mikson's defense and cancelled a planned visit to Israel. The Estonian suspect himself denied the charges and claimed that no Jews had been persecuted in Estonia during World War II.

In the following months, while our research continued, I learned of Mikson's celebrity status in Iceland, as the person who had introduced basketball to the island (a fact that I found particularly painful given my love of that sport); whose sons, Johannes and Atli, were stars of the national soccer team (Mikson had been the goalie of the Estonian national team during the years 1934–1938); and as the owner of a popular Reykjavik sauna and massage parlor frequented by leading politicians. Under these circumstances, it was obvious that I had to build the most powerful case possible to convince the Icelandic authorities to take action against him. Further complicating the situation were the facts that, as an Icelandic citizen, Mikson could not be extradited and that there was a local statute of limitations on all crimes except murder. Thus, the only legal option available was to have him prosecuted in Iceland for his crimes.

Luckily, two very bright, young Icelandic journalists, Thor Jonsson of Icelandic television's Channel Two and Karl Birgisson of the news-weekly *Pressan*, were assisting me on the research and media front, which was exceptionally helpful. We still faced formidable obstacles. A legal panel in Iceland, established by the government to clarify Mikson's status, reached the conclusion that the evidence they had received failed to prove that he had committed murder and that there was therefore no need to initiate an official investigation. It was absolutely clear to me at this point that the Icelandic government, which had hitherto made no effort whatsoever to obtain any evidence from Estonia, was seeking to dodge the issue and shirk its responsibility.

Under these circumstances, I realized that the only hope of getting Mikson on trial in Iceland was to go to Estonia to obtain the necessary evidence. Together with Shmuel Lazikin, an Estonian Jew living in Jerusalem, I traveled to Tallinn and met with the Estonian minister of justice, Kaido Kama, and the minister of the interior, Lagle Parek. Contrary to our expectations, we were granted access to the voluminous Mikson files in the KGB archives, which contained tens of witness statements on crimes committed by Mikson while he led the Omakaitse in the Vonnu district, including testimony from seven individuals who had seen him personally commit murder. Johannes Sooru, for example, related how Mikson had shot a young man from Piirsare and then decided that every third prisoner being held by the Omakaitse in Vonnu would be executed by his men. Raimund Punnar confirmed that the executions took place and described how Mikson had shot many of the victims himself. The most horrific testimony was that of Hilka Mootse, who described how Mikson had raped a Jewish mother and her daughter:

> While arrested in the Vonnu rural district I saw together with other prisoners through a window in the basement how Mikson with a

group of other Omakaitse members, about six or seven men, took two Jewish women out to the street, a mother aged about 40 and her daughter who was 17 or 19 years old, stripped them naked, put chains on their necks, tied their hands behind their backs, and began to make fun of them. The guards dragged the women on the ground, forced them to bend down and eat grass, then pushed them to the ground and raped them. I saw how Mikson raped the women first, and after him all the other guards did so as well. The women broke down, then they were dragged behind a shed and executed by shooting.[3]

In late January 1993, I went to Iceland to present the documents to the Icelandic judicial authorities and to try to make my case to a very skeptical Icelandic public. Accompanied by my strongest and most valued supporter, the New York businessman Aryeh Rubin, I met with Hallvardur Einvardsson, the director of public prosecutions, held a press conference at which I revealed the shocking testimony regarding Mikson's crimes, and delivered a lecture to a packed hall at Iceland University.

As confident as I was regarding the strength of the evidence against Mikson, I knew that we would have to enlist political support as well. Our New York office, headed by Rhonda Barad, coordinated a protest letter campaign, which generated 800 letters that Aryeh, Rhonda, and I submitted to the Icelandic consul Kornelius Sigmundsson in May 1993. In August of the same year, I sent David Oddsson the signatures of 85 members of the Knesset, in addition to over 6,400 letters of protest from Israelis, calling for Mikson's prosecution. The former obviously had an impact since, the very day after I announced that they had been sent to Prime Minister Oddsson, Einvardsson announced that an official criminal investigation had been opened against the former Estonian soccer star. Slightly more than four months later, however, on December 27, 1993, the investigation came to a halt—Mikson had died. According to family members, his health had suddenly deteriorated (which led to his family's accusations against the Wiesenthal Center). This would not be the last time that I would be accused of "killing" a Nazi war criminal.

THE MIKSON CASE was not our only investigation that related to Nazi war crimes in Estonia, but it is of special significance for two reasons. The first is that it clearly reflected the ambivalent attitude of the Estonian government to the issue of local Nazi collaborators. On the one hand, I was granted access to the KGB files, where I found extremely incriminating testimony against Mikson. On the other hand, if I recall correctly, the Estonian Foreign Ministry issued an official statement that asserted that Mikson was not guilty of any crimes, and least of all against the Jewish people, a total distortion of the historical facts. A second reason for the case's significance is that it led me to two additional suspects who had worked under Mikson in the Estonian political police—Martin Jensen, who had immigrated to Toronto, Canada, and Harry Mannil, who had escaped to Caracas, Venezuela. Jensen died on August 8, 1992, not long after I had notified the Canadian War Crimes Unit of his presence in Toronto. Mannil is still alive today, and his case has proved to be one of the most difficult that I have ever dealt with.

In theory, everyone is supposed to be equal in the eyes of the law, but being one of the richest Estonians in the world and a generous donor to Estonian cultural institutions apparently can help protect a suspected Nazi collaborator from prosecution in Estonia. Thus, all our efforts to facilitate the prosecution of Mannil for his alleged role in the arrests and interrogations of Jews who were murdered by the Nazis and their Estonian collaborators have until now been unsuccessful. Part of the problem stems from the fact that we have never been able to prove that Mannil personally committed murder. While there was testimony recorded by the Sandler Commission (which investigated the Baltic refugees who escaped to Sweden) that Mannil had killed as many as 100 Jews, we were unable to corroborate this accusation.

Over the years, we were able to record several victories against him. For example, I made sure that he was put on the American watch-list of individuals barred from entering the United States because of their purported Nazi past. Mannil was actually kicked out of the country upon arrival at a Florida airport at least once. (The list is secret and he had no idea that he was on it.) Another victory was the resignation of Henry Kissinger from the board of the Baltic Institute for Strategic and International Studies, which Mannil established in Tallinn. After I brought Mannil's past to the attention of the former secretary of state, he resigned from the board on January 24, 1994, and thanked me for informing him of the matter and bringing the relevant documentation to his attention. A third such victory, which was unfortunately short-lived, was Mannil's expulsion on February 4, 2003, from Costa Rica, where he had business interests and often visited, because according to the immigration director Marco Badilla, "His presence could compromise national security, public order, or way of life."[4] Nine months and three days later, however, Badilla secretly rescinded his original order, allowing Mannil to reenter the country.

In early 2001, I decided that our best bet to bring Mannil to trial was to try to convince the Estonians to do so. That summer, I met with the Estonian prime minister Mart Laar in Tallinn to discuss the possibility that the Estonians would open an official investigation against Harry Mannil and to persuade him to seek the assistance of the OSI, which I understood had obtained new documentation in the case. The investigation was eventually opened, but the visit, my first to Estonia in almost a decade, was marred by several ugly run-ins with the local media. In the course of an interview with the Estonian daily *Eesti Paevaleht*, I was asked whether any Estonian civilians had murdered Jews during the Holocaust. I answered in the affirmative, noting the murders carried out by the Omakaitse during the initial weeks following the Nazi invasion. Imagine my consternation the next morning when someone translated the headline of the interview. It read, "Nazi-hunter Accuses Estonian Nation of Murders,"[5] precisely the type of assertion that, besides being patently false, was certain to infuriate Estonian public opinion and increase its opposition to the prosecution of Harry Mannil and any other suspected local Nazi war criminals.

Another manifestation of the deep-seated local resistance to my efforts to hold Estonian murderers of Jews accountable was the most offensive caricature of me ever published anywhere, which appeared in the August 23, 2001, issue of *Eesti Ekspress*, Estonia's most popular weekly newsmagazine. It portrayed me as the devil, complete with horns, and holding a pitchfork upon which were impaled several discs with swastikas on them. In my other hand, I was holding a cup emblazoned with the inscription "Wiesenthal Keskus" (center), into which

Prime Minister Laar was seen pouring Harry Mannil's blood. The caption read, "Kutsumata Külaline" (unwanted guest).[6]

A YEAR LATER I clashed with the Security Police Board, the agency responsible for the investigation of Estonian Nazi war criminals. In 1998, Estonia, like its Baltic neighbors, had established an International Commission for the Investigation of Crimes Against Humanity, which was mandated to examine all crimes committed under the Communist (1940–1941; 1944–1991) and Nazi (1941–1944) occupations of Estonia. One of the surprising initial findings of the commission, which was published in 2001, was that on August 7, 1942, the 36th Estonian Security Police Battalion participated in the mass murder of the Jews of Nowogrudok, Belarus. Several months later, based on this information, I submitted to Juri Pihl, the director-general of the board, a list of 16 members of the unit who had been awarded the Iron Cross second class by the Nazis in December 1942 on the assumption that those decorated might have excelled in the murder of Jews. Less than two weeks later, the board informed the media that they had no information regarding the participation of the 36th Battalion in the murder of the Jews of Nowogrudok, a direct contradiction of the findings of the Estonian international historical commission.

I used this example in an op-ed piece I published in *Eesti Paevaleht* on August 7, 2002, the sixtieth anniversary of the murders, to demonstrate how Estonia was not facing its Holocaust past, and urged the government to designate a day to commemorate the annihilation of European Jewry. A date was decided on that same day, but the date chosen was January 27, the day of the liberation of Auschwitz, which, considering the fact that no Estonian Jews had been deported to that camp, only strengthened the opinion of many Estonians that there was no connection between their country and the Holocaust. An opinion poll held right after the decision confirmed the problem. Ninety-three of those polled opposed a Holocaust memorial day in Estonia.

IN THE CONCLUSIONS of the International Commission, there was an unequivocally negative evaluation of the activities of Evald Mikson, who was "particularly singled out," along with six other Estonian Nazi collaborators, as being "actively involved in the arrest and killing of Estonian Jews." He and three others—Ain-Ervin Mere, Julius Ennok, and Ervin Viks—were named as the ones who "signed numerous death warrants."[7] Not that these findings in any way convinced his children that their father had done anything wrong during the war.

As far as Mannil is concerned, as could be expected, the investigation was finally closed by the Security Police Board on December 30, 2005, after several years of investigation, with no charges brought against him. What made this decision particularly infuriating was that the Estonian investigation confirmed not only that Mannil had worked for the dreaded Estonian political police, but that at least seven persons (all named) whom he had arrested and interrogated had been executed by Estonian Nazi collaborators. This confirmed an important component of our original accusations, albeit with the exact opposite conclusion. In other words, those findings would have almost certainly been sufficient to have Mannil prosecuted in any country that treats Holocaust crimes seriously, but clearly Estonia is not such a country.

THIRTEEN

CROATIA'S PAST AND THE SEARCH FOR DINKO ŠAKIĆ

IN RETROSPECT, I have to admit that there were quite a few surprises in my career in terms of the results achieved in various countries and with different cases. In this regard, the country where I had the greatest number of successes, in absolute contrast to my extremely low initial expectations, was Croatia. Although I had never visited Yugoslavia while it existed, from the beginning of my studies of the Holocaust I had a very clear image of the Croatians as cruel, fanatic fascists who brutally annihilated their Jewish community almost in its entirety.

That image was no doubt reinforced by the Artuković case, during which I learned in greater depth of the cruelty of and horrible crimes committed by the Ustasha Croatian fascists. Andrija Artuković had served as the minister of the interior and minister of justice in the independent Croatian state established by the Nazis and their Italian allies in 1941. It was in this capacity that he established a series of concentration camps all over Croatia, in which hundreds of thousands of innocent Serbs, Jews, Gypsies, and anti-fascist Croatians were incarcerated, very often with lethal results. The most notorious of these concentration camps was Jasenovac, which was nicknamed "the Auschwitz of the

Balkans" and in which at least 90,000 civilians were murdered, although it is highly possible that the number of victims was much higher. In addition, the camp was notorious for the cruelty of the guards and the uniquely horrific tortures they devised for use on the inmates. Artuković had escaped to the West together with many other prominent Ustasha after World War II. Among them was their Poglavnik (supreme leader), Ante Pavelić, who eventually fled to Argentina. Artuković initially went to Austria and from there to Switzerland, from which he reached Ireland and, a few years later, the United States. He was one of the first Nazi war criminals discovered to be living in America, and Yugoslavia asked for his extradition as early as 1951. Artuković was finally deported from the United States in 1986 and sent back to Zagreb, where he was tried, convicted, and sentenced to death on May 14, 1987, by a Yugoslav court. The implementation of his sentence was postponed, however, due to ill health, and he ultimately died in a Zagreb prison hospital at the age of 88 on January 16, 1988.

My own active involvement in Croatia began a few years after Artuković's death, when we learned that several unprosecuted suspected Croatian Nazi war criminals were alive and well in various countries, including their newly independent homeland. The most prominent of these was Dinko Šakić, a former commandant of the Jasenovac concentration camp, who had reportedly returned to Croatia from his postwar haven in Argentina. Others on the list that I had compiled by 1995 were Ivo Rojnica, the Ustasha "governor" of Dubrovnik; Vinko Nikolić, one of the leading ideologues of the Ustasha movement who had been appointed to the Sabor (Croatian parliament); Mate Šarlija, an officer in the Ustasha movement; and Srećko Pšeničnik, Ante Pavelić's son-in-law, who had headed the émigré Croatian Liberation Movement.

In Jerusalem, in mid-June of 1995, I met a person who would play a very important role in what ultimately turned out to be one of our major successes—Dr. Milan Bulajić, the director of the Museum of Genocide Victims in Belgrade and an expert on the Jasenovac concentration camp. He had come to Israel to visit all the Holocaust museums in the country in order to help him establish his museum in Belgrade, which at the time of our meeting consisted solely of a team of researchers. (There was already a site for the project but they did not yet have sufficient funds to build the museum.) The focus of our meeting, however, was on what was happening at the site of the Jasenovac concentration camp. The Croatian president Franjo Tudjman was trying, according to Bulajić, to convert the camp into a memorial for all the victims of totalitarian regimes rather than for just those murdered by the Ustasha. I also asked him about the possibility of obtaining evidence against the Croatian Nazi war criminals who had returned to Croatia and those we had discovered elsewhere.

It did not take long before a dossier sent by Bulajic arrived in Jerusalem. It was the file on Dinko Šakić (File No. F-3376) from the "Yugoslav State Commission for the Crimes Committed by the Occupiers and their Collaborators," which was housed in the Yugoslav State Archives in Belgrade. The file outlined Šakić's crimes in his capacity as the head of the general department of Jasenovac (1942–1944) and the commander of the camp (1944–1945). It listed the names of 13 of his victims, noting that there were also several thousand unknown victims as well, and briefly described the crimes attributed to him, listing the names of the witnesses against Šakić and the dates (with one exception) of their interrogations. This information was to serve us well when we tried to facilitate Šakić's prosecution.

Several months later, I was given my first lesson in Croatian history by Igor Alborghetti, a journalist with the popular Croatian weekly news-magazine *Globus*, who came to Jerusalem in December 1995 to inter-view me. He was the first Croatian journalist to contact us regarding unprosecuted Croatian World War II criminals and was actually the first Croatian non-Jew I had ever met face to face. I have to admit that he opened my eyes to several important aspects of Croatian history that I was not aware of—for example, the large number of Croatians (among them Igor's relatives) who joined Tito's partisans and fought against the Ustasha. He also cleared up several misconceptions I had regarding aspects of the new democratic Croatia, explaining, for example, that the name given to the new Croatian currency (kuna) had its origins hun-dreds of years before the Holocaust and had merely been adopted by the Ustasha based on historical precedent. All this, while unequivocally acknowledging the guilt of the Ustasha in the mass murder of Croatian

Jewry. In short, he was able to present a somewhat more balanced picture of Croatia's World War II history and its current impact on the newly independent democracy, which helped me enormously in my subsequent dealings with Croatian officials and media. Igor, in fact, became a good friend and has been extremely helpful, in his role as editor of *Globus*, in our efforts to help Croatian society confront its Ustasha past.

The problem, however, was that Igor was not a typical Croatian, and just to remind me of this fact, the reaction in certain quarters to his interview with me in *Globus* was unbelievably outrageous. On January 11, 1996, Mirsad Bakšić, a political commentator for the Croatian daily *Slobodna Dalmacija*, which at that time pursued a very nationalistic position, accused me of heading and organizing all three pre–State of Israel Jewish underground movements, the Hagana, Etzel, and Lehi, all of which were disbanded even before I was born. He also accused me of leading the massacre of Palestinians in the Sabra and Shatilla refugee camps—an event that took place during the 1982 war in Lebanon and was carried out by Christian militias without the participation of a single Israeli. In other words, while Igor represented enlightened Croatian public opinion, there were other voices whose opinions fit the fascist image I originally had of Croatia before I began my hunt for war criminals in that country. Since leading Croatian public figures were among those fostering nationalistic sympathies and nostalgia for the Ustasha, it became increasingly clear that we faced a very difficult uphill battle.

THE PERSON WHO personified these problems more than anyone else was the Croatian president Franjo Tudjman, who had led Croatia to independence in 1991. Ironically, he had served with Tito's partisans during World War II fighting against the Ustasha, who had even murdered one of his brothers. But when he became a politician in the late 1980s, he adopted an extremist nationalist line that glorified the Ustasha and sent a very negative message to Croatia's minorities. In one of his more famous speeches he expressed his joy that "Thank God, my wife is neither a Serb nor a Jew."[1]

Tudjman was particularly active in attempting to shape historical memory in the new Croatia in accordance with his extremist nationalist views. One of his more outrageous proposals, which I mentioned earlier, was to turn Jasenovac into a national memorial for all the Croatian victims of political violence. Under his proposal, victims of Communism would have been buried at the same place where at least tens of thousands of Serbs, Jews, Gypsies, and antifascist Croatians were murdered by the Ustasha. Needless to say, this initiative enraged the Serbian and Jewish communities and was one of the factors in Israel's decision not to establish diplomatic relations with Croatia, although it did recognize its independence.

Another very important factor behind this decision was Tudjman's claim in his book *Wastelands of Historical Reality* that the Jews had intentionally exaggerated the number of the victims of the Holocaust from 1 million to 6 million and that the Jasenovac concentration camp had in fact been run by Jewish inmates. It was only after Tudjman took out these offensive passages (from the English edition of his book) that Israel finally agreed to establish diplomatic relations with Croatia in the summer of 1997. Apparently, one of the considerations involved in the Israeli government's change of heart was an extremely large deal to sell a million U.S. dollars' worth of arms to Croatia, a fact that I considered shameful and a betrayal of the victims of the Holocaust. This prompted me to write to Foreign Minister David Levy, urging the government to reconsider. Among my arguments was the shocking revelation that while Tudjman had removed the offensive passages from the English edition of his magnum opus, he had failed to do so in the Croatian edition as well as in the French and German editions, which clearly indicated his lack of sincerity in this matter. "Imagine," I wrote to Levy, "how embarrassing it will be for Israel and the entire Jewish world if Tudjman comes to Yad Vashem without having completely repudiated his comments casting doubt on the scope of the Holocaust and unequivocally admitting that what he wrote was factually incorrect and totally misleading."[2]

While our protest, which had considerable support from Israeli public opinion, did not stop Israel from establishing diplomatic relations with Croatia, it did help prevent a visit to Israel by Tudjman, which would normally have taken place shortly after the forging of diplomatic ties between Croatia and the Jewish state. This issue did not end here, and time and again I found myself marshaling whatever influence I could in Israel to ensure that the protofascist and Holocaust-denier Tudjman never actually set foot in Jerusalem. And at least in this respect, we won a resounding victory.

OUR SUCCESS IN preventing President Tudjman from visiting Israel was not the only victory that we can claim in Croatia. Even more important was our campaign to facilitate the prosecution of Dinko Šakić, who by the winter of 1998, we now knew, was living somewhere in Argentina (contrary to previous media reports that he had returned to Croatia). Our first step was to look for survivors of the Jasenovac camp in Israel. With the help of Sarajevo survivor Miriam Aviezer, we obtained a list of all the Israelis who had survived Jasenovac and also turned to the Yugoslav authorities through their ambassador in Tel Aviv, Mirko Stefanovic, to consider seeking Šakić's extradition to stand trial in Belgrade for his heinous crimes.

In the meantime, my colleague Sergio Widder, the director of our Buenos Aires office, was working with a local journalist named Jorge Camarasa to trace Šakić's current whereabouts. At the same time, in preparation for Šakić's exposure, I helped arrange for Camarasa to meet in Belgrade with survivors of Jasenovac. They shared their horrific experiences in the camp as well as their recollections of Šakić with the Argentinean journalist, preparing him for his encounter with the Ustasha Nazi criminal. In early April 1998, that critical information was obtained, and Šakić was found living in the seaside resort town of Santa Teresita, slightly less than 300 kilometers south of Buenos Aires on the Atlantic Ocean. Camarasa went to Šakić's house, accompanied by a television crew, without any prior notification, and the conversation recorded by the cameras of Argentinean television went something like this:

> CAMARASA (to the person answering the door): Are you Dinko Šakić?
> ŠAKIĆ: Yes.
> CAMARASA: I believe that you were the commandant of the Jasenovac concentration camp in Croatia. Can I ask you a few questions?

ŠAKIĆ:	By all means, come in.
CAMARASA:	(seated in Šakić's living room) Mr. Šakić, as a person who served as commandant of the Jasenovac concentration camp, how do you explain the terrible things that took place there?
ŠAKIĆ:	Jasenovac was a penal colony and all the people incarcerated there deserved to be there. It was actually a work camp where the Jews managed themselves. We never laid a hand on any of the prisoners in the camp.
CAMARASA:	But how do you explain the cruel atrocities which took place there, the terror, the executions?
ŠAKIĆ:	The people died a natural death. There was a typhus epidemic, for example, but there were no cremation ovens that killed anybody. I think that you are the one who does not understand. The real problem with Jasenovac was that we were not able to finish the job. I sleep like a baby. If I were offered the same post today, I would accept it.

This shocking exchange, which was filmed and broadcast on April 6, 1998, on the Channel 13 evening news in Argentina, along with an interview with me from Jerusalem, in a sense marked the public "breaking" of the story.

Once that happened, I went into high gear in order to try to make sure that Šakić would indeed "face the music." In that respect, exposing him publicly was a big risk since in theory, once revealed, he could try to flee, but I felt fairly certain that we had no real choice. The only way we could convince both the Argentineans and the Croatians to take the necessary steps in this case was to create a public scandal, which was exactly what happened. The interview with a totally unrepentant Šakić was shown together with footage on Jasenovac and interviews with survivors of the camp, whose testimony on the horrible conditions, barbaric executions, and the cruelty of the Ustasha camp personnel all made an enormous impression on the viewers and reinforced my call for the former commandant to be prosecuted for his crimes.

Yet as shocking as the initial broadcast was, a trial was a relatively remote possibility at this point, since Šakić obviously could not be prosecuted for his crimes in Argentina, which had no legal basis to do so, and it was not clear whether any country would seek his extradition. Our policy always was to give priority to the country in which the criminal committed his crimes. But in this case, the territory of the Jasenovac concentration camp was actually in two different countries (Croatia and the Serbian enclave of Bosnia-Herzegovina), and a third country (Yugoslavia), whose citizens had been murdered there, could in theory could also seek his extradition.

As noted earlier, I had already approached the Yugoslavs in this regard, but even though I was almost certain that they would jump at an opportunity to be able to prosecute and punish a commander of Jasenovac, I began to feel very strongly that we would be making a big mistake if we helped facilitate Šakić's extradition to Belgrade. If Šakić was tried in Serbia, such a proceeding would most likely have absolutely no impact in Croatia, the land of the Ustasha and the place where such a trial could fulfill the absolutely vital function of exposing Croatian society to the full scope of Ustasha criminality. If he was prosecuted in Belgrade, Croatians could simply ignore the entire proceeding as Serb propaganda, thereby robbing it of its incredible educational and moral potential.

Given these circumstances, I opted for a far more difficult option, but one that could have a watershed impact: extradition to Croatia, a country with a bloody Holocaust past and a Holocaust-denier president.

On the day following the broadcast of Šakić's interview, I wrote to the ambassadors of Argentina (Vincente Espeche Gil) and Croatia (Dr. Svjetlan Berković), calling upon the government of the former to immediately arrest him and upon the authorities of the latter to seek his extradition in order to prosecute him for his crimes, a step that was "an opportunity not only to achieve a measure of justice for the victims of that infamous concentration camp, but also to honestly confront the painful issue of Croatian participation in the crimes of the Holocaust."[3]

It did not take long for the Argentineans to take action. On the day of my letter to their ambassador, the minister of the interior, Carlos Corach, asked a federal judge to order Šakić's arrest, based on an order from President Menem in response to our request. But all of a sudden things went wrong. Šakić disappeared before he could be arrested by the Argentinean police. According to his wife, Nada, he had gone to Buenos Aires to seek the assistance of the Croatian embassy. Asked about his wartime role, his wife, who was the sister of the notorious Ustasha commander Vjekoslav (Maks) Luburić, who was responsible for running all the concentration camps in Croatia, replied that Dinko was as innocent as a newborn baby.

Šakić's temporary disappearance did not, however, stop the progress of the case. The Croatians, apparently afraid that Šakić might be extradited to Yugoslavia and awaiting the imminent arrival in Zagreb of Eytan Benstur, the director general of the Israeli Foreign Ministry, moved quickly to submit their own extradition request. (The Yugoslavs indeed submitted such an extradition request shortly after the Croatians sent theirs to Argentina.)

In the meantime, with the Šakić story making headlines all over the world, more and more information started coming to light regarding Šakić's life and political views. One of the things that emerged very clearly is that while he was virtually unknown outside his homeland, in Croatia it was no secret that he was alive and well in Argentina. In fact, slightly more than three years before we finally exposed him and pressed for his extradition, Šakić gave an extensive interview to the Croatian journal *Magazin*, in which he made the following comments:

1. I regret that we didn't do all that is imputed to us, for had we done that, then today Croatia wouldn't have problems, there wouldn't be people to write lies!
2. Jasenovac was a legal institution based on law, where all those proved to have worked for the destruction of the Croatian state, and who had been dangerous for public order and safety, were interned.
3. There are no states in the world that don't have prisons and camps, and somebody has to perform this thankless duty.

4. For the hundredth time I have to say that there were no mass executions in Jasenovac. Considering the duration and the population of
the camp, the death rate was natural and normal; at any time there
were 3,000 inmates in the camp.
5. If we shot people, we did it on the basis of the law. I only want to tell
you that the legal state and the rule of law was functioning.
6. ...Dr. Franjo Tudjman is, to put it metaphorically, on the top of the
cathedral and his horizons are wider and larger. Nobody in Croatia
is of his caliber.
7. I am proud of everything I did.
8. If I were offered the same duty today, I would accept it![4]

One would assume that such outrageous comments would have helped
pave the way for his prosecution, but in Tudjman's Croatia, the tendency was to glorify the Ustasha rather than hold them accountable for
their crimes.

For this reason, we were the ones who engineered Šakić's arrest in
Argentina (he was caught several days after he disappeared) and facilitated his extradition to stand trial in Zagreb, when, in effect, Croatia
should have dealt with his case many years previously. According to one
media report, President Tudjman himself met with Šakić during his
1994 visit to Argentina, and Šakić visited Zagreb in 1995, at which time
he easily could have been arrested. Since he gave an extensive interview
at that time regarding his role at Jasenovac, no one can honestly say
that they did not know who he was and where he was living.

The simple truth is that Croatia, like practically all the post-
Communist, and especially post-Soviet, societies of Eastern Europe,
has been extremely reluctant to take legal action against its own unprosecuted suspected Nazi war criminals. And while this is true to a very
large extent elsewhere in Europe as well, the situation in Croatia was
particularly problematic under the Tudjman regime, which actively tried
to glorify the NDH, the quisling satellite state run by the Ustasha.

As it turned out, the decision to prosecute Šakić did not exist in
a vacuum. Croatia was extremely anxious to establish full diplomatic
relations with Israel, which it considered critical to its main foreign
policy objectives of joining NATO and the European Union, and the

prosecution of Šakić was clearly perceived in Zagreb to be part of the price, besides the obligatory acknowledgment of Holocaust guilt and requisite apology for the participation of Croatians in the crimes. The timing and the political circumstances for what turned out to be the most significant trial of a local Nazi war criminal in post-Communist Europe were absolutely perfect.

FOURTEEN

A HISTORIC TRIAL IN THE LAND OF THE USTASHA

WHEN ASKED TO describe my job or how I carry out my work, I usually say that I am one-third detective, one-third historian, and one-third political lobbyist, all of which together combine to constitute a twenty-first–century Nazi hunter. The Šakić case is a perfect example of how I had to use all those skills to complete the job, the first part of which was finished on June 19, 1998, when Šakić was extradited from Argentina to Croatia, less than three months after his television interview was broadcast. He was imprisoned while awaiting trial, and I was really overwhelmed with cautious joy. For the first time, a Nazi was going to be judged in a country of the former Eastern bloc. It was a truly historic moment, but there always was the fear that the trial would not go as we hoped and that the criminal would be either acquitted or spared punishment. My first step, therefore, was to go to Croatia immediately to provide the prosecution with all the documents that I had concerning him.

On the evening of July 4, 1998, I was in Zagreb with my wife, Elisheva. The quarterfinal of the World Cup between Croatia and Germany was being played. Croatians were all glued to their television sets watching this match, which was taking place in Lyons, France.

With each goal, the crowd went so wild with enthusiasm that the earth seemed to tremble. Ninety minutes later, madness gripped an entire country: the Croatians had just won 3–0, qualifying for the semifinal of the World Cup. After the match, I suggested to my friends that we go out to witness the general euphoria. That was a big mistake: While we were walking around, a group of young men—seven, to my memory—came our way. Their arms linked, they were not chanting "We won! We won!" or cheering Davor Šuker, the magnificent striker who had scored the third goal. No, they had a single refrain in their mouths, which was so out of context and so atrocious that I could not believe my ears. These young men were chanting "Din-ko Ša-kić! Din-ko Ša-kić! Din-ko Ša-kić!" They were celebrating the former commandant of Jasenovac, the mass murderer of Serbs, Jews, Gypsies, and antifascist Croatians. And there I was, on that warm summer's evening, going for a walk with a *kippa* on my head.

They were glorifying one of the worst figures of the Ustasha regime and they were rapidly headed in my direction. I did not know what to do. I was afraid of being lynched. I removed my *kippa* and was about to put it in my pocket, when I hesitated. Changing my mind, I put it back on my head. I had never taken my *kippa* off and I was not going to do so then. I turned around and headed back to the hotel. Incredulous and horrified, I watched them go by. Why were they giving Šakić this accolade? Doubtless because in their eyes he embodied the Croatian spirit, of which they were so proud that evening. The trial that would soon begin was vitally important for this country.

The debate about Šakić would overwhelm Croatia more than any other that had occurred since independence, highlighting the profound division that still existed between fascists and antifascists. It would also allow Croatian society to learn the painful truth about the atrocities committed by the Ustasha during the World War II.

Innumerable articles in the press—often far from complimentary—were devoted to me. I met numerous personalities—religious (the archbishop of Zagreb, Josip Bozanić; the chief rabbi, Kotel Dadon), diplomatic (the American consul), and political (the Croatian ministers of foreign affairs and of justice)—but not Tudjman. I was often asked

the question, "Why won't you meet the president?" Each time, I gave
the same reply: "I have respect for his behavior during the war. But he
has, as head of state, denied the Holocaust. I want nothing to do with
people like him. And if I am asked whether or not he should visit Israel,
I oppose it."

THE TRIAL OPENED in Zagreb on March 4, 1999. I arrived there
the day before. In the courtroom, I stared at Šakić. Sometimes one
can discern in someone's features, in their expression and bearing, the
traces of the horrors they committed long ago. This was not the case
with Šakić. This man was a monster, and yet it did not show. He looked
like any other old man, an elderly average Joe. The atrocities of the
Holocaust were committed by ordinary people. That is one of the mad
elements that characterizes it. It is why, when Allan A. Ryan Jr., the
former director of the OSI, wrote a book on the hunting of Nazi criminals, he entitled it *Quiet Neighbors*.

On the opening day of the trial, I had succeeded in getting an
Israeli diplomat to come to the trial, to emphasize Israel's interest
and concern. Representatives of the Croatian Jewish community were
beside us. It was a historic day, the realization of so much effort, of
so many hours spent searching for him and researching his crimes,
of setting a trap into which he had stupidly fallen, and, above all, of
helping convince Argentina and Croatia to cooperate and carry out
his extradition.

There was, however, an initial delay. As could be expected, Šakić
tried to inspire pity. It is incredible how these old Nazis always try
to present themselves as sick and frail as possible as soon as they face
trial. Pronounced too ill to appear before the court, Šakić obtained a
suspension of the hearing until March 15, 1999. Once the trial began,
however, the proceedings were transformed into a veritable history
lesson, as the procession of survivors on the witness stand described
in detail the horrors perpetrated in the camp. The charges related to
the murders committed in Jasenovac under Šakić's command. He was
charged with crimes against humanity but not with genocide, which
was probably a political decision, perhaps to appease pro-Ustasha

elements, but which had no practical impact on the trial. Šakić pleaded not guilty, expecting his country's judicial system to give him favorable treatment.

THE TRIAL WAS punctuated by revealing incidents. One day, at the end of the afternoon session, the judge went into a corner of the room to talk to someone while Šakić, flanked by two policemen, prepared to return to prison. As he did every day, the defendant turned toward his supporters to look at them. When they saw that the judge had his back turned, they gave Šakić a fascist Ustasha salute (very similar to a Nazi salute with an outstretched arm), before my very eyes and in the middle of the courtroom.

Another remarkable moment in the trial, which I personally witnessed, was when Yaacov Finci, who refused to be photographed during his testimony for fear of possible reprisals, recounted how he had been arrested by the Ustasha during a roundup and deported to Jasenovac with several other Jewish teenagers from Sarajevo. Several days after their arrival in the camp, the boys were forced to gather up the bodies of prisoners who had been mutilated and killed by the Ustasha and to throw their remains into the Sava River. An appalled Finci, who had not yet totally grasped the laws of the concentration camp world, went up to a guard and dared ask him why they were being forced to carry out such an atrocious task. Finci reported the guard's reply: "Because you killed Jesus!"

Hearing Finci say these words on the witness stand, Šakić burst out laughing. He laughed a lot during the trial, as he listened to testimonies, each one more horrible than the last. At this latest outburst, Judge Dražen Tripalo was forced to call him sharply to order. After that incident Šakić did not laugh again but maintained an almost permanent sardonic smile on his face. It was only toward the end of the hearings, when the judge spoke of Šakić's 55 years of marriage to his wife, Nada, with whom Šakić had fallen in love in the camp, that his smile faded. The sadistic director of Jasenovac was overcome by just one thing: his separation, through his 16 months of imprisonment so far, from Nada, another suspected torturer whose committal to trial we would attempt to facilitate.

I N ONE OF the last sessions of the trial, when Šakić was given an opportunity to address the court, he focused primarily on Milan Bulajić, a Serbian historian who had assisted me during the case, and to me: "Behind everything that happened to me are Milan Bulajić, director of the Belgrade Museum of Genocide Victims and Efraim Zuroff, liar and marginal person better known in Croatia than in Israel...."[1]

The following day, October 4, the packed courtroom was divided in two: Šakić's supporters on one side and on the other side we, the Jews, and several other people convinced of the importance of the trial. For several hours, contradictory rumors circulated; the most persistent one was that Šakić would be acquitted, as his lawyer had sought. I was wracked with anxiety.

Finally, Judge Tripalo delivered the judgment. He declared Dinko Šakić, then aged 78, guilty, and sentenced him to the maximum penalty: 20 years in prison. Šakić would pay for murdering at least 2,000 people during the months when he was the head of the camp. The decades that had passed had not attenuated the guilt of the former commanding officer. Šakić burst out laughing and applauded. It was all an act, nothing more. But I couldn't care less. I was wild with joy. We had succeeded: The man who had headed Jasenovac would end his days in prison.

But we were not able to celebrate our victory for long. The atmosphere around the court was electric. When I left the courtroom, a man accosted me. In impeccable American English, he yelled: "You would have done better to concern yourself with Israeli criminals! And what are you doing about the millions of displaced Palestinians?"

Šakić's lawyer, Ivan Kern, told the press: "We are going to appeal the verdict and we will stress the fact that in the verdict the exact number of victims was not established, which could mean that there were no victims at all and in this case there was no crime."[2] At the same moment, some men knocked into Zoran Pusić, the director of the Croatian Civic Committee for Human Rights, a very important local NGO, who was a strong supporter of our efforts to bring Šakić to justice, and spat in his face before running off. The police intervened.

Another man approached me; this one was friendly. He was tall and
well dressed. He introduced himself as the brother of Dr. Mile Bošković,
who had been executed by Šakić himself at Jasenovac. This murder, a key
element in the prosecution's case, had given rise to one of the most dramatic testimonies of the trial. In September 1944, after two young Jews
had attempted to escape, Šakić assembled all the prisoners into the central courtyard and chose men at random. It was clear that these men were
going to be executed as punishment for the escape attempt. When he
pointed to Bošković, the man explained that he was from Montenegro,
where hanging was incompatible with the code of honor. Šakić then got
out his revolver and shot him where he stood. Three bullets in the head,
in front of everyone.

Mile Bošković's brother looked me straight in the eyes and said: "I
have only one word to say to you: thank you." It was an overwhelming, unforgettable moment—one of the most moving of my life. I had
fought for so long to ensure that the victims were not forgotten and to
obtain justice after their death. Nothing could give me greater pleasure
than this simple thank-you. That day, historic for Croatia, was a mem-
orable one for me, too. The journalist Igor Alborghetti, of the popular
weekly newsmagazine *Globus*, would later tell me that the Šakić trial
had been a watershed event in the history of Croatian democracy, an
assessment that I consider to be the highest possible form of compliment from such a knowledgeable observer of local society.

AFTER THE TRIAL, President Tudjman's HDZ (Hrvatska demokratska
zajednica) party suffered a first partial defeat at the elections and its
government was replaced by a coalition of liberals and social democrats.

Then Stjepan Mesić, one of the foremost antifascist political figures,
was elected president in 2000 in place of Tudjman, who had just died. He
gave me a warm reception on January 16, 2001, in his presidential pal-
ace, before traveling to Israel. That visit demonstrated the extent of the
change that had begun in Croatian diplomacy. During his stay in Israel,
Mesić gave a public apology, using unambiguous language, for the crimes
perpetrated by the Ustasha thereby opening a new chapter in relations
between the two countries as well as between Croatians and Jews.

Our work in Croatia did not end, however, with Šakić's conviction. I was informed that a street in Split bore the name of Mile Budak, the education minister and also deputy prime minister under the Ustasha. After a visit to Split and much lobbying, we succeeded in getting the street renamed, and a monument in Budak's honor was also later destroyed. I also lobbied to have an annual mass in honor of Ante Pavelić, the head of state of the NDH and the leader of the Ustasha movement, cancelled, another campaign that succeeded.

IN JUNE 2007, Marko Perković, known as Thompson, the most popular Croatian singer, gave a gigantic concert in Maksmir Stadium in Zagreb before of an audience of 50,000. Among the crowd, numerous spectators were wearing Ustasha uniforms and sporting their symbols, and others gave the fascist salute. Two years earlier, Perković, an ultranationalist, had sung a song called "Jasenovac-Stara Gradiška," the name of the women's camp at Jasenovac, which called for all the Serbs to be sent to camps and then killed. My protest to President Mesić set off a wave of complaints by nationalists who defended Perković, claiming that he was simply a Croatian patriot who loved his country and his people.

In response, on July 11, 2007 I published an open letter to the singer in Globus, calling upon him to denounce the crimes of the Ustasha and to tell his fans to stop glorifying the killers, that contrary to the opinion of the ultranationalists, one did not have to support the Ustasha to be a loyal patriotic Croatian.[3] Perković's failure to respond proved my point about his own unacceptable chauvinistic views, and at his next concert, held in Split on July 27, the police confiscated all Ustasha paraphernalia.

Despite these victories, the struggle for truth continues in Croatia, as was clearly seen in the wake of Dinko Šakić's funeral. Dinko Šakić died in prison on July 20, 2008. His body was dressed in his Ustasha uniform, and during the mass, Vjekoslav Lasić, the priest who had conducted the annual mass in honor of Pavelic, described him as an "example to all Croatians." No official representative of the Croatian state expressed anger at this exhibition or at these indecent declarations. I therefore asked President Mesić in a public letter to formally condemn the organizers of the ceremony, as well as the pro-Ustasha priest. In a press release, Mesić asked "all the institutions concerned to take the necessary measures to ensure that the burial of Dinko Šakić, shamelessly used to rehabilitate the Ustasha regime, does not undermine the worldwide reputation of Croatia."[4] Šakić did not get away with it.

FIFTEEN

A DIFFICULT BEGINNING

BUOYED BY THE success of the Šakić trial in Croatia, I set my sights on replicating it in as many post-Communist countries as possible. What better way to get these countries to face the complicity of their nationals in the crimes of the Holocaust than by having them prosecute those personally responsible in their own courts?

Progress was initially slow, however, partially because the Wiesenthal Center was increasingly focusing on the fight against global anti-Semitism, especially in the wake of the outbreak of the second Intifada in fall 2001 and the upsurge in attacks on Jews and Jewish institutions all over the world. This naturally meant that the efforts to bring Holocaust perpetrators to justice became less of a priority and therefore I was particularly pleased to receive a phone call from my good friend Aryeh Rubin in late 2001, with the offer of very generous financial support for a large-scale project which would seriously upgrade our efforts to bring Nazi war criminals to justice.

At this point, I had already known Aryeh for over 30 years. We first met in 1969, during my senior (and his sophomore year) at YU, when we were in the same dormitory, but our friendship began in earnest the year following, when both of us were in Jerusalem. I had made aliyah and was studying at Hebrew University and he was studying his junior year at the local *Merkaz ha-Rav* Yeshiva, but he spent a lot of time with his fellow juniors from the United States, among them my sister Elayne.

Apparently, one of the subjects that brought us together was our mutual interest in the Shoa. In Aryeh's case, it was definitely personal. Both of his parents had escaped from the Nazis. His mother fled Germany right before the outbreak of World War II and his father escaped from Poland to the Soviet interior ahead of the Nazi invasion. After he graduated from YU, in the early seventies, Aryeh spent close to a year on his own in Europe visiting the sites connected to the history of the Holocaust, long before such trips became a rite of passage for young Jews.

When Elisheva and I came back to the States in 1978, we reconnected with Aryeh, who by this time was a successful businessman living in New York City. He founded *Jewish Living*, a very innovative monthly magazine designed to reach out to all sorts of Jews in an effort to strengthen Jewish identity and unity in the spirit of the teachings of Rabbi Irving "Yitz" Greenberg, with whom both of us had studied at YU. In the summer of 1979, when I accompanied a group of young American Jewish high school graduates on their way to spend a year in Israel to the sites of the Holocaust, I had each of them keep a travel log that I edited into a collective diary, probably the first of its kind, that Aryeh published in the magazine. Unfortunately, for a variety of reasons, the magazine was not successful financially, and he had to shut it down. Always resourceful, Aryeh then launched a medical publishing company that he would sell several years later for a considerable sum. Today, he lives in Miami, where he runs the Targum Shlishi (www.targumshlishi.org), a philanthropic foundation which he founded to support a wide variety of initiatives, primarily in the field of Jewish education.

Throughout the past three decades, Aryeh and I continued to be in close contact, during which he always maintained an active interest in my Nazi-hunting activities, on several occasions underwriting overseas trips and in a few instances accompanying me to potentially hostile destinations such as Costa Rica, Iceland, and Croatia. In order to understand how important his companionship was on these journeys it's important to know that unlike government prosecutors, who invariably have the support of their local embassy, there are only a few countries in which I can enlist the assistance of local colleagues, so having a friend such as Aryeh at my side in diverse and often hostile places has been a real boon.

Over the years, Aryeh has proven his friendship and loyalty to my mission time after time, so when he called to discuss his latest idea on how to enhance our efforts, I was all ears. His proposal was relatively simple: He was willing to provide me with $100,000 to run a campaign to solicit information that would facilitate the prosecution and punishment of Nazi war criminals. The campaign would be based on rewards of $10,000, which would be given to any person who supplied information which helped lead to a conviction and punishment of a Holocaust perpetrator, in any country anywhere in the world, $10,000 per criminal, up to the sum of an additional $100,000, which we frankly never believed that we would reach. In other words, Aryeh was willing to donate $200,000 of his own money for the project, with the rest of my expenses covered, as always, by the Wiesenthal Center.

Needless to say, my response was extremely enthusiastic. It was a terrific idea. In fact, I had secretly dreamed of launching such a campaign—but without the extra financing, it had been out of the question. Aryeh offered me this opportunity. I would organize and coordinate the research, and he would finance the operation. All that remained was to find a name for our endeavor. A name that would evoke the notion of the hunt but also the passing of time. I suggested "Operation Last Chance," and he agreed.

TIME WAS RUNNING out. I therefore quickly began the necessary preparations. The first and most important decision was determining where to start. Normally, the most logical place would have been Germany. But due to financial reasons, and the fact that I wanted our primary focus to be on post-Communist Eastern Europe, the latter was a far better place to begin. So I decided to launch Operation Last Chance in the Baltics, where I believed that the project had unusually high potential due to two important historical factors and contemporary circumstances. The former were: the extremely high number of local Nazi collaborators and the fact that many of the participants in murder (who in theory were the best potential witnesses) had already been prosecuted by the Soviets and released after serving their sentences, which meant that they did not have to fear being prosecuted again due to "double jeopardy." Free of that concern, they could tell the truth and be handsomely rewarded (by Baltic standards) for the information. The other factor was that since Lithuania, Latvia, and Estonia were on the verge of entry into NATO and the European Union, there would be pressure on them to prosecute Nazi war criminals. The last thing they wanted at this point was to appear to be protecting Holocaust perpetrators.

Before we could begin, there were several technical matters which had to be prepared. The most critical was to find a local partner to cosponsor the project. Originally, I turned to the branches of the "Open Society" NGO in each of the three countries, but they refused to copartner. I then traveled to each of the countries to personally meet with the leaders of the Jewish communities to enlist their help. All three initially agreed, although in Latvia and Estonia they subsequently had a change of heart, as will be explained.

In early July 2002, Aryeh and I—accompanied by Elisheva and Aryeh's wife, Raquel, and his daughters—went to Vilnius, Tallin, and Riga for the start of the project, which we officially launched on July 8, 2002, in Vilnius. From the beginning, I applied a method that would remain unchanged, consisting of the following stages:

- Call a press conference in the local capital with the participation of the leader of the local Jewish community;
- Set up a telephone line to collect all types of information. We guaranteed anonymity to whoever wished it;
- Publish advertisements in the press announcing the payment of a reward of US$10,000 to anyone who had information that could lead to the arrest, trial, conviction, and punishment of a Nazi war criminal.

The ads that we published were especially important, since I specifically designed them not only to inform the public of the reward, but also to remind them of the horrific nature of the crimes committed by their country's nationals, as a means of arousing public discussion and debate on this issue. In Lithuania, for example, the photo I chose showed men in civilian clothes and in uniform who were busying themselves around corpses. It was a photo taken during the June 1941 massacre in the Lietukis Garage in Kaunas, during which a group of armed Lithuanian security personnel and vigilantes killed more than 50 Jews. Armed with crowbars, they beat some of the men to death and put fire hoses into the mouths of the others before turning on the water until their stomachs exploded. A crowd of men, women, and children witnessed the massacre, applauding as each Jew succumbed and died. After all the Jews had been killed someone took out an accordion, and the entire crowd joined in singing the Lithuanian national anthem. (The scene was immortalized by a German army photographer who also gave testimony on the event.[1]) In Latvia, I used one photo that depicted a crowd of deportees leaving the Riga ghetto, and another that showed two women, one completely naked, being led away brutally by a guard. In Estonia, I used an atrocious image of a row of corpses lying on their backs from the notorious Klooga concentration camp.

Captions accompanied these images: "The Jews of Lithuania Did Not Disappear. They Were Mercilessly Murdered in Paneriai (Vilnius), Fort IX (Kaunas), Kuziai Forest (Siauliai)...and Over a Hundred Other Places of Mass Murder..."; "This Is About Your Jewish Neighbors, the Ones Who Were Killed Nearby"; "During the Holocaust, Latvian Collaborators Helped the Nazis Murder Close to 100,000 Local and Foreign Jews in Latvia and Many Thousands Elsewhere"; "During the Holocaust Local Collaborators Helped the Nazis Murder Jews in Estonia and in Other Countries." Each message was written in the local language and was accompanied by the phrase "Help bring those responsible for these crimes to justice," the amount of the reward, and the telephone numbers to call—generally, the numbers of the headquarters of the local Jewish community, our own contact numbers, and those of the attorney general's office.

In some countries, these notices were published for us free of charge. In Romania during the summer of 2004, thanks to the fantastic assistance of the Tempo Advertising Company, we were given 250 billboards, as big as four meters by three meters, at locations all over the country. On many of them, we displayed the disturbing photograph of an aged and battered teddy bear with these words: "Mira Greenberg kept her best friend close to her heart until the last moment." Mira Greenberg was a four-year-old girl who was murdered with 9,000 other Jews at Iasi in 1941. In other countries, notably Austria, we had to pay huge sums of money to be able to publish these messages.

The rewards we promised in exchange for information aroused opposition in certain quarters. In Germany, for example, Micha Brumlik, the director of the Fritz-Bauer Institute—a center for the study and documentation of the history and consequences of the Holocaust—criticized our offer of a financial reward and declared that we were appealing to "the lowest common denominator of desire for material gain rather than to moral responsibility."[2] Others agreed that we should not offer any financial rewards. I feared that these good souls were deluding themselves. Without this reward, neither the public at large nor the press would have had any interest in our campaign, and no witnesses would have ever come forward.

A YEAR AND a half after the launch of the operation, we had already received the names of 196 suspects in Lithuania, 41 in Latvia, 6 in Estonia, and 13 in Ukraine. For each name, we created an information sheet containing as much detail as possible about the informant—when he or she was not anonymous—and about the suspect. The information poured in; after checking the credibility of the tips and verifying that the suspects were alive and healthy enough to stand trial, we went looking for evidence to corroborate the charges.

An inhabitant of Kedainiai, Lithuania, Eleonora Vilčinskiene, contacted us and explained that she wanted to make the truth known. I went to see her in her dilapidated apartment, typical of the Soviet era, with a film crew. She described a series of murders committed, she said, a few hundred yards away from her house in Rokiskis shortly before the

Nazis arrived on June 28, 1941. Lithuanian men had forced Jews to dig ditches, shot them dead, and then threw the bodies into the ditches. They had raped Jewish women before killing them and had pulled out gold teeth from some of the corpses. She recounted that afterward, the men had gone home, their boots covered in blood. She gave us the names of eight of them.

Another Lithuanian contacted us, writing that he wanted to tell us about something he had witnessed near the village of Panemunelis, a shtetl in which 100 or so Jews lived. One day in August 1941, he had seen a cart driving by with ten Jews on it—five from the Olkin family, five from the Jaffe family. They were accompanied by four armed Lithuanians, whom he named in his letter. Two hours later, the vehicle came back in the opposite direction. The four Lithuanians were still there, but the Jews had disappeared; all that remained was their clothes, piled up at the bottom of the cart. He said that several moments earlier, he had heard the sounds of rifle fire ringing out from a forest very near by. According to our informant, who began his letter by explaining that he sought no recompense, two of the four Lithuanians were no longer alive at the time of his writing. We looked into the matter and discovered that all four of them were dead.

A certain Justinas Jokubaitis, who lived in Klaipeda, Lithuania, wrote to us on November 11, 2002, about what had happened in his hometown of Gargzdai. He said that one morning in the fall of 1941, while he was at school, he had seen women and children being taken from their homes by Lithuanian guards. It turned out that they had been held in a barn during the whole summer. He gave us the names of three of the four guards: (1) Antanas Puzneckis, from the village of Saulazoles; (2) Lukauskas Ilde, from the village of Rudaiciai; (3) Salykla, a policeman in Gargzdai. He could not remember the name of the fourth man. This witness then described another scene. During the winter of 1941, he had played the accordion during a celebration that took place in his village. Antanas Puzneckis was present. He was drinking vodka, a lot of vodka, and began boastfully to recount his exploits, detailing how he had abused Jewish women and murdered Jewish children. On hearing this, the shocked villagers beat him up. The next day the police rounded up several of them, including the witness's father, who spent eight months in a prison camp. After the war, Justinas Jokubaitis denounced Puzneckis to the Soviet authorities who governed Lithuania at the time. According to him, his mother and brother were murdered shortly afterward, in what he described as bloody reprisals for having denounced Puzneckis.

He concluded his letter with these words: "If possible, publish this account in the newspaper so that people will know what happened here. I sympathize with the sufferings endured by your people. I have a deep respect for the Jewish people. I have seen and I continue to see those who look on you with contempt. But I hope that the heads of the Jewish community of Lithuania will read my letter attentively and appreciate the way in which the Jokubaitis [family] behaved towards the Jews."[3]

A **MONTH LATER,** I received a very long letter from one Andrius Gudzinskas, a lawyer. This how his account began: "In my native village of Kalnaberze lived a man, Pranas Žemaitis, whom we nicknamed 'the emperor.' During the war, he worked as a farmer, while his brother, Antanas, served in the security police force, which collaborated with the German SS." Our correspondent added that Antanas Žemaitis had been the head of the Kaunas prison and that he had tortured Jews before assisting in their murder. Further on in the letter, he gave us other names: "Edvardas Guoga, who was the member of a paramilitary battalion, participated in the murders of Jews in Lithuania and in Belorussia."[4]

I **N WRITTEN OR** oral form, we gathered the names of 260 suspects. All were meticulously examined. Could they really have been Nazi collaborators? Had they already been tried in the Soviet era? Were these people still alive? All fundamental questions.

In order to research these cases, I hired Rūta Puišytė, today the deputy director of the Yiddish Institute of Vilnius University, who was then working for the Jewish Museum of Vilnius. An extraordinarily courageous young woman, Ruta was one of the few "truth tellers" among ethnic Lithuanians, those who considered it their mission to research the crimes of their countrymen and teach about this important aspect of the history of the Holocaust in their homeland. We categorized suspects by letters: category A ("alive, living in Lithuania, known address"); category J ("deceased"); category C ("certainly alive, living in Lithuania, but address unknown"); or category G ("no indication of age, living outside Lithuania"), among others. We also grouped informants: (1) for "direct witness," (2) for "holds evidence," and (3) for "hearsay." Obviously, not all the allegations we received were credible and worthy of investigation, but quite a few seemed serious.

By July 2004, we had submitted 72 names to local prosecutors, including those of 46 Lithuanians. Dozens of investigations were opened by the judicial authorities, but unfortunately, to date, none of these suspects has been prosecuted. In addition, I encountered many negative reactions, especially in the Baltics. In Taurage, Lithuania, for example, a member of the local city council, Saulius Oželis, burned an imitation Israeli flag and rode around the center of the town in a car from which Nazi songs were blaring. Time and again, I was criticized for only pursuing Nazi criminals and not Communists. My reply always was that while I fully supported the prosecution of Communist criminals, the expertise and mission of the Wiesenthal Center were to focus on the crimes of the Holocaust. But why, I asked, hadn't any of the Baltic countries produced their own Simon Wiesenthal whose mission would be to bring Communist criminals to justice?

We also encountered our share of opposition from within the Jewish communities. For example, Arkady Suharenko, the president of the Jewish community in Latvia, who had initially given us his support, suddenly changed his mind in the middle of our joint press conference at the launch of the project and started criticizing Operation Last Chance. I can only explain his change of heart by his fear that our campaign would give rise to anti-Semitism that would hurt his community. His Estonian counterpart, Celia Laud, was no more helpful. She, too, was afraid to support the project publicly, but did agree to host our initial press conference at the Jewish community center.

Later on, in Germany, where more than 100,000 Jews live today, Stefan Kramer, the secretary-general of the *Zentralrat*, the representative organization of German Jewry, told me that "the time was not right" for Operation Last Chance in Germany. But there were other Jewish leaders who provided us with outstanding assistance, such as the president of the Lithuanian Jewish community, Shimon Alperovich, and the secretary-general of the Romanian Jewish community, Julian Sorin. They understood and appreciated our efforts, fully realizing that the best way to fight anti-Semitism was to encourage the government to take legal action against anti-Semites. The trials of suspected local Nazi war criminals that we hoped to facilitate were designed to serve the same purpose. In that respect, we knowingly ran the risk of causing a small amount of anti-Semitism to help thoroughly defeat the local anti-Semites by delegitimizing them in the eyes of their compatriots.

SIXTEEN

THE SHE-DEVIL OF MAJDANEK

AFTER WE LAUNCHED our mission in the Baltic countries, I decided to expand Operation Last Chance in fall 2003 to Poland, Romania, and Austria, each of which had its share of unprosecuted Holocaust perpetrators and posed difficult challenges to our project.

Approximately 3 million Polish Jews were murdered during World War II, the largest number in any European country. Although the Nazis refused to actively integrate Poles into the forces that carried out the mass murder of Jews, as they did elsewhere throughout Eastern Europe, many individual Poles helped kill Jews, a fact often denied or ignored by Poles, who prefer to view their country solely as a victim of Nazism.

In the summer of 2003, statements by the Romanian Ministry of Information, which claimed that "within the borders of Romania between 1940 and 1945 there was no Holocaust,"[1] and by president Ion Iliescu that "The Holocaust was not unique to the Jewish population in Europe,"[2] caused a general outcry that was ultimately to prove useful. A commission of inquiry to study the Holocaust was set up. Nothing was done, however, to inform the Romanian people of the crimes committed by the wartime government of General Ion Antonescu, who was still seen as a national hero in certain circles. Since democracy had come to Romania in 1989, not one alleged Nazi war criminal had been questioned, let alone put on trial, and several had even been exonerated. Under these circumstances, Operation Last Chance had a critical role to play.

With the generous pro bono help of the Tempo Advertising Company, we were able to spread our message regarding the project and the reward being offered all over the country, but the amount of concrete information we received on our special toll-free hotline was relatively small. In total, local informants gave us the names of 18 potential suspects. However, after researching the allegations, I reached the conclusion, in consultation with Otto Adler, the head of the local association of Holocaust survivors, who very ably assisted us in collecting the information, that only four cases were worthy of an official investigation by the prosecutor. I submitted our files on the four Romanians to the legal authorities there, but progress was very slow. Two years later, I met with Dr. Ilie Botos, the Romanian attorney general, to ask him why the investigations conducted by his department had still not been completed. Hesitantly, he told me that he was still waiting for additional research.

In spring 2006, I criticized Romania for its failure to prosecute alleged war criminals. As a satellite of Nazi Germany, Romania, under General Antonescu, had incontrovertibly helped implement the Final Solution and had caused the deaths of hundreds of thousands of Jews. In an open letter to the attorney general, I expressed my "deep concern" and pointed out that, with each passing day, more of these suspected criminals were escaping justice. To further complicate matters, that May, I was informed by Prosecutor Angela Nicolae that she was unable to obtain all the files necessary to complete her investigations of the four suspects whose names we had handed over to the authorities a few years earlier. I protested this inexplicable delay of justice and, in July, was finally informed that none of the suspects would be prosecuted since there was insufficient evidence to corroborate the allegations.

Of the four cases, the one that, I considered to have the best potential involved a person who had bragged to a neighbor (who had contacted our hotline) that, while serving in the Romanian army, he had participated in the shooting and burning alive of approximately 29,000 Jews in Odessa, an atrocity that was well-known to historians. While he was being investigated by the Romanian prosecutors, the suspect denied his personal participation, claiming that the Germans carried out the murders, although there is unequivocal evidence of the participation of Romanian soldiers in these murders. However, the question of his guilt soon became irrelevant, as he died during the course of the investigation.

Although we were unable to achieve a prosecution of a Romanian Nazi war criminal, we did help focus public attention on the collaboration of Romanians in the implementation of the Final Solution, a topic that has rarely been openly discussed in the country. We also were able to achieve an educational victory by creating, together with the Federation of Jewish Communities of Romania, a Romanian-language version of "Courage to Remember," our traveling Holocaust exhibit, which went on display in the National History Museum in Bucharest and included a specially added section on the Holocaust in Romania prepared by the local Holocaust historian Lya Benjamin with the help of the Culture Ministry adviser Irina Cajal. The exhibition was opened on January 26, 2004, by President Iliescu and Culture Minister Razvan Theodorescu and received very good media coverage.

IN FALL 2003, we launched Operation Last Chance in Austria, where we encountered the most difficult conditions I had ever experienced. Nowhere else had I faced such a flood of insults through telephone calls, e-mails, anonymous letters, and postcards sent to my Jerusalem office. As soon as our advertisement seeking witnesses appeared in the *Kronen Zeitung*—the most popular daily in the country, openly right-wing, with a circulation of more than 1 million—it triggered an avalanche of anti-Semitic messages. Of course, we had not pulled our punches: "Die Mörder sind unter uns" (The murderers are among us), our message read in bold letters, against a red-and-white background, the colors of the Austrian flag. It also said: "War criminals are still alive and some of them are living in Austria. Please help us find them." It was accompanied by a terrible image. On the left was a group of men lined up by a ditch, about to be shot in the back. On the right were authentic instruments of death and torture: a pistol, a knife, a rope, a canister of Zyklon B, a syringe, and pincers. Desperate times call for desperate measures: Austria's record in terms of prosecuting alleged Nazi criminals was absolutely awful. Not a single criminal had been convicted in over three decades.

Austria has long preferred to present itself as Hitler's first victim, rather than dare confess it was a devoted accessory to his crimes. There were many Austrians among the main perpetrators of the Final Solution—Adolf Eichmann; Franz Stangl, the commanding officer of Treblinka; Artus Seyss-Inquart, the Nazi official who ruled the Netherlands; Odilo Globocnik, Gauleiter in Vienna, head of the SS in the Lublin district, whose main task was to implement "Operation Reinhardt," the plan for the mass annihilation of the Jews in Poland; and, of course, let's not forget the Führer himself: Adolf Hitler, born on April 20, 1889, in Braunau-am-Inn, Austria.

Nearly 95 percent of the telephone messages to our toll-free line (the number was given at the bottom of the advertisement) were insults. Christine Schindler, an employee of the Austrian Resistance Documentation Center based in Vienna, volunteered to collect and transcribe all these messages, writing up a record for each one. For example: "The action is disgusting; one cannot denounce old men." "It is a scandal to offer a reward for hunting our grandfathers, very old men." "The Jews are a world power suppressing the whole world." "It's a shame that such an ad is possible in Austria. The Jews are so greedy." "Innocent Austrians have paid enough to the Jews." "There are two murderers: Ariel Sharon and George Bush." "The real murderers are in Israel." "My grandfather died at Auschwitz, he fell off the watch-tower."

ONE DAY, OUT of all this abuse, a gold nugget emerged. It came to us through the mail: a simple letter, handwritten and dated May 8, 2004, signed by a Mrs. Martha Waninger, who lived in Vienna.

> Dear ladies and gentlemen at the Wiesenthal Center,
> I was interested to read your advertisement a while ago, "The murderers are among us," published in the *Kronen Zeitung*. It reminded

me of a person known as "the she-devil of the women's camp." This person's name was Wallisch, Erna. She used to live in Vienna at 100, Schiffmühlenstrasse. I cannot tell you if she has been brought to trial or not for what she did. For my part, I am writing to you to fight the Holocaust deniers and neo-Nazis. I hope I have helped you. Martha Waninger.[3]

I hurried to my telephone and called Dr. Stefan Klemp, our researcher in Germany, to get him to quickly check the Austrian yellow pages and the German records to find out if this Erna Wallisch really did exist and who she was. I had to be both cautious and suspicious in proceeding. The worst thing possible was for us to make a false accusation, and we had already received tips that were clearly inaccurate and had been submitted to make trouble for people.

A Nazi hunt can sometimes begin in the simplest, most obvious way: by checking the telephone directory. Erna Wallisch existed, and she still lived at the address we had been given. The first hurdle in the long verification process had been cleared. However, we found no trace of Martha Waninger, the writer of the letter, who had also indicated that she did not want the reward before vanishing into thin air. She may have been afraid of reprisals from Wallisch's friends or family.

I gradually followed up the Wallisch lead and discovered that Mrs. Waninger's information was accurate. Here is a summary of the initial in-depth report that Stefan Klemp sent me after searching the German archives:

Born in February 1922 in Germany, [Wallisch] volunteered to work as a guard at Ravensbrück concentration camp in May 1941. In October 1942, she was transferred to the Majdanek death camp, where she met Georg Wallisch. Was four months pregnant in November 1943. After the war, she was questioned twice by investigators in Austria, on January 14, 1965, and November 30, 1972. The first time, she denied all knowledge of the gas chambers. The second time, she admitted having escorted deportees into the gas chambers. In the Stasi[4] archives there is a statement made in 1971 by a deportee, Tatiana Marta Targalska, who describes Wallisch as a well-known sadist who helped select prisoners when they arrived at the camp. However, she only appears once in these records. Strange. So I have three recommendations: contact survivors from Majdanek; contact the Austrian authorities; try to find a photo of her.[5]

Despite exhaustive research, in different countries and for several years, we were never able to get hold of any pictures of Wallisch in her concentration camp days. However, we did find evidence of her time at Ravensbrück and Majdanek. Like Auschwitz, Majdanek was a concentration camp in Poland that was also used as an extermination center. Located on the outskirts of, and in clear sight of, the city of Lublin, it was divided into five quarters. Quarter I was the women's camp.

Gas extermination operations began in Majdanek in October 1942 and continued until the end of 1943. Seven gas chambers were used to kill prisoners with carbon monoxide or Zyklon B. The Majdanek SS carried out regular selection operations. Prisoners judged unfit for work were executed by shooting or in the gas chamber. After the destruction of the Warsaw ghetto in May 1943, some 18,000 survivors of the uprising were transferred to Majdanek. On November 3, 1943, special SS and police units sent to Lublin executed 18,000 Jews from Majdanek outside the camp. The massacre, which took an entire day, was part of "Aktion Erntefest" (Operation Harvest Festival), the code name for the extermination of the surviving Jews of Majdanek and the Trawniki and Poniatowa labor camps. During the executions, loudspeakers played music into the camp.[6] It was the first major concentration camp to be liberated, on July 24, 1944, by the Soviets.

It was in this hell that Erna Wallisch made her mark. Our inquiries confirmed the initial information supplied by Stefan. We searched Polish, East German, and Austrian archives, collecting as much information as possible. We needed incontrovertible proof and direct witness testimonies before moving on to the next stage of operations: contacting officials, organizing a press conference, and demanding a trial in Austria or extradition.

Stefan tried to contact the suspect, using an assumed identity. Generally, my foreign contacts pretend to be history students when they call our suspects. The ruse often works, but not this time. Wallisch replied and was polite, but wary, refusing to discuss the subject. She said she no longer wanted to talk about the war.

O**N MARCH 22,** 2005, I sent the information regarding Wallisch to Dr. Kurt Hengel, the veteran Austrian ambassador to Israel, with a request that her case be reopened in view of the incriminating evidence regarding her activities in the camp. On the same day, I also wrote to Professor Leon Kieres, the president of the Polish Institute of National Memory, which is responsible for the investigation of Nazi and Communist crimes, to inform him about the case and ask for his assistance in the investigation. A month later, I met personally with Professor Kieres and his colleague Dr. Witold Kulesza, director of prosecutions, in Warsaw to discuss how best to ensure that Wallisch would indeed be held accountable for her crimes.

Stefan's research showed that in 1972, Wallisch (who seven years earlier had denied knowledge of any gas chambers during her time at the camp) admitted she had escorted inmates, especially women and children, to their death. She was questioned again in 1978 by the Austrian authorities and accused of being an accessory, but the charges were soon dropped because of the Austrian statute of limitation on such crimes.

I wanted Austria to reopen the Wallisch case and was determined to find some way to do so—but it was not easy. New difficulties arose in January 2006. Austria announced that Erna Wallisch would not be tried in that country. The investigators had come to the conclusion that she could only be accused of "passive complicity in genocide," but that this crime was unfortunately subject to the existing Austrian statute of limitation. Thus, the minister of justice informed us that in the absence of new criminal charges, the information supplied by the Wiesenthal Center had not changed Erna Wallisch's situation. There was now no legal possibility of reopening the investigation into Erna Wallisch, a decision backed by many Austrians, not least by most of her neighbors, apparently none of whom knew anything of her horrific history. "All that's in the past and should be forgotten. People should learn to forgive,"[7] one of them said, sighing.

At a press conference I held on February 1, the day after my meeting with Justice Minister Gastinger, I declared that "The law in this country does more to protect Nazis than to bring them to justice." And then I came up with a phrase that hit the nail on the head: "There is a system here that makes Austria a paradise for Nazi war criminals, plain and simple."[8]

All the country's newspapers and television channels repeated those words, which had an absolutely explosive effect. Pursued by journalists, the minister of the interior, Liese Prokop, refused to comment on my words, while the minister for justice could not be contacted. Was it provocation on my part? Not at all. If I had to do it again today, I would.

While Austria is making serious efforts to teach the history of the Holocaust and, in some measure, to confront its responsibility for the crimes of the past, almost nothing has been done in recent years about tracking down Nazis and bringing them to justice. There has not been a single conviction in the past 30 years in Austria, despite the fact that Stefan Klemp's research clearly proves the involvement of many Austrians in the German police battalions responsible for mass crimes against civilians, mainly Jews.

EVERY YEAR SINCE 2002, I have published an annual report on the state of the investigations into and prosecutions of alleged Nazi war criminals around the world. Each time it is released, the document is reported on by media worldwide. This report is a great asset in my efforts. In the 2006 report, I ranked Erna Wallisch seventh of the ten most wanted Nazis in the world, the only woman to appear on the list.

My annual report also included a second listing that ranked countries, ordered in seven categories, from those that had made the most efforts to prosecute Nazi war criminals—the United States and, to a lesser extent, Italy—to those that had completely failed in this area, mainly due to lack of political will. I obviously placed Austria in that last category.

Since the Austrians were refusing on legal grounds to prosecute Wallisch, I set out to find additional evidence of her crimes. On February 8, 2006, I appealed again to the Polish authorities to do everything in their power to help me find more information on her, and also asked them to consider seeking her extradition based on the fact that she had committed her crimes in Poland and against Polish citizens. Meanwhile, in September 2007, Wallisch spoke briefly to journalists, telling them: "I knew nothing about the gas chambers. Anyway, I don't know anything else about all that and I don't ever want to know anything else."[9] The woman was lying, and I would soon have proof.

IN THE FALL of 2007, our investigation finally got somewhere. The Poles had found what we needed: statements from survivors of the camp. There was already a terrifying account from a former prisoner, Jadwiga Landowska. Quoted in the British daily the *Telegraph*, she said she had never forgotten the "monstrous pregnant Nazi who sometimes went crazy and was never put on trial with the other Majdanek executioners in Düsseldorf after the war. Once, she hit a young man lying on the ground in front of me, hit him with something harder than a whip. Blood was spurting from the poor man's head. He seemed to be dead, but she carried on hitting him. I'll never forget that monster's sweaty, panting face."[10]

There were five other testimonies that told of this tall, pregnant, very beautiful blonde guard who would also beat old women. "When she came, terror reigned," recalled one of the survivors. The six statements I received all described a sadistic, terrifying woman, capable of beating prisoners to death and treating deportees, including children, in a particularly inhuman way. One of the prisoners also described how she had seen Wallisch beat a small child and then toss the body away "like a piece of wood."[11]

After the discovery of these new statements, the Polish judiciary announced its intention to request that Wallisch be extradited and put on trial. Dated November 27, 2007, a letter from the attorney of the special commission dealing with crimes against the Polish nation informed me that he meant to prosecute Erna Wallisch for crimes committed at the Majdanek camp. Now all we had to do was convince Austria. More meetings. More pressure.

A long article about the case was published in the Austrian weekly *Profil*.[12] Since the disclosure of the Wallisch affair, not a week had gone by without the press taking an interest in her. The effect was disastrous for Austria—but it was to our advantage, for in this way perhaps the government would finally give in. Then the unbelievable happened.

ON JANUARY 28, 2008, the Vienna district attorney's office announced the launch of a new preliminary investigation into the actions of Erna Wallisch, 85, suspected of murder when she was a guard at the Nazi concentration camp of Majdanek. Due to the statute of limitations, only one murder charge was upheld—very little given the accusations against her, but enough to bring her before a court. "We're trying to establish whether the witness statements from Poland are sufficient to identify this woman. It's obviously difficult more than 60 years later,"[13] a spokesperson for the district attorney, Gerhard Jarosch, told a reporter for Reuters. I appealed to the Austrian authorities to handle the case with great urgency, given the advanced age of the suspect and the importance of the case. As I explained in a letter dated January 29, 2008, to Maria Berger, the Austrian minister of justice:

> I...urge you to do everything possible to expedite the investigation in Vienna so that justice can be achieved...Erna Wallisch ultimately was dismissed from her duties at the Majdanek death camp after she became pregnant in the course of a sexual relationship with a fellow guard. The idea that an individual was conducting sexual relations while hundreds of thousands of innocent civilians were being murdered is one which is so obviously repulsive, and yet another indicator of the total disdain of the guards for their unfortunate victims, a situation which only made it easier for them to participate in the orgy of mass murder which took place at Majdanek....People like Erna Wallisch do not deserve any sympathy. The fact that they have not previously been convicted is a travesty of justice which can now be corrected. Doing so will send a very powerful message that Austria has finally ceased being a haven for the perpetrators of the Holocaust.[14]

IT WAS A huge victory. Four years of battles, procedures, research, controversy, and sleepless nights would end in Erna Wallisch's prosecution and punishment in Austria, the first conviction of a Holocaust perpetrator in Austria in more than 30 years! The court case there would be a worldwide sensation. A woman, a guard from the Majdanek camp on trial: a first in over a quarter of a century.

My joy was very short-lived. On February 21, 2008, as I was coming out of Hadassah Hospital in Jerusalem, where I had just undergone surgery, I received a call from Dr. Norbert Hack, the deputy ambassador of Austria in Israel. Erna Wallisch had died five days earlier in a Vienna hospital. She would never stand trial. The Wallisch case was closed.

It would be incredibly hard to describe the maelstrom of emotion that engulfed me, a combination of deep anger, frustration, and helplessness. Instead of going right home to begin my convalescence, I headed for the office and issued the following statement:

> Erna Wallisch and her family can thank the decades-long failure of successive Austrian governments for the fact that she ultimately was never punished for her role at the Majdanek death camp and Ravensbrück concentration camp. The fact that a woman who admitted taking people to be gassed and guarding them so that they could not escape was never held accountable for her heinous crimes is a badge of shame for Austria and stark proof of the decades-long lack of political will in Vienna to bring Austrian Holocaust perpetrators to justice. Her death should serve as a reminder to all the governments that are dealing with the cases of Nazi war criminals that they had best expedite these prosecutions while justice can still be achieved.[15]

The angel of death had snatched a last victory from the men and women who had helped me over those five years. Ours was supposed to have been a victory over lies, against the erasure of memory and the refusal to admit crimes, one that would have enabled the dead not to be avenged, but simply recognized and finally respected as they deserved. But it was not to be.

SEVENTEEN

CHARLES ZENTAI

THE CHARLES ZENTAI case began with an appeal for help sent to me from Budapest shortly after I launched Operation Last Chance in Hungary on July 13, 2004. It was sent on behalf of Ádám Balázs, a retired pharmacist who was almost 80 years old. The launch of Operation Last Chance in Hungary had inspired him to continue the efforts started by his father, Dezső, who had died in 1970, and who had never stopped demanding justice for his son, Ádám's brother, Peter. Ádám Balázs wrote to the Hungarian historian László Karsai, asking him to pass the information on to me. The information was about a man called Károly Zentai, who Balázs believed was responsible for his brother's death.

In this letter, he stated that the Foreign Secretary of Hungary had requested the extradition of Charles Zentai who was residing in the American occupied zone in Germany.

I had never heard of Károly—or Charles—Zentai when I received this letter. As a consequence, the letter triggered a real effort to find out more about him. I began by going through the documents Ádám Balázs had collected: one was a brief letter by his father, Dezső. Dated June 24, 1948, it was addressed to the American Legation in Budapest.

According to Dezső, he and his family were living in hiding in 1944, but Zentai recognized his son Peter on a tram and took him to a barracks where Zentai and two accomplices beat him until he died, that same day. In this same document, he stated that a captain named Béla Máder brought six other prisoners to witness Peter's last breaths, threatening them that they would be killed the same way. He then named a second man, Nagy, who he claimed assisted Zentai in disposing of Peter's body, which was never found. It was only three years after his death, in 1947, during the trial of one of Zentai's accomplices, that the Balázs family found out for certain what had happened to Peter.

The accompanying documents, including six pages of testimonies, are yellowed and worn with age, and I preserve them very carefully in my archives in Jerusalem. In a second document, a letter to the American military headquarters in Germany, Dezső Balázs recounted with overwhelming precision the atrocious suffering that his son was subjected to.

Dezső Balázs then explained what had happened to Zentai's two accomplices: Béla Máder had been sentenced to life imprisonment in March 1946 and Lajos Nagy to the death penalty two years later. But Zentai had not been tried.

"There is no pain on earth greater than that of the parents who have lost their child," Peter's father continued. "The sore wound inflicted upon us with the death of my son: upon myself, my wife...and upon the lame twin-brother is never going to be healed. Our nights are still haunted by his picture and...Meanwhile the murderer is peacefully living in Bavaria and getting on quite well. But this bloodshed is appealing to Heaven! This terrible crime must not remain unpunished...I want my son to be avenged!"[1]

I was able to confirm that what Dezső Balázs had said in his letter was correct. His description of the crime fit the pattern of the manhunts and murders of Jews carried out by Hungarian soldiers and members of the fascist Arrow Cross in Budapest following the establishment of the government of Ferenc Szálasi on October 15, 1944. By this point, practically all the Jews living outside the capital had already been concentrated and deported to Auschwitz by the Hungarian gendarmes, so the focus of the anti-Semites turned to the approximately 100,000 Jews in the Hungarian capital, many of whom were caught and murdered. After the war, some of those responsible for these crimes were prosecuted, among them Máder and Nagy. In the course of the latter's trial, the fact that Zentai had apparently played a role was revealed.

I immediately went to Yad Vashem to search for Zentai in the files of the ITS. He was listed and I lost no time in getting hold of the documents concerning him. First name: Károly. Date of birth: October 21, 1921. Nationality: Hungarian. Sex: Male. Status: Married. Profession: Chauffeur. Peter's father was right: the soldier Zentai, born Steiner, had fled Hungary after the war. He went to Germany—first to the zone occupied by the Americans, then to the zone occupied by the French—where he claimed to be a refugee. His first son, Tomas, was born there in 1949. On January 30, 1950, the Zentais left for Italy. On March 2, they sailed for Australia on board the *Fair Sea* from the port of Naples.

Dezső Balázs's poignant letter to the occupying authorities in Germany is dated May 30, 1948, slightly less than two years before Zentai's departure. Unfortunately, it did not succeed in getting the authorities to try Zentai for Peter's death. Not only was Zentai not prosecuted for the crime, he was able to depart without any difficulty to start a new life on the other side of the world. From 1950 to 2004, he lived in western Perth. Working as a psychiatric nurse, television salesman, and real estate agent, he lived quite comfortably in an affluent residential area with his wife and children.

I NOW HAD in my possession the details of the events that had led to the death of young Peter and believed I knew the identity of the killer and his accomplices. I also knew what escape route the killer had taken after the war and that he had settled in Australia. But all that information was from the 1950s. I did not know whether Zentai was still alive and whether he was still in that country.

Following my tried and trusted method, I passed the baton to my contacts on the ground. I immediately wrote to Dr. Colin Rubinstein, the director of AIJAC, presenting him with the facts. Having learned my lesson from Milivoj Ašner's escape from Croatia to Austria, I asked him to proceed with the greatest discretion. I also called a journalist I trusted, to whom I promised a nice scoop if he found something.

The journalist did not waste time in getting back to me: "I have your man!" He had managed to speak to Zentai on the phone. Zentai seemed to be in perfect physical and mental health, and, he said, it was difficult to believe he was over 80 from the sound of his voice. Zentai was living in a nice suburb of Perth, alone since the death of his wife. We now had his address, his telephone number, and all the necessary information to move on to the next stage, but in order to be 100 percent certain regarding his health, I made a deal with Channel 9 to film him secretly. Sure enough, Zentai was filmed driving his car, a sure sign that he was healthy enough to be put on trial.

Thus the stage was set to contact the governments that would be called upon to take legal action against him, Australia and Hungary. In the case of the latter, if we were to succeed, it would be the first-ever trial of a suspected Hungarian Nazi collaborator since the transition to democracy. Like the rest of post-Communist Europe, Hungary was also having trouble facing its role in the crimes of the Holocaust. As luck would have it, an extradition treaty existed between Australia and Hungary, which theoretically paved the way for Zentai to be put on trial in Budapest. I therefore contacted both the Australian and Hungarian authorities to inform them of Zentai's crimes in 1944 and his current residence in Perth. Shortly thereafter, Zentai was exposed on national television by Channel 9. In response to the allegations leveled against him, he said that he was prepared to go to Hungary and prove his innocence. My reaction was to say that it was an excellent idea and I looked forward to him doing so, a step that would save the Australian and Hungarian taxpayers a small fortune.

In April 2005, Budapest officially requested the extradition of Charles Zentai, and that was the last anyone heard that he was willing to voluntarily go to Budapest to stand trial. This was undoubtedly an important first victory. Another occurred several weeks later, when the Australian justice minister accepted the request. In July, Zentai, who would be the first Australian extradited for alleged war crimes, was arrested in his home by the police, before he was placed on probation.

I quickly informed Ádám Balázs, Peter's sole surviving relative, who was now 82 years old. He was approached by numerous journalists, but he declined all requests for an interview. Even with us, he was very cautious. Still traumatized, 65 years later, by his brother's murder, he said that he feared Zentai might send his followers to his home to kill him and his family. Nonetheless, he was comforted by the good news I had brought him. The previous few months had been painful for him, forcing him to plunge back into that tragic family past and those old, atrocious memories. His other brother, Paul, Peter's twin, who had died in 1991, had never gotten over their brother's death. Ádám alone remained to fight for the family cause. He thanked me and added sadly that Peter could have had a wonderful life since he was a talented, responsible, and generous lad.

I didn't want him to be disappointed, which would be cruel, so I warned him that the game, although well under way, was not yet won.

Zentai could appeal the extradition request, a move that would take months or even longer. And that is indeed what he did, making use of a technical legal tactic, whereby, with complete legality, he teamed up with an Irishman who was facing extradition to Dublin for fraud to challenge the competence of the local court in Perth to deal with matters of extradition, claiming that only a federal court would be able to make the judgment. It took over two years before the Australian high court on June 13, 2008, dismissed Zentai's case and finally gave the Perth court the responsibility to rule on the extradition request from Hungary.

In the meantime, my lobbying work continued. I informed the Hungarian authorities that Zentai was protesting to all and sundry his desire to return to his native country to defend his honor. As for the Australian authorities, I gave them a failing grade in our 2006 Annual Report on the worldwide investigation and prosecution of Nazi war criminals. This naturally was very bad publicity for them that was reported all over the world and that the Canberra government would gladly have done without. As for Zentai, I put him in ninth place on the list of the ten most wanted suspected Nazis in the world, between Soeren Kam, a Dane suspected of having murdered the anti-Nazi editor Carl Henrik Clemmensen and of having stolen the register of Danish Jews to enable their deportation to a Nazi concentration camp, and Algimantas Dailide, a suspected former member of the Lithuanian security police, responsible for the arrest of numerous Jews and Poles who were subsequently murdered.

Zentai was a strange man. Initially, he had announced his willingness to go prove his innocence in Hungary but, in fact, he did everything to avoid a trial. He even sent his children out on the front lines in his defense, starting with one of his sons, Ernie, who did the media rounds advancing an argument that he thought irrefutable, that his father left Budapest the day before Peter Balázs was murdered. The day before was November 7, 1944. That sounded like an improbable coincidence. And yet Ernie did not give up: "Like hundreds of other people, my parents left on November 7. They remember the date perfectly because they had just gotten engaged. What is more, November 7 is the day my mother saw her parents and brother for the last time."[2] True, he acknowledged that he was not able to provide the least proof of this, but his father had talked to him so much about this particular day that he believed his word.

IN FEBRUARY 2006, Zentai's children learned that I was coming to Perth and asked to see me. I had no desire to meet with them, feeling that it could lead to nothing positive—I would not succeed in convincing them of their father's guilt, and there was no chance they would shake my own certainties. Eventually, I agreed to a meeting in Perth, organized by a journalist from the *Australian*, Paige Taylor, who had been following the case closely from the beginning. I did not know what they might do when faced with the man who was publicly accusing their father of being a murderer and, consequently, I had a small degree of apprehension, but my friends from the Jewish community of Perth who accompanied me and Paige reassured me that I had nothing to fear.

Ernie Steiner (the children all used their father's real name) arrived late, accompanied by his brother and sister. He had just spent the past 18 months of his life collecting documents on his father—becoming, in a sense, his lawyer.

To my surprise, the meeting was relatively calm and civil. I had said to myself that if I could avoid shaking their hands, I would do so. But when he arrived, Ernie held his out to me warmly. He then gave me a text that he had written, narrating his version of the facts, and asked me to read it right there. I responded politely that I would do so later and that I was there to hear him speak. So he asked me: "Why are you doing this? Our father would not survive a trial in Hungary." I replied that his father had to be tried and that if the court found him innocent, I would acquiesce to its judgment.

It was on this point that our opinions were totally divergent. In their eyes, their father's innocence was so obvious that there was no need of a trial. "When I spoke to him at length about this affair, I saw in his eyes that he was telling the truth," said Ernie—an argument that, in my view, did not hold much weight. His brother, Gabriel, added: "I have never heard our father say the least negative thing about any community or minority. On the contrary, he is a very tolerant man." And once again, they assured me that their parents had left Budapest the day before Peter Balázs's death. They wanted to believe it.

I could not find much to say to them, other than that, from a certain perspective, I sympathized with them. I absolutely would not like to be in their shoes. They were roughly the same age as I and were confronting a stranger who was accusing their father, the person they loved most in all the world, of being a war criminal, a murderer, and a liar. A stranger who was ruining their father's last years and, in doing so, their own lives. A stranger who was soiling their family name.

Their stubbornness was only natural. How would I react in their place? Would I have the courage to confront these allegations or would I prefer, like them, to put this challenge aside and take refuge in denial? All three children refused to accept what I had to say to them. For them, Charles Zentai was the victim of a huge judicial mistake—worse, of a plot. They refused to examine the evidence or to have even the slightest objectivity.

That was one of the most difficult moments of my career. The suspects I had found until then never expressed any regrets or composed confessions. But I hoped for a different attitude from their children. A healthy courage. It wasn't there. Like the sons of Mikson in Iceland, Zentai's children did not want to know the truth. If they asked to speak to me, it was simply with the aim of changing my mind. I adopted another tactic: I explained to them that I had no doubt that their father was an elderly gentleman who was good in every way and who had been a loving and attentive father to them. But what I wanted them to understand was that during World War II, men who had until then been irreproachable had committed horrific crimes, before once again becoming normal, widely respected people when the war was over. I added that their father was not the only one. That they were not the only ones. In many families, big secrets had remained buried during the postwar years before resurfacing. But that should not deprive the victims of justice. These bloody parentheses in otherwise uneventful lives should be exposed in a court of law.

After an hour, the meeting was going around in circles. I brought it to an end by saying that if their father was innocent, he had only to prove that before a court. In his native country, before a Hungarian judge, he would have the right to a fair trial that would establish whether his arguments stood up against an exposition of the facts.

As I left the meeting, I remembered the incredible phrase that had been slipped in during the course of the discussion: "You know, we do not doubt the historical reality of the Holocaust!" What did they think? That I would fall on them in gratitude for this acknowledgment? For them, that constituted a concession. A compromise.

AFTER HIS CHILDREN, Zentai recruited his parish priest, John B. Flynn. In a letter sent to the minister of justice, this man of the church wrote: "I have known Charlie for over 30 years. He is a good man, a good citizen, a good husband, a good father, a good family man, a good worker, a good Catholic, a good Christian, and a good parishioner." Then the priest turned detective and posed all sorts of questions on the circumstances of the crime of which Zentai was accused: "Where is the gun? Where are the bullets? Where are the fingerprints? Where's the DNA? Where are the living witnesses?"[3] What weapon or bullets was he talking about? DNA traces for a murder committed in 1944? As for witnesses, they existed. Some of them had already spoken at the trial of Zentai's accomplices, just after the war.

The high court decision to dismiss Zentai's case and give the Perth court responsibility for deciding the extradition case came on June 13, 2008. The extradition hearing would begin on August 18. We had to wait another two months, a situation that was very annoying to me and extremely frustrating. At least Zentai's position was not improving. On June 15, the Australian judicial authorities refused him the legal aid he had requested for the August hearing, and although he was on the verge of financial ruin, the old man would have to pay his lawyers from his own pocket. He also had to pay AUS$200,000 to the state after his appeal was turned down, a sum that would be added to the AUS$100,000 he had already spent on defending himself since the first revelations about his past.

As the date of August 18 approached, I was largely hopeful that the court would validate the extradition request, but I worried about the attitude of the minister of internal affairs, Bob Debus, who had the power to cancel that decision because of Zentai's health. In the past, I had observed to what degree war criminals who had been hale and hearty weeks before their trial were often subsequently victims of a sudden weakening that was likely to move a judge or minister. If Debus refused to sign the extradition order, everything would collapse.

On Wednesday, August 20, I was overcome with joy: the Perth magistrates' court authorized the extradition of Charles Zentai to Hungary. I was euphoric; to journalists, I talked of "a decision that is a giant step on the path of historical truth." I thought of the family and friends of Peter Balázs. However, I could not totally give free rein to my delight because the Australian minister of internal affairs still had to sign the document. If he opposed it, the court decision would be null and void.

In the meantime, Zentai was able to launch yet another appeal against his extradition, and the process has therefore not yet reached its final stage. Time after time, Zentai's lawyers have been able to find ways to delay his extradition and thereby spare him prosecution. It's a sickening situation in which the legal system is practically being abused by a defendant who deserves no sympathy.

WHILE WE AWAIT the final decision, it is important to mention an unexpected, indirect product of the Zentai case—the exposure in Australia of Lajos Polgár, an alleged Hungarian Nazi collaborator who found refuge in Melbourne. Polgár was the youth leader of the Arrow Cross movement and, during the Szálasi regime, was in charge of party headquarters, the so-called House of Loyalty, at 60 Andrassy Street in Budapest, where numerous Jews were tortured and murdered. He was initially named by *Magyar Elet*, a local Hungarian magazine, in August 2005, and his case was then publicized by the Australian Labor MP Michael Danby. Polgár, who never denied his role in the party, although he claimed to be innocent of any crimes, explained that "everybody in Hungary was anti-Jewish," and that none of the Arrow Cross leaders executed for war crimes after World War II were in any way guilty. "At that time," according to Polgár, "you could not do anything because everybody was in the hands of the Jews. They just hanged them. Completely, completely innocent people."[4]

Two days later, I learned that Polgár had been assisted in Australia by the family of the former Prime Minister Malcolm Fraser, who viewed him as an innocent refugee from Communism. In fact, Fraser himself called me in Jerusalem to clarify the issue, and I explained the nature and basis of the allegations against Polgár, whose citizenship application Fraser's family had supported.

As soon as I learned that Polgár was alive in Melbourne, I called upon the Hungarian and Australian authorities to investigate his activities during World War II and began research into the case. The center issued a worldwide call for survivors from Budapest with knowledge of the crimes committed at the Arrow Cross headquarters to contact us. We were assisted by the journalist Natasha Robinson of the *Australian*, who was able to obtain documents from Hungarian archives that proved Polgar's close relations with Josef Gera, an Arrow Cross leader executed after the war for war crimes. In late November 2005, on the basis of documents I submitted to Dr. Andras Gyenge, the Hungarian ambassador in Tel Aviv, the Hungarian authorities announced that they had opened a full-scale investigation against Lajos Polgár.

Soon, there was more news. Several weeks after we issued our call for witnesses from Budapest, I received an e-mail from Melbourne in which Judy Rogers informed me that her mother, Susanne Nozick, had been tortured together with her own mother (Judy's grandmother) in the cellar of Arrow Cross headquarters at 60 Andrassy Street. Less than a month later, in late January 2006, I sent the Hungarian prosecutors a copy of the shocking video testimony that Susanne Nozick gave at the Melbourne Holocaust Center on April 22, 1993, as well as trial protocols of proceedings held in Budapest in 1948 that detailed the atrocities committed by Hungarian Nazi collaborators at Arrow Cross headquarters.

In mid-February 2006, I was in Melbourne to deliver the Annual Hans Bachrach Memorial Oration as a guest of AIJAC and the Jerusalem College of Technology and had the opportunity and privilege to meet Susanne Nozick in person and hear her story.

In the winter of 1944–1945, she and her mother were caught hiding in a hospital in Budapest, trying to pose as non-Jews, and were taken to the cellar of Arrow Cross headquarters at 60 Andrassy Street, where they were repeatedly beaten, tortured, and raped over the course of three days, along with dozens of other Jewish and Gypsy prisoners. The Arrow Cross guards forced the Gypsies to rape the Jewish women prisoners, some of whom, like Nozick, also had sticks shoved into them by the guards.

Throughout this entire ordeal, all the prisoners were kept naked. After three days, during which quite a few of the prisoners had died, 40 to 50 of those still alive, including Nozick and her mother, were marched naked to the banks of the Danube under the guard of Arrow Cross men. There they were shot, and all of them fell into the river. Susanne Nozick, who luckily was not wounded, was the only survivor. She emerged from the river after all the Arrow Cross had departed the scene. She was found by Hungarian soldiers who eventually brought her to the Budapest ghetto, which was liberated three days later by Soviet troops.

Susanne Nozick not only survived the war but had the courage to speak about her Holocaust experiences and relate the details of the terrible ordeal she and her mother suffered at Arrow Cross headquarters. Given the particularly sensitive and horrifying aspects of her torture at the hands of the Arrow Cross, I found her bravery incredible and drew inspiration from her willingness to share the details of her ordeal with the public in order to help bring Polgár to justice. Despite the ostensible desire of Holocaust survivors to see justice done, some are reluctant to testify against perpetrators due to the deep trauma they suffered and their desire not to relive their horrible experiences. Susanne Nozick is, therefore, in my eyes, a special heroine.

Two months later, in early April 2006, I met in Hungary with Dr. Richárd Szoboszlai, the deputy chief prosecutor of Budapest, and his team of lawyers to discuss the Polgár investigation and received the bad news that Susanne Nozick's testimony would not incriminate Polgár since he had apparently left his post before she and her mother were brought to Arrow Cross headquarters in January 1945. This was very painful news, but the investigation, I was informed, would continue, and I promised that the center would do its best to help find potential witnesses.

On July 13, 2006, the Polgár investigation came to an end when the former Arrow Cross youth leader suddenly died at the age of 89 in his home in Ferntree Gully, Melbourne. As happens so often, we were blamed for his death. His son, Lou Polgár, asserted that "the stress of being 'outed' as an alleged Nazi-linked war criminal had played a 'big part' in his death. It weighed on him like a bloody lead anchor,"[5] an accusation that frankly leaves me unmoved, in view of Polgár's service with the notorious Arrow Cross, his collaboration with the Nazis, and the unabashed anti-Semitic views he held to his dying day.

Thus, Australia is left with one case, one last chance to take successful legal action against a suspected Nazi war criminal who found refuge in the country. I only hope that, in contrast to its record to date, Australia will finally extradite Zentai so that he can be held accountable for his alleged crimes, and thereby at long last produce a small measure of justice for the numerous victims of the killers who found a refuge down under.

EIGHTEEN

DR. HEIM, THE MOST WANTED NAZI IN THE WORLD

WHAT MAKES A person the most wanted Nazi war criminal in the world? The factors that determine one's place on my most wanted list are the scope of the crimes, the degree of responsibility, and the details of one's specific role in the killing process. For many years, the number-one slot belonged to Alois Brunner, Eichmann's right-hand man, who was responsible for the deportation to death camps of a total of 128,500 Jews—47,000 from Austria, 44,000 from Greece, 23,500 from France, and 14,000 from Slovakia. A fanatic Nazi, Brunner was interviewed in 1985 in Damascus by the Austrian magazine *Bunte*, and in response to the question whether he had any regrets, he said that his major regret was that he had not been successful in killing more Jews.

In Spring 2008, we received information from a reliable source, who had served in Syria as an intelligence agent for a major Western country, that Brunner was dead. We have not yet been able to conclusively confirm this, but given his age (he was born in 1912) and the fact that he was the victim of two letter bombs that maimed him, it is reasonable to assume that he is no longer alive, and we therefore placed him in a special category of his own.

The person who replaced him at the top of my most wanted list was Dr. Aribert Heim, the notorious "Dr. Death" of Mauthausen, whose case was high on Simon Wiesenthal's agenda for many years. I remember that in 1987, when the center consulted Mr. Wiesenthal regarding a most wanted list, which we wanted to publish to help gain access to the files of Nazi war criminals in the archives of the United Nations, he insisted that Heim be given a high ranking. We placed him at number four.

BORN IN RADKERSBURG, Austria, on June 28, 1914, Aribert Heim was in the vanguard of Nazism. A real fanatic, he joined the then-illegal Austrian National Socialist Party at 21, before joining Heinrich Himmler's SS in 1938 (membership number 367,744). He occupied his first post as a concentration camp doctor in 1941 at Sachsenhausen, 30 kilometers north of Berlin, before leaving for Buchenwald, another camp of lugubrious memory. Shortly thereafter, he took on a third posting in Austria, at Mauthausen, to which around 200,000 people were deported—and from which almost 120,000 never came back. It is in Mauthausen that he became most notorious and acquired the nickname of "Dr. Death." According to numerous witnesses, he personally killed numerous camp inmates by injecting them with poison or by using them as guinea pigs for abominable pseudomedical experiments.

Heim was a sadist and a criminal of the worst sort, a despicable creature. During his seven weeks at the camp, Heim, also known as "the Butcher of Mauthausen," carried out numerous amputations without anesthetic. He removed organs one after the other to see how long the victims survived. He injected their hearts with phenol (gasoline), and recorded the time it took them to die.

Karl Lotter, an inmate who worked at the Mauthausen clinic while Heim was there, reported the following incident in postwar testimony given to the Austrian authorities, which was made public by the Associated Press. An 18-year-old Jew had been sent to the clinic with a foot inflammation. Instead of treating him, Heim "cut him open, castrated him, took apart one kidney and removed the second.... The victim's head was removed and the flesh boiled off so that Heim could keep it on display. He needed the head because of its perfect teeth."[1]

Many of the medical records kept by the German doctors in the camps were recovered after the war. Day by day, with terrifying precision, they recorded all the operations carried out by the SS doctors. In Heim's case, numerous operations were an almost daily occurrence. Everything was typed up: the day, the month, and the year, and then, line by line, the number of operations carried out that day, followed by the surname and first name of the medical practitioner. Page after page, all identical, today kept in the archives of the German Ministry of Justice.

Here are a few excerpts:

> October 8, 1941: Dr. Aribert Heim, 18 operations, 11 deaths, all Jews;
> October 9 1941: Dr. Heim, 7 operations, 12 deaths, all Jews;
> October 10, 1941: 7 operations, 19 deaths, all Jews;
> October 16, 1941: 11 operations on Aryan prisoners, 13 deaths, all Jews;
> October 30, 1941: 8 operations on Aryan prisoners, 11 deaths, 10 Jews, 1 Pole;
> November 5, 1941: 6 operations on Aryan prisoners, including one Spaniard, 8 deaths;
> November 17, 1941: 15 operations 6 by Dr. Krebsbach, 9 by Dr. Heim, 3 deaths;
> November 27, 1941: 8 operations on Aryan prisoners, 4 deaths, no Jews.[2]

IN THE LATE fall of 1941, Heim was transferred out of Mauthausen. After brief stops in southern Germany and Austria, he was assigned to the 6th SS Division serving in Finland, and later in France. Then—something that remains incomprehensible to this day—when Europe was liberated, Heim managed to escape prosecution. True, he was arrested on March 15, 1945, by the Americans and did two years of forced labor in Germany, but curiously, he was released in 1947. He was not prosecuted alongside the other commanders and staff of Mauthausen in the huge trial that opened in Dachau in March 1946, at the end of which several of the 61 defendants were executed.

The only explanation for this very strange turn of events lies in the context of the Cold War, since at that time the hunt for Hitler's loyalists was no longer a priority. Certain Nazis obtained immunity in exchange for information on the Soviets, and Heim may have benefited from that arrangement. This theory was advanced by the German magazine *Der Spiegel*, which carried out extensive research into his case.[3]

"Why has the SS doctor Aribert Heim never been arrested?" my friend Stefan Klemp asked with mock astonishment in an article published in the *Süddeutsche Zeitung*. "A Nazi war criminal whose appearance is completely unmistakable? There is only one possible answer to that question: for 60 years, Heim has been and continues to be protected."[4]

Heim was released on December 21, 1947, and settled first in Vienna and then in Bad Nauheim, Germany, where he became a star player on the ice hockey team, then in Mannheim (where he married a doctor in 1949), and finally in Baden-Baden. He resumed his medical career under his real name and opened a gynecological practice. He lived in a beautiful white two-story house, surrounded by a large garden full of flowers. His patients knew nothing of his past. Germany was barely de-Nazified; one did not ask too many invasive questions. Many Germans had things on their conscience they did not want to talk about, and people did not risk prying into their neighbors'—even less their doctor's—personal histories.

Years went by without the lucky Dr. Heim being disturbed, until 1961. His name reemerged during the trial of a former Nazi in Wiesbaden, when a witness spoke about "the Butcher of Mauthausen." A year later, in September 1962, when the German authorities had located him and were about to arrest him, Heim disappeared.

Although Simon Wiesenthal had tried to find Heim, I did not pay much attention to his case until 2004, when the German police contacted us to solicit our help. They heard that we planned to launch Operation Last Chance in Germany and asked whether we would be willing to name Dr. Aribert Heim as our primary target. It turns out that one of Heim's sons had committed a financial crime of some sort, which had prompted the police to investigate all of the family's bank accounts. Imagine the investigators' surprise when they discovered a bank account in the name of Aribert Heim in a Berlin bank, with approximately 1.2 million euros in cash and 800,000 euros in stocks and bonds. Their conclusion was that if his children (2 sons in Germany and a daughter from his mistress living in Chile) had not taken the money, he must still be alive, which led to a decision to set up a small task force to find him. They were the ones who called us.

So it was that on January 26, 2005, I launched Operation Last Chance in Germany, together with Stefan Klemp and Aryeh Rubin at a press conference held in the Bundestag (German parliament), where I named Dr. Aribert Heim as our primary target. Since that day, we have received word of hundreds of "sightings." A good part of the interest in the case stemmed from the fact that the reward offered for his capture was much bigger than the others. We originally promised 140,000 euros (around US$190,000) for information that would lead us to *Doktor Tod* ("Doctor Death"): 130,000 euros donated by the German government and 10,000 euros raised by the Wiesenthal Center. I urged my colleagues in Los Angeles to add to the reward and also put pressure on the Austrian government to do so, but they were initially reluctant to collaborate with us—even though Heim was born in Austria and had committed the worst horrors on their territory in Mauthausen. If Vienna did not want to hear about it, we would try our best to arouse world public opinion. Thus one of the reasons adduced to prove my accusation that "Austria is a paradise for Nazi war criminals" was their failure to add to the reward for Heim in contradiction to the Germans who were offering so much money. It took a year and a half, but, finally, Vienna gave in.

In April 2006, I was invited to lunch by the new Austrian ambassador to Israel, Michael Rendi, his number two, Dr. Norbert Hack, and members of a delegation of officials who deal with Holocaust-related issues. We went to Little Italy, a delicious kosher Italian restaurant where I often go, a stone's throw from my office in Jerusalem. I reminded them that three months earlier, during a trip to Vienna, their justice and interior ministers had given me a personal assurance that they would participate financially in the hunt. Three months had gone by and not a single euro had been added to the reward. It was beginning to frustrate me, and I told them so openly. The two diplomats tried to reassure me. If they were to be believed, I had nothing to worry about. Ambassador Rendi and Norbert Hack were speaking the truth, as it turned out: More than a year later, on July 13 (coincidentally, the day our second granddaughter, Aviya, was born to our son Itamar and his wife, Yael), Austria announced it was donating 50,000 euros to this cause. It was a miracle. This, together with the contribution from the Wiesenthal Center, which, in February 2006, had risen from 10,000 to 130,000 euros, brought us up to a total of 310,000 euros we could give the man or woman who enabled us to catch Heim and take him to court. This was an unprecedented occurrence in the history of Operation Last Chance—in no other case had we been able to offer such a large reward.

We utilized the media to publicize the following identifying characteristics: Heim was six-foot-four, his shoe size was 12.5, and he had a V-shaped scar on the corner of his lips. We even had a copy of his fingerprints, taken by the Americans in 1945, which I had received from Simon Wiesenthal's office in Vienna. We distributed three pictures of the fugitive: the first dating from 1950, the second showing him in a tuxedo in 1959—the most recent image that we had of him—and the third a simulation produced by German police experts of what Heim might look like in the present, as a man in his nineties.

In the wake of the publicity regarding the reward, a large number of messages poured into my office. One thing struck me immediately: the huge majority of these messages came from Spain. We would explore this trail as seriously as we could, with the invaluable help of a lawyer, Gloria Trinidad, who had offered to assist our campaign. At the request of the German police, the Spanish authorities also carried out an inquiry. It was a revolution—for the first time in its history, Spain, which under Franco (but afterward as well) had served as a haven for many Holocaust perpetrators, was participating in the search for a Nazi war criminal.

AN ISRAELI ON holiday in Ibiza, Spain, came across an old man in a souvenir shop with a pronounced German accent. Upon hearing the Israeli speaking Hebrew, the old man turned to the shopkeeper and cracked an anti-Semitic joke. A Frenchwoman traveling by bus in Spain sat next to a man with a strong resemblance to the pictures published in the press. Back in Ibiza, we were told about the owner of an apartment who rented it out to tourists. He went by the troubling nickname "Mengele," was German, and had said he had been a doctor during World War II. Elsewhere in Spain, another person claimed he heard a tall, elderly gentleman with a German accent say he was distrustful of Jews.

The Spanish daily *El Mundo* claimed that Heim was in Costa Brava and stated that he had entered the country in 1985 before going into hiding in the region of Roses in Catalonia.[5] In Roses, an elderly German who called himself Emil Hubert came to our attention. We investigated him and had him watched, but it was a false trail. In Cadaqués, another German, aged 93 and called Schilibeck, was denounced by a neighbor who erroneously swore he had found our man. Retired in Marbella, the Norwegian ex–Waffen-SS officer Fredrik Jensen, 86, was accused of having helped Heim go into hiding, which he denied. He also declared to a journalist for a Norwegian daily: "I do not regret for a moment that I enlisted for German service on the eastern front as an 18-year-old. We managed to prevent the Communists from taking over all of Europe, and have been subjected to great injustice after the war."[6]

During the fall of 2005 the sightings proliferated: several hundred, distributed between Spain and the rest of the world. Some of these sightings were clearly fantasies: "I am not absolutely certain but I think I saw Heim in the Venezuelan jungle 17 years ago," a Dane wrote to me once. Others were motivated solely by desire for material gain—people who wanted to get their hands on the reward. Certain correspondents even went as far as harassing me, declaring that they deserved to receive all or part of the reward. There was a Scotsman, for example, who wrote to me in September 2007 that he was 99 percent sure he knew where Heim lived, in Southern Spain, but would not reveal the location until he was guaranteed the money. He contacted me again on November 8 insisting that he knew where Heim was and that he wanted his reward. This man had a lot of nerve. The inquiries of the Spanish police revealed that his supposed revelations were total fantasies.

Fortunately, many of the messages we received were legitimate. They were often serious, well argued, and written with the sincere aim of helping me. Some people even sent me photos taken in secret, while others provided physical descriptions. Someone told me he had seen Heim on a railway platform in Mouscron, Belgium. Another saw him in Denmark, others still playing at three-card poker in Monte Carlo; in Toronto a certain very old and very tall Dr. Lang was brought to our attention; and there were reported sightings at the airport in Phoenix (Arizona), in Bolivia, in Venezuela, on a ferry in Ireland, in the restaurant of a Geneva hotel. Even in Japan, in a bar on the quays of Yokohama.

THROUGHOUT THIS ENTIRE period, we were in very close contact with the officers of the special German police unit of Baden-Wurtemburg, the LKA (the Landeskriminalamt). Based in Stüttgart, the unit was in charge of the efforts to find Heim. I alerted them every time I received a credible message.

In the spring of 2008, I returned to the offices of the LKA in Stüttgart. One of the officers drew up a list for me of the countries in which inquiries about Heim had been opened: Argentina, Austria, Belgium, Bolivia, Brazil, Canada, Chile, Costa Rica, Denmark, Ecuador, Finland, France, Israel, Italy, Mexico, Netherlands, Paraguay, Spain, Switzerland, the United States, Uruguay, and Venezuela. In five of these countries (Argentina, Austria, Chile, Spain, and Switzerland), investigations were still under way, but there were serious difficulties in carrying them out, especially in South America, where the local police forces were initially slow to respond to requests from the German police for investigations in the case. In Chile, for example, where the Supreme Court had to approve certain aspects of the operation, there were legal problems that hampered the ability of the authorities to respond to the LKA's request for collaboration, as well as leaks to the media that made it difficult to carry out what was, of course, supposed to be a clandestine campaign. Once the media found out that a request for help in finding

Heim had been sent to Santiago, there was a strong risk that the doctor would become aware that he was being actively sought by the local police in addition to the Germans and the Wiesenthal Center.

Surprisingly, the difficulties experienced by the LKA police officers also originated from their own country, Germany, where Judge Hans-Richard Neerforth in Baden-Baden, Heim's last known residence, seemed to continually hamper their investigation. Several of their requests to tap the phones of Heim's family and friends living in Germany were turned down, as were the requests for warrants to search the houses of his ex-wife and his niece, with whom he had always been close. On June 27, 2008, I publicly criticized the attitude of the judge. It was the 94th birthday of the former SS doctor, and I publicly accused Judge Neerforth of obstructing the investigations, noting that: "The fact that he has hereto not been caught is unfortunately at least partially a result of the obstruction of the presiding judge in the case at Baden-Baden."[7]

The response of the German judicial authorities was not slow in coming: On June 30, Heinz Heister, the spokesman of the Baden-Baden court, rejected my accusations on the grounds that the requests made did not meet the legal standards required in Germany. "Investigative measures—even in the case of a person urgently suspected of many counts of murder—are held to certain boundaries by the constitution and the laws." Nonetheless he asserted that "the highest effort is being put into the search, in accordance with the particular importance of these criminal proceedings,"[8] citing the 11 requests for legal assistance filed with foreign countries since 2005. Unfortunately, our criticism did not change the judge's attitude, and he has continued to be a serious obstacle in the investigation.

IN THE FALL of 2007, a book came out in France entitled *Ni oubli, ni pardon: Au coeur de la traque du dernier nazi* (published in English as *The Secret Executioners* [London: John Blake Publishing, 2009]) by an ex-colonel of the Israeli air force, Danny Baz, who claimed to have been part of a commando called "The Owl," which had found and executed Heim in 1982. The media gave much credit to his claims. If his claims were true, I had apparently been chasing a ghost, a man who had died years before, and was engaged in a false manhunt, going to Germany, Chile, and Argentina even though the operation was destined to fail because "Dr. Death" was no longer alive.

On paper, Baz's story is fascinating: This secret American organization took on the mission of tracking down the last Nazis hiding on the American continent. The air force colonel, Baz, said he had captured Heim in Canada after a two-year hunt before the war criminal was "tried" and then executed on the island of Santa Catalina off the Californian coast. "The Owl" had supposedly found and liquidated a dozen Nazi criminals in this way. Working in total illegality, the commando enjoyed the support of high-ranking officials in the CIA, FBI, and the Israeli secret service. Baz also claimed that the organization had been created by a survivor of Mauthausen who had made his fortune in Alaskan oil. Under the pseudonym "Barney," this businessman supposedly financed the organization in installments of US$6 million, symbolizing the 6 million Jewish victims of the Holocaust.

As soon as the book appeared, I wasted no time in refuting its claims, stating publicly that the story was pure fiction, nothing more than delirious ravings. Serge Klarsfeld and I were in agreement. The founder of the Association of Sons and Daughters of Jews Deported from France described Danny Baz's book as "total fantasy." He had "never heard of 'The Owl'; if this organization existed, you would think I would have heard of it!"[9] Baz had already made similar declarations in the Israeli press five years earlier, claiming that his group had executed 25 Nazis on the American continent, without providing the names of any of these criminals nor the slightest proof in support of his declarations.

And, once again, he provided no formal evidence, nothing tangible that would back his arguments.

BESIDES THE FACT that Baz had not proven Heim's death, there were numerous reasons to believe that the doctor was certainly alive long after 1982. One was, of course, the huge amount of money in his Berlin bank account, which his children had never even attempted to claim. But it was not this matter of inheritance alone that made me think that Heim was alive and that, in any case, he had certainly not been executed in 1982. Very reliable witnesses had given us assurances that they saw him first in Spain, then in Uruguay, well after 1982. In addition, in 2005, Stefan Klemp found a 100-page report on Heim in the Stasi archives, which made it clear that the former East German political police had begun looking into him in 1979. The Stasi had also attempted to strike him off the medical register, without success. I had made the same request in 2005 to the Austrian health minister and was equally unsuccessful.

The Stasi had spied on Heim's family for many years. A report dated 1986 (in other words, four years after Heim's supposed execution by Baz), proved that the East German services had tried to question him that year when he was due to clandestinely meet his family. Surveillance was put in place in Austria, in Switzerland (where the Heims owned property in Lugano), and in France, but in the end, the family had found out they were being followed and had made for Italy instead, without being spotted, where the reunion apparently took place, brief but undisturbed.

What is more, Heim's lawyer, Mr. Steinacker, had in early winter 2008 asked to see all the latest information concerning his client. If Heim had really been dead for 26 years, why would his lawyer make this curious request?

Finally, Waltraud, the daughter whom Heim had with his mistress, Gertrud Böser, and who lived in Chile, had gone several times over the previous two years to Bariloche in Argentina, a well-known haven for former Nazi war criminals. All these trips, the lawyer's interest, the credible witnesses, the unclaimed inheritance—without question, there was a lot going on for this phantom.

IN AUGUST 2007, in Jerusalem, I received a very interesting message from a man who lived in Puerto Montt in Chile. He said he had seen Heim, who allegedly was visiting his daughter there, and knew where he lived. He provided his cell phone number, explained that he only spoke Spanish, and signed his name as Juan F.

I immediately enlisted the help of Yitzchak Safdie, the owner of our local health food store, who made aliya from Argentina and gladly volunteered to be available day or night to serve as my interpreter, a task which proved to be critical over the next few weeks as I attempted to follow up what appeared to be a potentially very valuable lead. That night he called Juan F., who provided us with the following details: he had known the individual in question for 35 years and had run into him not long before, with Waltraud. He was tall and thin, over six feet tall but walking slightly hunched. It was likely that he had been several inches taller in his youth. He was very old and had worn a beard.

Our informant worked in a bakery. He had obviously heard about a reward. I asked him to be more precise, and he immediately replied: "The exact address is in an isolated field in the Valdivia province. In order to get to the place, I will have to take you there myself. The person who will come [on your behalf] will have to bring documents that he is connected to you."[10]

The following day we exchanged several e-mails. To my question "When was the last time you saw him? What name does he use?" the man replied: "The last time I saw him was two years ago but I know that he still lives in his house. My son, who is friends with him, saw him very recently. He lives in an isolated house very near the sea, in the place called Chan Chan. His property measures a hectare. The name of this gentleman, who was a doctor, is officially Kurt Lenz."

I immediately passed this valuable information on to the police officers of the LKA. They replied to me the evening of August 29:

> Efraim, I agree with you that this is a very serious lead. We have to treat this trace absolutely confidentially. (I think that you can inform our friend Dr. Klemp, if you want.) I will pass this information directly to our connection officer so that we can avoid the information being leaked to journalists by unreliable diplomats.
>
> At first I will try to identify this suspect with the assistance of my German colleague who is responsible for Argentina and Chile....If this person is our Dr. Heim, I will try to secure an intended arrest....But let us proceed step by step...We remain in contact....[11]

One of the policemen spoke to Juan F., my informant, who declared himself impatient to meet the intermediary on the ground in Chile. But then things got complicated. The Germans' contact did not succeed in meeting the informant. In addition, the informant told us that he would not participate in a joint operation of Chilean and German police; he did not trust his own country's police. Then, Juan F. changed his attitude. While still very suspicious, he agreed to provide us with a photo of the man he thought was Heim. As soon as he had managed to do so, he would give the photo in person to an envoy from the LKA; they would meet each other at the Chilean-Argentine border, on the Argentine side. The German policeman would pay for our informant's travel expenses. "This was the only way to secure the anonymity of the reference giver,"[12] the German police informed me on September 28, 2007. Two weeks later, the LKA envoy posted in Buenos Aires went to Bariloche, where he met Juan F.

The picture he gave us was of very poor quality. It was a copy of a photo from 2004, in which Lenz was posing with his granddaughter. The LKA envoy was unable to say whether the person in the photo was indeed Aribert Heim. But Juan F. gave him other details about this Lenz. They had known each other since 1968 but had lost contact over the past few years. In Lenz's home, they listened to German music ("Lili Marleen") and German military marches, and read German literature, notably Goethe. Lenz had never spoken to him of his past. In fact, they had not seen each other since 2004, not 2005 as he had initially told me. The Germans immediately alerted me; I was increasingly worried. Realizing this, they tried to reassure me: "Have some patience. As soon as I have further information in this affair I pass it to you."[13] That was around the time I arrived in Latin America to launch Operation Last Chance.

I have to admit that the slow progress of the investigation had me very worried. I also knew that, because of the formalities required, it would take weeks before the LKA's request that the Chilean police investigate Lenz would even reach Santiago Interpol, let alone be carried out. Each such request had to be approved by a judge, then sent to the German

Foreign Ministry, which in turn would send it to the Chilean embassy in Berlin, which would transfer it to the Chilean Foreign Ministry, which would send it to a judge for legal approval and from there to the Chilean police, a process that took a minimum of six weeks. I decided, therefore, in the middle of the meeting I had in Santiago in November 2007, with Sergio Widder, our director for Latin America, and Joel Hernandez, the head of Chilean police investigations, to try to expedite the matter by giving Hernandez all the information directly, without any intermediaries. In other words, instead of waiting for weeks for the request from the authorities to arrive, why not carry out the investigation of Lenz based on the information I could give him? Hernandez agreed, and I breathed an enormous sigh of relief and anticipation, hoping that we were finally on the verge of tracking down Heim.

Unfortunately, we were not allowed to accompany the police officers sent to carry out the investigation, so Sergio and I continued our planned itinerary in Santiago, masking our anticipation and anxiety from the media. On December 5, we received the bad news.

Lenz was not our man; we had been following a false lead. This tall, elderly man whom the investigators had finally visited was not Aribert Heim. He was called Kurt Heinz Schlenz Hiebel. True, the suspect was German, but he was much younger than our suspect, aged just 74. He was a farmer, the father of two children, and in possession of a residence permit since 1980. His fingerprints did not match those of our target and he had done nothing wrong. I spoke to the head of Interpol in Santiago, who told me that he too had believed in this lead until the last moment. He had thought that the German police and I were closing in on Heim. But we had gotten it all wrong, and now we had to start from scratch. My disappointment was very palpable.

MEANWHILE, THE TESTIMONIES from Spain continued to flood in. All of much the same kind: "I am certain that my neighbor is Aribert Heim!"

The Spanish police had not closed the case. I learned in September 2007 that they were continuing to question men whose appearance corresponded to the wanted notice (over 90, very tall, German accent), each time taking their fingerprints. I was grateful to the Spanish investigators for pursuing their mission with such professionalism but, in my view, the most promising hunting ground remained Latin America.

I decided to return to South America. On July 6, 2008, I took off from Tel Aviv for Chile, then Argentina, on a two-week assignment tracking Aribert Heim. I knew the hunt promised to be a hard one: South America is twice as big as Europe, I don't speak Spanish, and it was 104 degrees Fahrenheit in Jerusalem when I left, while in South America it was winter and 39 degrees Fahrenheit, under continual rain or snow. But the excitement is always at its height when I begin a mission of this type, and in this case it was even more intense than usual. For the first time in my life, I was going to Patagonia, that region at the end of the world where so many Nazis have received a warm welcome.

Also for the first time, I was going to Puerto Montt, where Heim's illegitimate daughter, Waltraud Böser, lived. Sixty-six years old, she had been settled in Chile for 30 years, where she had married a businessman. I was convinced more than ever that she was the key to this mystery, the person who would lead us to the fugitive. The only problem was that this fugitive happened to be her father and that Waltraud would not be hurrying to expose him to a Nazi hunter or the police.

I arrived, exhausted, in Santiago, where I met Sergio, who of course would be with me throughout the trip and without whose help it would have been impossible to carry out our mission. A crew from the BBC headed by director Dov Freedman, followed us during the two weeks of the trip to film a documentary. I needed several hours' rest but it was impossible: The meeting I had arranged for the afternoon with senior police officials had been pushed up to noon.

The meeting was friendly, and the investigators communicated their latest information to us, assuring us of their support. But how could we know whether these promises would actually be followed up and whether Arturo Herrera, the chief of Chilean general intelligence, would really help us find Heim? According to our information from the LKA, the Chileans had not done everything they could to find

Heim, and who knew what kind of local issues might influence the investigation? In that respect, the terrible past record of countries like Chile (in the case of Walter Rauff, the designer of the gas vans used by the Nazis) and South America in general in offering a haven to Nazi war criminals was always in the back of my mind throughout the trip.

That evening, we met the Israeli ambassador in Chile, David Cohen. Three weeks earlier, someone had called the embassy declaring that they had essential information, and the ambassador, who realized its potential, wanted to personally deliver it to Sergio and myself. Once we heard the story, both of us became quite excited. The person in question, we'll call him Juan B., had grown up with Waltraud's husband, Ivan Diharce, on the island of Chiloe, opposite Puerto Montt. Several months earlier, he had met Diharce on the island, carrying bags of groceries, which Diharce claimed he was taking to an elderly relative living on the island. But according to Juan, Diharce did not have any elderly relatives living on Chiloe, which aroused his suspicions (and ours). Could this "old relative" be "Dr. Death"? After the meeting, we immediately called Juan B. to set up a meeting with him upon our arrival in Puerto Montt.

The following day, July 8, I held a large press conference at the Jewish community center in Santiago. There were many journalists present, all quite well informed and aware of the charges against Heim. Their reports would cause a stir in Chile, as well as in Argentina, where people rushed onto the Internet, Heim's name being cited thousands of times on search engines. Then, one of the young men in charge of security at the Jewish community center asked me if I would meet with a group of very committed young people who had helped work on this and related security issues before I arrived. The meeting with these dedicated young Jews moved me very much and gave me the reassuring knowledge that these young people were willing to take over the baton. That afternoon, Sergio and I went shopping in the Jewish neighborhood of Santiago for enough kosher food to tide me over in Puerto Montt, where there was no local Jewish community. We could now take off for Patagonia.

WE LEFT SO early on Wednesday, July 9, 2008, that I did not even have time to recite my morning prayer at the hotel, and so I prayed at the airport. Praying in the airports of New York, London, or Paris is an easy, habitual occurrence for a Jew; less so in Santiago, Chile. When we touched down in Puerto Montt, dozens of journalists were waiting for us. My smallest gestures were immortalized by a horde of photographers. I had a single desire, to take immediate refuge in my hotel—unfortunately, the journalists followed me there, too.

On our way into the hotel, I was accosted by a local neo-Nazi, who told me to leave the country since "Chile is a land of peace." When I asked in reply if this meant offering refuge to people who committed mass murder, he started shouting at me that Israel was guilty of genocide against the Palestinians. I made it clear to him and to the crowd that had gathered around us that he obviously did not understand the meaning of the term *genocide* and that indiscriminately launching lethal rockets at civilian targets such as the city of Sderot was closer to the definition.

I would have no peace in this gloomy town, one of the most drab I have ever been to in the world. Puerto Montt is a large port of about 150,000 inhabitants in southern Chile, 1,000 kilometers from Santiago, the capital. While the town is physically very unappealing, the surrounding region is quite beautiful, with lakes, large forests, and mountains. One can fish, swim, and ski there. Established by German immigrants in the mid-nineteenth century, it still has a distinctive German flavor with many German restaurants and other reminders of the country of origin of its founders.

Shortly after our arrival at the hotel, Sergio and I met secretly with Juan B. and another informant. Juan's story seemed credible, and he added new facts about an isolated house on land owned on Chiloe by the Diharce family. But it would take time until we were able to organize a search on the island, and the last thing we wanted to do was to draw any attention to any potential local hiding place of Heim. The day after my arrival in Puerto Montt, I organized a press conference at which I brandished the wanted notice, entitled in Spanish "Operacion Ultima Opportunidad." I informed the journalists that we had received some interesting information from various sources that had been checked and found to be reliable.

I also made sure to repeat my mantra regarding the issue of Heim's age, citing the four points of my standard response to the question that had been posed to me by hundreds of journalist over the years:

1. The passage of time in no way diminishes the guilt of the murderers.
2. People do not deserve a medal simply because they reach an elderly age.
3. The practical implication of a chronological limit of prosecution is that if a person is rich enough, lucky enough, and/or smart enough to escape justice until they reach that age, they will never be held accountable for their crimes, which is a terrible travesty of justice.
4. Every victim of the Nazis deserves that a serious effort be made to find and punish the person(s) who turned them into victims.

Much of the evidence we gathered indicated that Heim was probably in this region, between Puerto Montt and Bariloche in Argentina. Over the previous two years, Waltraud Böser had gone several times to Bariloche, another ideal spot in Latin America for all those nostalgic for the Tyrol and Bavaria. Bariloche has a cable car, as well as typically Alpine architecture and restaurants serving fondue and game.

I said to the journalists: "We believe that there is someone in this region who without doubt holds the key that will enable us to catch Heim." So that the media did not serve up the same old story about the suspect's advanced age—he was 94—I reminded them of the atrocities he had committed: "He castrated prisoners and used parts of the human body to decorate his office! I am not giving you such details to be sensational but just to make you understand how important it is to catch this murderer." The South American media were fascinated by the hunt for Heim. During the press conference, I showed caution by explaining that "the aim of this trip is not necessarily to leave with Heim in my suitcase. What we want is for people to become aware of the importance of this search and to convince them to give us details that will enable us to locate him."

The local papers printed the three photos, from 1950 and 1959, as well as the aged image produced by the German police specialists. That same morning, we went with several journalists to the home of Waltraud Böser, for what would basically be a staged encounter for the benefit of the media.

A large dog, a German shepherd, was yapping behind a gate. I sent two journalists to knock at the door of the chalet to try to persuade Waltraud to meet me. A man opened the door, saying he was the cleaner and that he was alone. His employers had gone out. Two cars belonging to the owners were parked very close by but he said no more. Smoke was emerging from a chimney; perhaps Waltraud was hiding in another room? What disconcerting discretion and astonishing behavior on the part of people who claimed to have done nothing wrong. We left the scene with the disappointed journalists in tow but it was exactly as I had expected—I had been certain that neither Waltraud nor Ivan would be at home when our media armada turned up in their garden.

ON JULY 14, Sergio and I crossed the Andes in the snow and passed the Argentine border to go to Bariloche. As I went through the border post, I could not help imagining Heim doing the same during recent years or even months, probably even several times. In that respect, I was disappointed that there were no "Wanted" posters for him hanging on the walls in a conspicuous place. After all, it was people crossing the border who might be able to provide us with the critical information on his current whereabouts.

In Bariloche, we held another press conference. Again, I declared that there was absolutely no proof that Heim was dead: "On the contrary, many clues indicate that he is alive and that he is in this region." We were approximately 1,000 miles southwest of Buenos Aires. Puerto Montt was on the other side of the border, over 200 miles away. Waltraud Böser had made this trip numerous times—had she come here on holiday or to meet up with a beloved father hiding in this German enclave, considered one of the main Nazi sanctuaries after the fall of the Third Reich?

I had the feeling that we were making progress, getting closer than ever to the truth about Heim.

The mayor gave us a warm welcome while the local newspaper published a special supplement devoted to our hunt. Other testimonies flooded in. A parking lot attendant was certain that he had seen him, this very tall, very elderly man, who was getting out of a car licensed in Chile. But he had not taken the license number. I felt that the noose was tightening.

Then, in Buenos Aires, Sergio and I met the minister of justice, Anibal Fernández. He assured me that, if Heim was arrested in his country, he would be immediately extradited to Germany. He seemed very determined to help us—and was more convincing, I have to say, than the officials we had met in Santiago.

While waiting to board the flight back to Tel Aviv, I thought of the two weeks I had just spent in South America. I had not captured Heim. But that was no surprise, at least not to me. Sergio Widder and I wanted above all to increase our chances of capturing him one day, as soon as possible, by informing as wide a public as possible about his crimes and the 310,000 euros reward, and by distributing his picture in the area where we thought that he was probably hiding.

BACK IN ISRAEL, on August 18, 2008, I received a letter addressed to the Simon Wiesenthal Center. It was from Waltraud Böser! She wrote: "I am the illegitimate daughter of Aribert Heim,"[14] and asked me to let her live in peace. I replied to her, with Stefan Klemp helping me translate the letter. He wanted to use the customary German formulas of politeness but I refused. I simply requested a meeting so that we could talk face-to-face, something we had never done. To my enormous surprise, she accepted and asked me to meet her at her lawyer's office in Innsbruck, Austria.

In early September 2008, I flew to Frankfurt, where I met Stefan Klemp. Together, we went to Stuttgart to meet with the LKA investigators for a comprehensive briefing on every possible aspect of the case. For practically an entire day, we sat at police headquarters reviewing every detail of Heim's relationship with his mistress, Gertrude Böser, Waltraud's mother, as well as all the problematic or questionable details of an interview that Waltraud had relatively recently given to the Austrian police, who in the opinion of the LKA had treated her far too gently. All of us, for example, were singularly unconvinced by Waltraud's claim that she had never met her father and that, until 2004, had no idea that he was a war criminal. We left there fairly confident that we had all the information we needed for the intriguing encounter with Heim's daughter and took a train to Austria.

On Tuesday, September 9, at 10 AM, we presented ourselves alone— Waltraud Böser having stipulated that no journalist be present—at the lawyer's office. Her half-brother was also there. She stood there in front of us and greeted us in a very friendly manner. A strange meeting, I must confess; I had been anxious about the idea of shaking her hand but, to my surprise, I ended up joking with the three of them. But we did more than joke. To tell the truth, I was disturbed by her attitude. According to her, Waltraud had never even met her father and until the Chilean media reported for the first time on the search for him several years previously, had no idea of his sordid history during World War II. Her mother had repeatedly told her that her father had never come back from the war, and until recently that had been the end of the story, as far as she was concerned. "I have never set eyes on my father," she declared, her eyes looking straight into mine. Was she telling the truth? Why not? But my intuition told me that she was not telling us everything that late summer Tuesday in Innsbruck.

When I asked her, "If your father walked in this door right now, what would you say to him?" she replied: "Where have you been all this time?" Very touching perhaps, but I was not convinced by her version of the events; nor was Stefan. I could not believe, for example, that many years previously, when the Austrian police came to question her mother about Heim, and she was in the house at the time (claiming to be ill, which is why she was not present at the questioning), she never asked her mother why the police had come to speak to her. In short, we did not receive convincing answers for many of the questions we posed to Dr. Death's love child.

As months passed, information continued to reach our office, but there were no dramatic breakthroughs until February 5, 2009, when

I received a telephone call from ZDF (German TV Channel 2) while on vacation at the Carmel Spa, my favorite hotel in Israel. According to the caller, there had been a "very important development regarding Nazi war criminals," which ZDF wanted to discuss with me, so we set up a time for a conversation shortly after Elisheva and I left the hotel to visit her parents in nearby Kfar Haroe.

Nothing prepared me for the shocking information I received. An informant, whose name they refused to reveal, gave ZDF and the *New York Times* information that had led them to conclude that Dr. Aribert Heim had died in Cairo in 1992. The story had been confirmed by the doctor's son, Ruediger, who a mere six months previously had claimed that he had not had any contact with his father since his disappearance in 1962, and now asserted that he had visited him in Egypt several times and had been with him when he died in the Egyptian capital in August 1992.

What a shock! I felt as if someone had punched me hard in the stomach. But was it true? Did all the facts fit? The more I thought about the ZDF/*New York Times* version of the events, the more holes I found in the story. And the fact that Heim had supposedly been buried in a mass grave for paupers, which made finding his corpse virtually impossible, only strengthened my doubts. If there was absolutely no way to carry out the necessary forensic examinations to unequivocally confirm his identity (DNA and teeth), we could not possibly close the case. In fact, we would not be doing our job properly if we did.

So as dramatic as the revelations were about Heim's life, including his conversion to Islam and adoption of the name Tarek Hussein Farid, and as tempting as it is to resolve the mystery of his disappearance, there are important unanswered questions that prevent us from closing the case. Thus, for example, if Heim indeed died in 1992, why did his children never even attempt to take the 2 million euros in his Berlin bank account? Further, Stefan subsequently found a transcript of a trial held in Berlin in 2001, in which a lawyer representing Heim tried to obtain a reduction on his income tax (from his apartment building) and claimed that he was in close contact with his client, who was living abroad. Obviously, if he was alive in 2001, he could not have died in Cairo in 1992. So while I accept the fact that Heim apparently did live in Egypt, a fact that Simon Wiesenthal himself claimed in 1967, the serious question marks regarding the latest "revelations" give me some reasonable hope that our efforts in this ever-so-important case were not in vain. The Heim case, therefore, remains open until conclusive forensic evidence can be produced to prove that he is no longer alive.

NINETEEN

KÉPÍRÓ

THE SUSPECTED NAZI WHO LIVES OPPOSITE A SYNAGOGUE

ARTUR ROSENSTEIN WAS only six years old at the time, but he remembered it all. Years later, he could recount all the details of that horrible day—January 23, 1942—when he and his parents were marched to the banks of the Danube to be shot by the Hungarians. To this day, this event in Novi Sad is referred to as "the Razzia," or the raid.

The operation had commenced two days earlier, as the Hungarian army and gendarmerie combed the area around Novi Sad, arresting and murdering Jews, Serbs, and Gypsies in the region, ostensibly as a reprisal against the local resistance to their occupation of the Voivodina province of Yugoslavia. On the third day, January 23, the Hungarians began the operation in the city, which was divided into sections, each with a Hungarian officer in charge of the roundups in that area. Thousands of men, women, and children were taken to Sokolski Dom, the main cultural institution of the town, to be interrogated, after which their fate was decided. Some lucky people were released, but thousands of others were marched to the Danube to be shot. The temperature that day was minus 22 degrees Fahrenheit, and the Hungarians had to bring in a cannon to break the ice on the river so that those shot, but not killed, would drown in the freezing Danube.

Artur Rosenstein was in the crowd with his parents, carried in his father's arms. They advanced slowly in rows, walking toward their own death. Soon, it would be their turn to be shot. "When the Hungarian police came to look for us, they told us to take only the bare minimum, and they took us in small groups to the banks of the Danube," he recounted to me in a crowded Budapest café 64 years later. "There was a large crowd there. In the distance, we heard the sound of machine guns. We were queuing up, waiting our turn to be killed." They had not more than a quarter of an hour left to live. Suddenly, a plane landed. Officers got out. They spoke a lot, shouted. The order was given to stop the executions, and the Rosensteins' lives were saved. But when they returned home, they found the corpses of Artur's grandfather and his wife, who had been murdered. In total, during those three days of horror, 3,309 Jews, Serbs, and Gypsies were killed in the region, including 141 children. In Novi Sad (Ujvidek in Hungarian), two-thirds of the victims were Jewish.

PEOPLE'S BOASTFULNESS HAS sometimes been very helpful to me. I received an e-mail in February 2005 from a Scotsman living in Aberdeen, who I will call A.M., explaining that he and his Hungarian girlfriend organize and attend reunions for Hungarians living in Scotland. According to the e-mail, one of the attendees at these gatherings, a man called Istvan Bujdoso, who had changed his name to Steven Brandon, would often talk of having being a member of the Csendor (gendarmerie) and of his own participation in the mass Jewish deportations to Auschwitz in 1944.

I immediately replied to A.M. and asked him several questions: This Istvan Bujdoso, or Steven Brandon, what was his date of birth? Where was he posted during the war? What was his current address? Two days later, A.M. wrote back to me. He was unable to answer my first two questions, but he provided me with a photo of Bujdoso and specified the rank that he had had in the Hungarian police—staff sergeant—and also sent me his current address.

I went to Yad Vashem to consult with my friend Dr. Gavriel Bar-Shaked, an expert on the Holocaust in Hungary. He studied all the documents likely to tell us more about this policeman but, despite moving heaven and earth, we found nothing about him or about possible witnesses able to enlighten us. We were lost. Several months later in Israel, I met a journalist from the *Glasgow Herald*, Michael Tierney, who had come to write a cover story for his paper's weekend magazine about "Nazi hunters." I spoke about Budjoso to Michael, admitting our difficulties in pinning down this fellow, not even knowing where he was posted during the war. He agreed to investigate and to try and meet this Hungarian ex-gendarme, now a pensioner living in the south of Scotland.

Several months later, Michael Tierney made contact with the suspect. He had to be careful not to insist too much or Budjoso was likely to get suspicious. Michael pretended that he was writing a feature article about the Hungarians in Scotland. He went to the ex-gendarme's home, engaging in casual conversation and winning his confidence. Very nonchalantly, the journalist asked the pensioner about a photo that was on display behind him, showing a Hungarian gendarmerie officer in uniform. Budjoso did not say anything very interesting about himself— perhaps he was finally wary. All he said was that he had been posted to Miskolc, a large town in present-day eastern Hungary, where a large Jewish community lived, victims of mass deportations in 1944. Now we knew where to go and look for witnesses. But Budjuso made a more interesting revelation when he spoke about the man in the photo, a fellow officer, who had been a captain in the gendarmerie. A good colleague, a friend even, who had come to visit him two years earlier and to whom he spoke regularly on the phone. His name was Sándor Képíró.

I RETURNED TO see Dr. Gavriel Bar-Shaked at Yad Vashem. I told him of the latest developments and explained that we had identified a Hungarian gendarmerie officer who was also still alive, a captain named Sándor Képíró. Upon hearing this news my friend almost fell off his chair. "What? That son of a bitch is still alive?" He was clearly in shock. Bar-Shaked is a very religious man, not at all in the habit of swearing, so to hear him use such strong language was not only astonishing in itself but, more than that, showed that we had discovered a very big fish. He then proceeded to explain that Képíró was one of the Hungarian officers who had organized the large-scale massacre in the Serbian city of Novi Sad in 1942 and had even been prosecuted and convicted two years later for his role in the operation. But in the wake of the Nazi invasion that took place shortly after the conclusion of the trial, his conviction was cancelled and he never served his jail sentence.

There was, however, one very important piece of the puzzle that was missing. Bujdoso had not indicated *where* Képíró was living, and without that information, we would not be able to do anything. I immediately contacted Michael Tierney, who at my request got in touch with Budjoso again to find out where Képíró lived and was told that he was in Hungary. Afraid that Budjoso would get suspicious, we did not ask him for any further details.

We had to proceed with great discretion, avoiding at all costs giving Budjoso and Képíró any hint of our intentions. In situations like this, I always turn to my two loyal helpers in Hungary, two teachers who also work at the Holocaust Museum in Budapest, Szilvia Pető-Dittel and Tibor Pécsi. Both are members of the "Faith Church" in Hungary, one of Europe's largest neo-Protestant charismatic churches, and great lovers of Israel and the Jewish people. Ever since I met them at a Yad Vashem seminar for teachers from Hungary, where I lectured on the efforts to bring Nazi war criminals to justice, they have been incredibly helpful on all matters concerning Hungary. So, of course, my first phone call was to Szilvia, who is my liaison, since her English is better than Tibor's. My advice was simple: Start with the Budapest telephone directory. If you can't find him there, we'll hire a detective.

Their search in the telephone directory yielded three names. The first did not reply, so they left a message on his answering machine. The second was a famous painter who obviously was not our suspect. The third number was in the name of a Mrs. Sándor Képíró. Tibor called her, passing himself off as a student. He asked her if her husband had indeed served in the gendarmerie during World War II. She said yes. Had he been posted to the Ujvidek (Novi Sad) district? Yes. The noose was tightening. Would it be possible to speak to him? No. Her husband had died two years earlier. Tibor, forgetting that Bujdoso had said that he was *still* in regular phone contact with Képíró, e-mailed that apparently we were too late. I e-mailed back that that was not the case, and within a short time, the real Képíró phoned Tibor in response to the message he had left on his answering machine.

On July 18, 2006, Tibor again claimed to be a student writing a thesis on the Hungarian gendarmerie during World War II. And the man spoke to him. It was him! We had him. Szilvia immediately e-mailed in big capital letters: "EFRAIM PLEASE CALL ME, NOW WE REALLY FOUND THE PERSON FOR YOU!!!!!"[1] Half an hour later, I received the following information from Tibor and Szilvia:

> Dr. Képíró, Sándor, police captain. 92 years old. Posted in Miskolc (from July 1 1944). Before that he was a district officer in Koloszvar (Cluj). Even before that in Novi Sad (Ujvidek)....He was a graduated lawyer already back then. Because the Russians were looking for him he immigrated to Austria (for 3 years), then went to Argentina for 48 years! Returned back to Hungary in 1996. According to his testimony, his job as a gendarme was 90 percent teaching and training. He isn't willing to meet personally (too old) but ready to "help" any time on the phone....Believed our story of making a research paper at the Peter-Pazmany University (Catholic, right-wing school)![2]

I ARRIVED IN Budapest on July 31, 2006, after arranging a meeting with the local prosecutors to inform them of our latest find. I have to admit that I had not been that nervous in a long time. For several weeks, I had been having terrible stomach aches, the type in which you feel your guts being wrenched continuously with no relief in sight. As bad as the pain was, however, I was certain that what I was suffering from was not a medical problem, but rather a case of work-related nervous anxiety. After all, it's not every day that you are on the verge of bringing an important suspected Nazi to trial. And this time, the case practically fell into our hands, completely out of the blue.

I met up with Szilvia and Tibor right away, and they took me for a walk in town. I did not know where we were going; they said they wanted to surprise me. Thus, that afternoon, I found myself aboard a tram that crossed the Danube from Pest to Buda. We got off and started walking north along a nondescript street of apartment buildings of various sizes and ages. A quick look at the street sign triggered a vague memory. Frankel Leo utca sounded familiar. Wait a minute friends, isn't that the street on which our suspected Nazi war criminal lives? Tibor and Szilvia smiled sheepishly, like schoolchildren caught in some act of mischief. OK, you're right, at what number does he live? At this point I was stumped, but they cheerfully supplied the data, and off we went, a bit apprehensive, not knowing what to expect. At this point, we did not have any specific plan, at least none that I was aware of, and Szilvia and Tibor did not strike me as particularly daring types. So we walked to the building and lo and behold, there was his name on the bell—plain and simple, as if he were an average law-abiding resident of Budapest and not an escaped war criminal with the blood of hundreds, if not thousands, on his hands.

It was clear that we were not going to knock on his door—he had refused to accept any visitors—and we had no other plan ready, so we just stood around for a few minutes, experiencing that odd but historic moment. All sorts of thoughts went through my head, including one or two of a particularly ominous nature. What could have been easier than to get into his apartment and execute the bastard? In this case, after all, he was not a suspect, but a convicted war criminal with hundreds of dead Jews and Serbs to prove it. What could be easier? A frail, as I imagined him, 92-year-old. A piece of cake.

Thoughts of revenge did not linger and certainly did not convince. The arguments remained the same in this case, as in every other. Killing him would be counterproductive in the long run and ruin our efforts elsewhere. What we had to do was get Hungary to put him in jail for life, however long that might turn out to be. Looking around us, a large building across the street caught our attention. Could it really be? A synagogue, right across the street from Képíró's house. What a sight for a Nazi mass murderer.

Tibor explained that this was the Sephardic synagogue of Budapest, which was only in partial use these days. We crossed the avenue to take a closer look, but as we were leaving, I saw a youngish woman walk out of the building. I immediately urged Szilvia to engage her in conversation, hoping to get some pertinent information about our man. In the meantime, Tibor and I went over to the synagogue, which was locked, so we stood outside and read the various signs. By the time Szilvia rejoined us a good five minutes later, we were dying of curiosity to know if she had been able to extract any information of value. She was all smiles, as if she had won some sort of jackpot or lottery, which only increased our curiosity. It turns out that the woman knew our criminal very well, having lived in the building for the past 30 years. According to her, he was fully active and in reasonable health. In fact, the residents would occasionally conduct parties for all those living in the building, and it was good old Képíró who actually did the organizing. Not only did our suspect attend parties, he actually organized them. What better proof that he was healthy enough to be sent straight to prison? Hallelujah, we were on our way to victory. Now if we could only ensure that he did not run away again...

I wanted to rush to announce the good news to the prosecutor, with whom I was scheduled to meet the following day. I had come to Hungary with a thick dossier on Képíró, which I submitted to the prosecutor. I also spoke to him about Bujdoso, the gendarme staff sergeant who claimed a role in the deportation of Jews from Miskolc to Auschwitz and who lived in Scotland. I demanded that investigations into the two suspects be opened or reopened and that the original sentence against Képíró, that of 1944, be applied.

In front of Képíró's house, as if under some magic spell, I felt fine. My unbearable stomach pains suddenly disappeared. Everything seemed to be going so well. Képíró was in fit condition and could be tried. We had found him. The prosecutor met me and listened to me with a great deal of interest. He explained: "If he did indeed commit war crimes, he can be arrested immediately because there is no statute of limitations for that type of crime. On the other hand, if he was convicted for other crimes, that will be more difficult." How much time was needed to take a decision? Between one and two months. It was too good to be true.

During the whole month of August, I continually badgered the Hungarian legal and diplomatic authorities to act, because nothing appeared to be happening. Even if Képíró was in good health, he was still 92 years old, and we did not have a minute to lose. Several times a week, I telephoned or wrote to them. I wrote it all down in my notebooks: August 14, 15, 22, 24, and 28 and September 6 and 8. Still nothing. I wrote to the prosecutors that since Képíró is very old, we request that every possible legal measure be taken, including his immediate arrest, obviously before checking his real state of health. It made no difference. I started getting the feeling that things were not headed in the right direction, that in fact they had come to a standstill.

ON SEPTEMBER 11, 14, and 22, I mounted a fresh attack, to no avail. So then I started planning to expose Képíró, phoning and e-mailing Rabbi Tamas Vero, who was in charge of the synagogue across the street from Képíró's house. I reminded him of the facts, who Képíró was, and what he was accused of having done at Ujvidek-Novi Sad:

> About two months ago, we gave all this information about him to the Hungarian authorities, but it appears fairly certain that they do NOT want to punish him, perhaps due to his old age [We asked that his sentence be implemented, not that he be put on trial again.] We are planning a press conference for this coming Thursday, September 28, at which we expect about 20–25 journalists at most and want to know whether it would be possible to hold it in your synagogue. [By coincidence, the person in question lives close to the synagogue.] All the information in this communication is CONFIDENTIAL.[3]

Rabbi Vero sent me his email reply that same day: "Dear Mr. Zuroff, we will be happy to support your work and give our place to serve as the home of your press conference."[4]

On September 28, there were more journalists than we had predicted. The synagogue was packed. I was taking a calculated risk: I was aware of the scandal that would erupt when the press put a name and a face to the war criminal we were chasing. But I chose to reveal his identity—knowing he might copy Milijov Ašner and immediately escape—because Képíró was older and, above all, I knew that he had no safe havens nearby. He was not going to return to Argentina at the age of 92. The journalists immediately understood the impact of the scoop

I had just given them. Then, innocently, I said to them in conclusion: "Oh, in case you're wondering where he lives, just take a look out the window at that building right across the street. All you have to do is ring the bell; his name is on the doorbell!" I watched from a distance as they immediately rushed over to the other side of the street.

Képíró was not at home, but the journalists waited, and he soon arrived at his apartment building. His welcoming committee was certainly a surprise. But he is no fool. He understood that he had nothing to gain by shoving past the photographers and shutting himself inside his home. Such behavior would be tantamount to acknowledging his guilt. He cleverly played the hand of transparency and replied to questions, improvising a press conference that would last almost an hour. His line of defense was to admit that he had been involved in the roundup of civilians, which preceded the massacre at Novi Sad, but denied any criminal responsibility. According to Képíró, it was Hungarian soldiers, not gendarmes like him, who did the shooting.[5]

A big article appeared in the *New York Times* soon thereafter: "Nazi Hunters Identify Convicted War Criminal." Another was published in the *International Herald Tribune*. Képíró's name was now known throughout the entire world, and his previously peaceful retirement was no more than a distant memory. And yet the Hungarian authorities still did not act. I again approached them on October 16, November 8 and 20, and on December 6 of that year. To no effect. Battle weary, I tried to get around the problem by turning to Serbia, since Novi Sad was now in its territory.

On August 7, 2006, I had made my first trip to Serbia, where I had meetings with the president of the Republic, Boris Tadić, and with senior officials of the Justice Ministry and asked if they would request the extradition of Képíró from Hungary. They replied that that was impossible, since Hungary and Serbia had signed a mutual agreement preventing the extradition of their citizens and since, unlike Ašner, the genuinely false Austrian, Képíró was indeed Hungarian. They promised to help me as best they could by giving me better access to the war records. So many meetings in these two countries. So much effort devoted to a single man, Sándor Képíró, whom I put at number five in the list of the most wanted Nazi war criminals in the 2007 annual report of the Wiesenthal Center.

I visited Serbia again in late January 2007, this time for the commemoration of the 65th anniversary of the Razzia. At the request of the mayor Maja Gojkovic, I was the guest of honor at the ceremony. We gathered on the banks of the Danube, very close to where most of the victims fell under the bullets of the Hungarian soldiers and gendarmes. Present were Dr. Ana Frenkel, the president of the local Jewish community; Yitzchak Asiel, the chief rabbi of Serbia; and Monsignor Irinej, the archbishop of the district of Backa. Overcome with emotion, I gave a speech in which I launched a solemn appeal to the Hungarian authorities to bring Sandor Képíró to justice, an appeal that, unfortunately, did not yield any concrete results. And despite the yeoman efforts of Ana Frenkel, we were unable to find any survivors of the massacre who remembered Képíró. At least in Serbia, I felt that my efforts in this case were genuinely appreciated, a fact clearly reflected in the honorary citizenship of Novi Sad bestowed upon me in a very impressive ceremony exactly two years later.

Less than two weeks after the 2007 memorial in Novi Sad, I learned that Képíró had been invited to take part in a conference in Budapest on the Hungarian gendarmerie and that he had chosen to entitle his contribution "How I became a 'war criminal.'" The event was due to take place in an official building—the center for education in the Ministry of Justice—which deeply angered me. I managed to help get this conference moved and postponed, and then finally canceled outright. Képíró withdrew from the conference, on the pretext of health problems—entirely diplomatic ones in my view.

In the meantime, I utilized the occasion of the visit to Israel, on January 30, 2009, of the Hungarian minister of foreign affairs, Kinga Goncz, to issue a public welcome to her in my own way, in an opinion piece published by the *Jerusalem Post*. In my op-ed, I asked her how Hungary could have let Képíró return peacefully to the country from Argentina without asking him any questions about his past. Worse: knowing very well who he was. I also asked her if it was true that Hungarian diplomats had assured him he would be left in peace once back in his native country. No response.

In February 2007, the court of Budapest ruled that, contrary to my request, Képíró's previous conviction of 1944 could not be applied but that an investigation should be reopened into his involvement in the massacres of Novi Sad.

SZILVIA DITTEL HAD few illusions about Sándor Képíró being indicted. She warned me not to get my hopes up too high and that most likely the Hungarian justice system would drag its feet, hoping that Képíró would die a natural death and afraid that such a trial would stir up the past. As for Képíró, he threatened to sue me, which he eventually did. I have lost count of threats of that kind, there have been so many.

A year later, still nothing had happened. Képíró had not been placed in detention for a single minute. He had not even been questioned by the police or by a magistrate. This kind of impunity makes one want to throw in the towel, to give it all up for good. An alleged Nazi collaborator who had taken part in a mass-murder operation, who had already been convicted for crimes but never imprisoned, had been identified, rediscovered, and located, and no one had come to question him? What on earth is going on here?

But there are always the victims to consider. I remember the words, written in response to an article published in Israel on my exposure of Képíró in Budapest by a woman, Chava Schick, who lives in Israel in Kibbutz Lehavot Haviva. A survivor of the massacre, she expressed her gratitude to me for my efforts to expose one of the alleged perpetrators and bring him to trial.

> From someone who was there [on the banks of the Danube in Novi Sad], when she was only 5 years old, with her twin sister and her parents....All honor to those who have been trying for all these years and finally succeeded to expose this terrible murderer...[6]

Three years after I submitted his name to the Hungarian prosecutors, Képíró—95 years old but in relatively good health—was still living at 78 Frankel Leo utca, probably organizing parties for his neighbors. But on September 14, 2009, there was surprising good news from Budapest. Dr. Sándor Képíró had been arrested and interrogated regarding his alleged complicity in the murder of four civilians in Novi Sad by members of his patrol on January 23, 1942. Now we have to hope that he will be healthy enough to stand trial. Needless to say, I will be praying especially hard every day for his good health.

TWENTY

CONCLUSION

TO BE FRANK, I have had my share of disappointing moments: when, upon leaving the hospital after surgery, I was told of Erna Wallisch's death; when I learned that the Hungarian authorities, after endless delays, would not implement the original verdict against Sándor Képíró, despite the hundreds of deaths at Novi Sad on his conscience; when I realized that the old German living alone in his house in Patagonia was not Aribert Heim; when I saw Milivoj Ašner, supposedly a doddering and helpless old man that the Austrian authorities were unjustly protecting, parading up and down the streets of Klagenfurt in the middle of the European soccer championship.

I know that time is against me. In July 2008, Chilean journalists again asked me, as I was leaving Waltraud Böser's home empty-handed, "How can you be sure that he [Aribert Heim] really is still alive?" What a question! Unless I had met him in the street that very morning, yes, indeed, how could I know? Irritated, frustrated by the sight of the empty house, frozen by the cold of the Chilean winter, I replied to them rather curtly: "Yes, you are right! Perhaps he died five minutes ago!" Why not?

More recently, the most irritating question I was asked by journalists is why I have refused to close the Heim case after the *New York Times* and ZDF ostensibly proved that he died in Cairo in 1992. I accept the fact that Heim indeed lived in Egypt. In fact, in June 1967, Simon Wiesenthal even named him as one of the Nazi war criminals living in the Middle East. But given the family's vested interest in ending the investigation, how can we be sure of the veracity of this story without a corpse to examine?

With the passing of time they will all die, one after the other, like Wallisch, who died one week after I succeeded in getting the Austrian authorities to reopen the case—a fact that very likely would have led to her conviction. My targets are invariably old. That is a fact of life. Some are even over 90. There is not a minute to lose; as I often say: "I'm running out of time."

When will I stop? The only answer I can give is this: When I am convinced that nothing more can be done to facilitate the prosecution of the perpetrators of the Holocaust. That is likely to take some time, even if I acknowledge that I am approaching the end. Barring some last-minute surprise, it is doubtful that I will undertake any more long journeys to South America in search of war criminals. The one I took in summer 2008 was most probably the last. I acknowledged this during my trip to Chile: The end of Operation Last Chance is rapidly approaching.

As hard as it is for me to believe, I am already over 60. My two daughters and two sons are grown up, and I have not seen as much of them as I would have liked over the past few years. I do not want to deprive myself of seeing my grandchildren grow up; the fourth one, Shira, the daughter of our son Elchanan and his wife, Talia, was born on September 7, 2008, while I was in Germany, at the Frankfurt airport, and we already have a fifth grandchild, Michael, and more on the way. I do not know if it is linked to my grandchildren, but since their arrival, my repeated excursions into the horrors of the Holocaust have affected me more. My eyes mist over more often when I read the accounts of the crimes perpetrated by the Nazis, particularly against children. Perhaps my armor is beginning to crack a little, after a long fight of 30 years. I am still strong, but the years have taken their toll.

I AM, HOWEVER, one of those privileged people who get up each morning with a smile on their face, happy to go to work, always intellectually and emotionally engaged in the task at hand and con-vinced of the importance of my mission. I expended a lot of energy on Operation Last Chance. I knew when I launched this operation, unique in the world, that it would not be easy, but perhaps I did not realize what formidable obstacles I would have to overcome. The ensuing dis-appointments, frustrations, political masquerades, and isolation took their toll. But I will not stop until justice, however limited, has been achieved for the victims of the Holocaust.

I have never allowed the Nazis I was chasing to ruin my life. I have never turned this quest into a personal obsession focused on the per-sona of the individuals I was trying to bring to justice. In fact, I have felt nothing but contempt and disdain for my targets. They have never interested me as individuals, and I have never dreamed of them at night. They have interested me solely from a strictly legal point of view. They have committed appalling crimes and yet they have hereto escaped human justice—and I have never been willing to accept this. I have not tracked them for my own pleasure, to satisfy some thrill of the chase on my own part, or to gain recognition. I have never wanted to take the law into my own hands. I have done what I had to do, the best that I could. Faithful to Simon Wiesenthal, I have not forgotten the victims of the Holocaust. I have pursued their murderers, many of whom could and should have finished their days in prison, if the political and judi-cial powers that be had had the political will to put them behind bars.

THE QUESTION OF the future is naturally of concern. In the meantime, there is still work to accomplish. The flow of information to our office continues, and every month, new names are added to my list of suspects: 1 Croat (in Argentina), November 2007; 1 Hungarian (in the United States) and 1 German (in Brazil), January 2008; 1 Latvian (in Australia) and 2 Austrians, February 2008; 2 Germans, March 2008; 1 German (in Chile), 1 German (in the United States), April 2008; 1 Czech, June 2008; and 15 additional suspects since my trip to South America in the summer of 2008. I have also not finished publishing my annual reports on the worldwide investigation and prosecution of Nazi war criminals. The final one will probably be published in the summer of 2010 or 2011.

At the end of June 2008, I was involved in an initiative, together with Spanish lawyer Gloria Trinidad and "Nizkor," a human rights NGO, to get the Spanish government to demand the extradition of four guards who served in Flossenbürg, Mauthausen, and Sachsenhausen. These men, Ivan Demjanjuk, Johann Lepprich, Josias Kumpf, and Anton Tittjung, all four of whom had taken refuge in the United States, had served in camps during the war in which barbarous acts had been committed against Spanish citizens persecuted by the Franco regime. The American authorities had authorized their deportation, but as no country was willing to admit them, they were still there, safe from all prosecution, as their crimes had not been committed on American soil. The Spanish judicial authorities indicated their willingness to proceed, but in the meantime, the U.S. government was able to deport Ivan Demjanjuk to Germany to stand trial for his alleged crimes at the Sobibor death camp in Poland, and to deport Josias Kumpf to Austria, so this initiative will not include these cases.

I AM A historian of the Holocaust. When the hunt for Nazi war criminals ends, we will still have to make sure that those seeking to deny and/or distort the events of the Shoa will not be able to change or manipulate the historical record. This task has already begun, but as we get further in time from the events of the Holocaust, the likelihood of denial and attempts at distortion will only increase. We have already seen how the Baltic countries of Lithuania, Latvia, and Estonia have consistently tried to hide or at least minimize the highly significant role of their nationals in Holocaust crimes, and they are leading the dangerous campaign to equate Nazi and Communist crimes.

So there is much to be done and my training and experience as a Holocaust historian and my efforts of the past three decades have prepared me for this task. Once again, in the spirit and tradition of Mr. Wiesenthal, I will be able to say that I did not forget the victims or the survivors and I remain committed to the making sure that the Holocaust will neither be forgotten, nor ignored, nor denied, nor distorted and that the historical record of its crimes that we leave to future generations will be as accurate as humanly possible.

NOTES

Chapter One   Milivoj Ašner, A Suspected Nazi at Euro 2008

1. Brian Flynn, "Soaking Up Atmosphere, the Nazi Who Sent 100's to Death Camps," *Sun*, June 16, 2008, pp. 4–5.
2. *Hrvatski drzavni arhiv, Zagreb (HDA)*; HDA Zagreb, Zemaljska komisija za utvrdjivanje zlocina okupatora i njihovih pomagaca, ZKRZ Zh. br. 29555, kut. 389; HDA Zagreb, ZKRZ, Kartoteka zločinaca okupatora i njigovih pomagača u Zagrebu, kartica na ime: Ašner Milivoj.
3. "Undated and Unsigned Letter Mailed to Office of the Civic Committee for Human Rights-Zagreb," text received July 16, 2004, Simon Wiesenthal Center-Israel Office Archives [hereafter-SWC-IOA], Operation Last Chance-Croatia, file I, February 23–August 31, 2004.
4. Tia Goldenberg, "Croatia to Assist Wiesenthal Nazi Hunt," *Jerusalem Post*, July 7, 2004.
5. Tzadok Yechezkeli and Gil Meltzer, "Ha-Nimlat," *Yediot Achronot*, August 5, 2005, pp. 32–38.
6. Emil Bobi, "Ach dieser Jude, ein Lump," *Profil*, November 8, 2004, pp. 44–45.
7. "Summary of Meeting with Croatian President H. E. Stjepan Mesić— July 5, 2005," July 10, 2005, SWC-IOA, Operation Last Chance-Croatia, file III, July 1, 2005–May 31, 2006.
8. Email from Tomislav Jakić to SWC-IO, May 8, 2007, SWC-IOA, Operation Last Chance-Croatia, file IV, June 1, 2006–May 31, 2007.
9. Letter of Efraim Zuroff to Austrian Minister of Justice Dr. Maria Berger, June 16, 2008, SWC-IOA, Operation Last Chance-Croatia, file VI, February 1–July 31, 2008.
10. "Gesuchter Kriegsverbrecher in Klagenfurter Fanzone," *Der Standard*, June 17, 2008.

11. "Justiz zu Fall Asner: Oesterreich ist nicht Guantanamo," *Die Presse,* June 18, 2008.
12. "Haider: Wir schatzen diese Familie sehr," *Der Standard,* June 18, 2008.
13. "Asner: Who Was Not Loyal, Had to Leave," *Javno,* June 20, 2008.
14. Flynn, "Soaking Up Atmosphere."
15. "Croat war crimes suspect admits deporting Jews during WW II," *Ha-Aretz,* June 20, 2008.
16. "Penny-pinching Keeping Ašner Extradition on Hold," B92, February 11, 2009.

Chapter Two   First Encounters With the Holocaust

1. In Europe, the family name was Zar, but for some reason unknown to me, my grandfather called himself Sar in America, even though all his brothers continued to be called Zar in their countries of immigration.
2. The spelling of my father's family name was the subject of a debate in his family. Both his father and brother spelled the name with an "i," whereas he insisted on spelling it with an "o."
3. As hard as it may seem to believe, during my years at Yeshiva College (1966–1970), one could not major in Jewish history.

Chapter Three   "I Did Not Forget You"

1. "Poland," *Encyclopedia of the Holocaust* (New York and London, 1990), pp. 1155, 1174.

Chapter Four   The Office of Special Investigations and the Case of Kazys Palčiauskas

1. "Memorandum of Decision" and "Conclusions Of Law," United States of America, Plaintiff vs. Kazys Palciauskas, Defendant, Case No. 81-547-Civ-T-GC, March 23, 1983, p. 5, 16–17.

Chapter Six   Nazis Down Under

1. Tom Bower, *Blind Eye to Murder: Britain, America and the Purging of Nazi Germany; A Pledge Betrayed* (London: Granada, 1983), pp. 69–70.
2. Letter of Rabbi Marvin Hier to Prime Minister Bob Hawke, September 30, 1986, SWC-IOA, Australia, file I, April 5, 1986–September 22, 1987.

3. "Review of Material Relating to the Entry of Suspected War Criminals into Australia," submitted to Special Minister of State Michael J. Young by A. C. C. Menzies, November 28, 1986, p. 7.
4. Konrads Kalejs, Petitioner v. Immigration and Naturalization Service, Respondent, CA No. 7 (INS), no. 92-2198, decided November 17, 1993.
5. "Ex-Nazi Guilty of Manslaughter," *International Herald Tribune*, December 20–21, 1997.

Chapter Seven Nazis in Great Britain

1. Letter of Rabbi Marvin Hier to Right Hon. Mrs. Margaret Thatcher, M. P., October 22, 1986, SWC-IOA, England, File I.
2. Letter of Charles Powell to Rabbi Marvin Hier, February 12, 1987, SWC-IOA, England, file I.
3. "The Wiesenthal File," *The Times* (London), March 3, 1987.
4. "Case for Inaction," *Daily Telegraph*, March 4, 1987, p. 16.
5. Peter Simple, "Zealots," *Daily Telegraph*, March 4, 1987.
6. First name unknown.
7. Letter of Gebietskommissar Carl to Generalkommissar Minsk, October 30, 1941, Nuremburg Document 1104-PS, *Nazi Conspiracy and Aggression* (Red Series), Vol. III, Washington, 1946, pp. 785–789.
8. *War Crimes; Report of the War Crimes Inquiry*, July 1989, p. 92.
9. Ibid., p. 94.

Chapter Eight Nazis under the Maple Leaf

1. Jules Deschenes, *Commission of Inquiry on War Criminals: Report, Part I*: Public, Ottawa, 1986, p. 17.
2. Ibid., p. 59.
3. See for example, Case nos. 8, 21, 24, 39, 45, 53, 65, and 76, ibid., pp. 279–325.
4. Ibid., p. 254.
5. Robert Sarner and Steve Leibowitz, "Under the Maple Leaf," *Jerusalem Post Magazine*, November 22, 1996, p. 8.
6. Transcript of interview conducted by "Salvatore Romano" (Steve Rambam) with Antanas Kenstavičius in the latter's home at 615 Thacker, Hope, British Columbia, January 3, 1996, SWC-IOA, Canada, file V, February 1, 1995–November 21, 1996.

228 OPERATION LAST CHANCE

Chapter Ten Lithuania: A Struggle for Justice and Truth in the Land of My Forefathers

1. "Adress [sic] by Gediminas Vagnorius, Prime Minister of the Republic of Lithuania on 20 June 1991 at Dedication Ceremony of Monument at Ponar," SWC-IOA, Lithuania, file III.
2. Robert D. McFadden, "Soviet Turmoil; Lithuania's Prosecutor Denies Rehabilitating Nazi War Criminals," *New York Times*, September 8, 1991.
3. "Speech by the President of the Republic of Lithuania," delivered at the Knesset in Jerusalem at 4 PM, March 1, 1995, SWC-IOA, Lithuania, file XIII, March–June 1995. Ironically, in the English translation of the speech it referred to the "persecution" of Nazi war criminals, rather than their prosecution.

Chapter Eleven Latvia: A Mass Murderer as a Contemporary Hero

1. Vaire Vike-Freiburga, "Remembrance and Understanding of the Holocaust in Latvia," January 27, 2000, SWC-IOA, Latvia, File VI, January 9–February 16, 2000.
2. "Address by H. E. Vaira Vike-Freiburga, President of the Republic of Latvia, at the International Forum Preventing Genocide: Threats and Responsibilities, Stockholm, January 26, 2004," SWC-IOA, Latvia, file XVII, October 21, 2003–February 19, 2004.
3. Efraim Zuroff, "Misleading Comparisons of 20th Century Tragedies," *The Baltic Times*, February 19–25, 2004.
4. Gunita Nagle and Nora Drike, "Nav tiesāts, tomēr nav arī nevainīgs," *Diena*, May 17, 2005.
5. "Israel Foreign Ministry Condemns Kirstein's Statements," LETA news agency, May 27, 2005.

Chapter Twelve Estonia: The Best Justice Money Can Buy

1. All quotes from Lynn Jolly, "Nazi Link Killed my Dad," *Paisley Daily Express*, March 31, 2009.
2. Letter of Yaakov Kaplan to Efraim Zuroff, 17 Marcheshvan 5752 [October 25, 1991], SWC-IOA, Iceland, File I, October 1991–September 1992.
3. Testimony of Hilka Mootse, June 12, 1961, criminal case 15-61, former KGB Archives, Tallinn, Estonia.

4. "Former Immigration Director Authorized Return of Nazi Collaborator," *Inside Costa Rica*, May 27, 2007.

5. Antti Oolo, "Natsikutt suudistab eesti rahvast mõrvades," *Eesti Paevaleht*, August 22, 2001, pp. 4–5.

6. Aet Suvari and Pekka Erelt, "Kutsumata kulaline," *Eesti Ekspress*, August 23, 2001, p. 5.

7. "Phase II-The German Occupation of Estonia, 1941–1944, Conclusions of the Estonian International Commission for the Investigation of Crimes against Humanity," www.historycommission.ee/temp/conclusions.htm, pp. 5–6.

Chapter Thirteen   Croatia's Past and the Search for Dinko Šakić

1. David Binder, "Tudjman Is Dead; Croat Led Country Out of Yugoslavia," *New York Times*, December 11, 1999.

2. Letter of Efraim Zuroff to Foreign Minister David Levy, August 27, 1997, SWC-IOA, Croatia, File I.

3. Letter of Efraim Zuroff to Dr. Svjetlan Berkovic, April 7, 1998, SWC-IOA, Croatia, File II.

4. Aleksa Crnjaković, "Dinko Šakić: Obavljao Sam Svoju Duznost," *Magazin*, February 1995, pp. 26–30.

Chapter Fourteen   A Historic Trial in the Land of the Ustasha

1. D. Romac, "Šakić: Žrtva Sam Lažnih Svjedoka I Kommunističke Propagande," *Novy List*, September 30, 1999, p. 5.

2. Verdana Bobinac, "Dinko Šakić proglašen krivim i osuđen na 20 godina zatvora," *Vjesnik*, October 5, 1999, pp. 1, 7.

3. "Zuroff: Moje pismo Thompson," *Globus*, July 11, 2007, pp. 30–32.

4. "Zuroff traži od Mesića osudu organizatora Šakićpokepa," *Večernji List*, July 29, 2008; e-mail of Tomislav Jakić to Simon Wiesenthal Center-Israel Office, SWC-IOA, Croatia, File XXII.

Chapter Fifteen   A Difficult Beginning

1. Ernst Klee, Willi Dressen and Volker Riess, *Those Were the Days: The Holocaust As Seen by the Perpetrators and Bystanders* (London, 1991), pp. 31–32.

2. Anna Lehmann, "Letzte Chance, bevor der Tot sie holt," *Die Tageszeitung*, May 18, 2004, pp. 7–8.

3. Letter of Justinas Jokubaitis to Jewish community of Lithuania, November 11, 2002, SWC-IOA, Operation Last Chance, Lithuania, File I, March 1–November 30, 2002.
4. Letter of Andrius Gudzinskas to Efraim Zuroff and Aryeh Rubin, November 28, 2002, SWC-IOA, Operation Last Chance, Lithuania, Cases/Suspects, File I, July 10, 2002–February 23, 2003.

Chapter Sixteen   The She-Devil of Majdanek

1. Alison Mutler, "Romania Denies Domestic Holocaust," Associated Press, June 13, 2003.
2. Grig Davidovitz, "Romanian President: Holocaust 'not unique to Jews,'" *Haaretz*, July 25, 2003.
3. Letter of Martha Waninger to the Wiesenthal Center, May 8, 2004, SWC-IOA, Operation Last Chance, Austria, File II, December 14, 2003–December 31, 2004.
4. The Ministry of State Security, or Stasi, was the service of the political police, intelligence, espionage, and counterespionage of the Democratic German Republic (RDA).
5. E-mail of Stefan Klemp to Efraim Zuroff, March 7, 2005, SWC-IOA, Operation Last Chance, Austria, File III, January 1–December 31, 2005.
6. Richard Rubenstein and John Roth, *Approaches to Auschwitz, the Holocaust and its Legacy* (Louisville, 2003), p. 202.
7. Michael Leidig, "Elderly Woman Is Wanted Nazi War Criminal," *Telegraph*, October 22, 2007.
8. "Nazi-Hunter Brands Austria a 'Paradise' for Nazis," Reuters, February 1, 2006.
9. Marianne Enigl, "Hitler in Altersheim," *Profil*, September 10, 2007, p. 30.
10. Leidig, "Elderly Woman Is Wanted Nazi War Criminal."
11. "Statement of Eva Kozlowska," March 29, 2007, SWC-IOA, Operation Last Chance, Austria, File V, January 1, 2007–January 31, 2008.
12. Martina Lettner, "Opfer der Zeit," *Profil*, January 28, 2008, p. 33.
13. "Vienna Investigates 85-Year-Old Nazi Camp Suspect," Reuters, January 29, 2008.
14. Letter of Dr. Efraim Zuroff to Dr. Maria Berger, January 29, 2008, SWC-IOA, Operation Last Chance, Austria, File V, January 1, 2007–January 31, 2008.
15. "Wiesenthal Center: Austria's Decades-Long Failure to Prosecute Majdanek Guard Erna Wallisch Ultimately Allowed Her to Escape Justice

Despite Recent Re-Opening of Her Case," press release of Israel Office of Simon Wiesenthal Center, February 21, 2008, SWC-IOA, Operation Last Chance, Austria, File VI, February 1–July 31, 2008.

Chapter Seventeen   Charles Zentai

1. "Letter of Dezső Balázs to American Military Headquarters in Germany," May 30, 1948, SWC-IOA, Operation Last Chance, Hungary, File II, July 21, 2004–January 19, 2005.
2. "Son of War Crimes Suspect Claims Evidence Flawed," ABC Online, July 25, 2005; letter of Ernie Steiner to Dr. Efraim Zuroff, February 13, 2006, SWC-IOA, Operation Last Chance, Hungary, File IV, July 1, 2005–July 31, 2006.
3. Letter of Fr. John B. Flynn to Minister Chris Ellison, July 9, 2005, SWC-IOA, Operation Last Chance, Hungary, File IV, July 1, 2005–July 31, 2006.
4. Natasha Robinson, "Wartime Fascist Denies Targeting Jews," *The Australian*, August 23, 2005.
5. Chris Johnston, "War Crimes Suspect Dies Amid Controversy," *The Age*, July 13, 2006.

Chapter Eighteen   Dr. Heim, The Most Wanted Nazi in the World

1. "Concentration Camp Doctor Aribert Heim Tops List of Wanted Nazis," *Haaretz*, April 30, 2008.
2. "Operationsbuch," Mauthausen concentration camp, SWC-IOA, Operation Last Chance, Dr. Heim, File I.
3. Georg Boenisch, Markus Deggerich, Georg Mascolo and Joerg Schmitt, "Es geht mir gut," *Der Spiegel*, August 29, 2005, p. 46.
4. Stefan Klemp, "Der KZ-Arzt und seine Freunde," *Süddeutsche Zeitung*, April 18, 2006.
5. Félix Martínez and Nando García, "A la casa del ultimo Nazi," *El Mundo*, October 30, 2005.
6. Jonathan Tisdall, "Accused of Hiding 'Docter Death,'" *Aftenposten* (English), June 6, 2007.
7. "On 94th Birthday of 'Dr. Death' Aribert Heim, Wiesenthal Center Calls For End Of Obstruction Of Investigation By Baden-Baden Judge," June 27, 2008, SWC-IOA, Press Releases, File II.
8. David Rising, "German Court Rejects Criticism of Role in Nazi Hunt," *Miami Herald*, June 30, 2008.

9. "Wanted Nazi Death Camp Doctor Killed, Book Claims," *Ynet*, October 13, 2007.

10. E-mail from J. F. to Israel Office of Wiesenthal Center, August 27, 2007, SWC-IOA, Aribert Heim, File III.

11. E-mail of "X" to Israel Office of Wiesenthal Center, August 29, 2007, SWC-IOA, Aribert Heim, File IJI.

12. E-mail of "X" to Israel Office of Wiesenthal Center, September 28, 2007, SWC-IOA, Aribert Heim, File III.

13. E-mail of "X" to Israel Office of Wiesenthal Center, October 18, 2007, SWC-IOA, Aribert Heim, File III.

14. Letter of Mag. Waltraut Diharce to Simon Wiesenthal Center Jerusalem, August 7, 2008, SWC-IOA, Aribert Heim, File V.

Chapter Nineteen Képíró: The Suspected Nazi Who Lives Opposite a Synagogue

1. E-mail of Szilvia Dittel to Simon Wiesenthal Center, Israel Office, July 18, 2006, SWC-IOA, Operation Last Chance, Hungary, File IV.

2. E-mail of Szilvia Dittel and Tibor Pécsi to Efraim Zuroff, July 18, 2006, SWC-IOA, Operation Last Chance, Hungary, File IV.

3. E-mail of Dr. Efraim Zuroff to Rabbi Tamas Vero, September 25, 2006, SWC-IOA, Operation Last Chance, Hungary, File V.

4. E-mail of rabbi Tamas Vero to Dr. Efraim Zuroff, September 25, 2006, SWC-IOA, Operation Last Chance, Hungary, File V.

5. "Wiesenthal Centre traces suspected Nazi war criminal to Budapest," *Deutsche Press-Agentur*, September 28, 2006.

6. Talkback by "someone who stood there" [Chava Shick] to Ronen Bodony, "Hungariya: Nechsaf Posheya Nazi she-Ratzach Alafim ba-Shoa," *Ynet*, September 28, 2006.

INDEX

CPSIA information can be obtained
at www.ICGtesting.com
Printed in the USA
LVHW041444120623
749529LV00004B/13

9 780230 108059